WHAT OTHERS A
FACE

Facedown is a jaw-dropping example of God's redemptive ʒʊ
out in the life of Donnie Foster. Through this vivid account of Donnie's journey, you can see how pain, anger, rebellion, and carnage can be
replaced with faith, hope, submission, and love. No one is able to outrun
the reach of a jealous God. If you have somehow forgotten that God is
in the business of changing lives, making beauty from ashes, this story
will make you a believer again and cause you to fall facedown before the
almighty God and glorify His Son forever.

—*E. Scott Feather*
Dean of Chapel and Global Ministries
Grace College, Winona Lake, Indiana

This is the most compelling story I've experienced. You find yourself
taking a trip with Donnie through his incredible life. It is a story of
tragedy and triumph. God's grace and love unfolds within these pages.
This book is a must read!

—*Douglas J Ballard*
World Champion Highland Athlete
Bloomington, Indiana

Do we all not have a cycle in our lives (mental, physical, or spiritual) that
needs to be broken? Harvard Business School says the best way to teach
a principle is to model it. *Facedown: The Donnie Foster Story,* wonder-
fully chronicled by Aletha Smithson, takes us through the horrifying
and sobering account of a life thrown into a terminal downward spiral
only to be resurrected tenderly by Christ. In one small way or another,
this is our life and to see hope modeled gives us strength. This book viv-
idly brings us to a fresh awareness of lives that need to be saved. It gives
us encouragement to be part of the answer. This is a real page-turner
that will help us to inspire and aspire.

—*Dr. Steve Connor*
Director, Sports Outreach International
Bloomington, Indiana

FACEDOWN

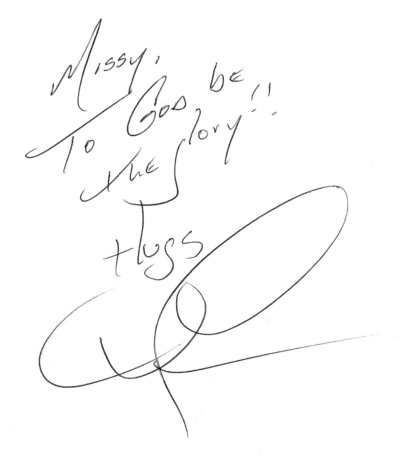

Missy,
To God be
the glory!!

Hugs

FACEDOWN

THE DONNIE FOSTER STORY

ALETHA V. SMITHSON

YorkshirePublishing
www.yorkshirepublishing.com
Write Now.

DEDICATION

Donnie's personal dedication to sharing his story:

This book is an offering of my life's dedication to God the Father and Jesus Christ, his Son, whose tender mercy saved my life and redeemed my soul.

To Kelly, my beautiful, dove-eyed wife whose love helped me to see my own worst enemy was *me*.

To my children, Tara, Cameron, and Shana. To them I dedicate the end of passing down the sins of the father (Exodus 20:5). My dedication to them is that the end of abusive generations has come.

To Brother Bob Kurko and his lovely wife, Virginia.

To Wyatt and Carolyn Mullinax, my mentor and friend.

To the dear lady in the story known as Millie.

To persons I have not personally met but know through the cries of needful and desperate hearts: slaves to abuse and their abusers, addicts, the unforgiving, the unforgiven, the guilty and the hopeless.

DONNIE AND KELLY FOSTER

ACKNOWLEDGMENTS

Thank you, Donnie, for giving me the privilege to pen your story. Thank you, Tom, for your encouragement to take on this adventure and your patience in seeing it through.

Special thanks:

> I want to extend a very special thank you to Donnie's mom, known in the story as May. This has not been an easy submission for her. It required that she relive years of painful memories and oppression that she kept hidden for fear of ramifications from a past society sparsely prepared to offer help. It was an era when people simply lived the life they were dealt, when child abuse was an issue kept silent and never talked about. Fear itself was the determining factor guiding the thought process, requiring desperate decisions to be made and hurting hearts to remain silent. In a sense, the underlying story of her life is somewhat told behind the scenes. Her courage is part of making this book possible. Thank you for giving us the opportunity to share Donnie's story with a needful world.
>
> —Aletha Smithson

Forgiveness is the fragrance the violet sheds on the heel that crushed it.

—Mark Twain

TABLE OF CONTENTS

INTRODUCTION

Let this be recorded for a generation to come,
So that a people yet unborn
May praise the Lord...
From heaven the Lord looked at the earth,
To hear the groans of the prisoners,
To set free those who were doomed to die.

Psalm 102:18–20 (RSV)

The story you are about to read is dark... very dark. The first quarter of the book will be very depressing and perhaps difficult to read, but it is Donnie's life told to me. In most instances, dialogue, color, and entities have been created to depict the narration of Donnie's life, a testimony of misery to ministry victory. Names and descriptions are all based on the lives of real people. Events told are actual events that took place in Donnie's life.

Please be advised that although Donnie shares his life story, the story to be told here is not about him but about God and his rescuing love and his power to change lives. It is Donnie's concern that you, the reader, not set your heart or your focus on him personally.

Neither does he desire the reader be absorbed by the abuse nor the dark episodes in the book as his cry for attention. *The focus he wants you to have as you read his story is to understand the spiritual warfare among mankind today, the warfare between the forces of good and evil, the power of God and his mercy against the destruction of Satan.*

Donnie shares only his memories as seen through the eyes of a terrified and hurting child; he recalls being sucked into the world of drugs and alcohol as a teen and reveals the enemy's deceptive lies of dependency that lead to self-destruction; he recalls the hopeless and evil world of addictions, anger, and hate that becomes a reality in a life void of love.

"So many times my life could have been snuffed out without so much as a whimper from anyone. Time and time again God spared my life in miraculous ways. There is only one answer to the obvious question of why. Because God had a purpose, and he is working out that very purpose today."

Donnie continues, "My heart is heavy because I know first-hand the trauma the abused are experiencing.

"I see the addict on the street and know the desperation he feels until he can make another buy to carry him through another night, all the while believing the lie that one more fix will solve his problem.

"I see the bruised and battered woman whose fear keeps her from seeking help. Mothers are often caught in the middle between an angry husband and father trying to protect her children and yet avoid abuse herself. A catch-22: fear of more abuse because she sought help or fear of more abuse because she did not.

"Like the Apostle Paul, I mocked everything God ordained as pure. I thought nothing of doing anything and everything I had to do to stay alive, do what I wanted, have what I wanted, be what I wanted. I had no conscience to contradict it until I found myself *facedown,* facing my own destruction. Like Paul on the Damascus Road, I had no place to lift my face but up into the face of my Redeemer."

Donnie's mom gave birth to five boys, of which, Donnie was the second. Because they lived under the threats of abusive alcoholic father figures, Donnie didn't know life could be any different.

Donnie also states, "I know how the angry alcoholic affected my life as a child. The spouse is not immune to the same kind of behavior from the alcoholic just because he or she is a spouse. Whatever my mother endured has taken years for her to talk about. So many things I never understood as a child. Lack of understanding created hatred, anger and bitterness that governed my thought process as I grew."

As only God can heal relationships, there has been restoration between Donnie and his mom since the beginning of the writing of this book. Because of God's healing power, Donnie's mom is currently a very significant part of Donnie's life today, as well as his youngest half brother. The destiny of the fourth son will be told as the story unfolds. Donnie's third oldest brother died at an early age. He is sure there were times his mom intervened to protect all of her children and took the wrath intended for them.

Donnie continues his motive for sharing. "If you get nothing else from the book, please understand this one thing: *I had to live the life I lived so that I could know firsthand the hearts, minds, and spirits of those to whom God has called me to minister to today.* I can identify with them on whatever level they are on and know their mind-set and thought process. These are my people. I don't ever want to forget the feelings from which I have been set free."

—Aletha Smithson

PRELUDE

Remember my affliction and my misery;
The wormwood and the gall.
My soul continually thinks of it
And is bowed down within me.
But this I call to my mind,
And therefore I have hope.

Lamentations 3:19–21 (RSV)

I closed my eyes and turned the other cheek against the tarmac, away from the hot sickening breath of mid-July, partly because the heat against the asphalt sweltered with a choking filth that clung to the moisture in my mouth like a sickening fungus but more because the awareness of death, spit, and stench of urine was driven through my nostrils with every breath. The back of my throat tasted of toxic waste that filtered up from turf saturated with blood pools from seldom acknowledged knife attacks in the prison yard.

This was just another riotous disturbance on the grounds that sounded the alarm for discipline. Inmates of C yard, level three, hit the deck facedown, prone out while steel-tipped batons danced above our heads. As soon as this was over and lights were out I would still carry out my plan to end it all.

I opened my eyes to see where the guards were standing. Instead of heavy boots intimidating of ruthless authority, I saw the tiny feet of a fallen sparrow less than a yard from my face. I could almost smell its sickening carcass, yet I couldn't take my eyes from the stiff and lifeless form. I wanted to kick it free for having died in this hellish place, but I was in no way free to respect its remains. It was a bird, a dead bird! Why was I so drawn to stare at something so worthless? To make the slightest move was the dumbest thing I could have done while lying facedown, spread eagle on the ground. It was a good way to be reminded of the humility pressed upon us, the prostrate, facedown, horizontal men of Corcoran State Prison, Corcoran, California.

I have to believe God's eye was on that sparrow, and looking back, I know he watched over me.

THE AGE OF FEAR

Just as you do not know...
How bones are formed in the womb of the pregnant woman,
So you do not know the activity of God
Who makes all things.

Ecclesiastes 11:5 (NASB)

Nobody fully understands the details surrounding the events on March 9, 1958. Everyone agrees the contractions maintained their persistent fight to free the babe in the womb.

I never got an accurate account by those in attendance. Some seem a bit confused about why it might have been better if this birth had not taken place on this particular day.

Some say my mother simply fought to not release my tiny frame from the security of her body. Perhaps she knew where life would take us. She knew her world would become my world.

Somewhere, a plan had been set in motion. If there ever was a God in heaven, I have to believe he was paying close attention on March 9, 1958.

Hi, my name is Donnie.

This is my story.

A plan had been set in motion all right. Anyway, they tell me that's how it happened.

Mom was married at a very young age and already had one son. Now I imposed myself right into an already dysfunctional household.

I remember very little about my birth father. I learned, only in recent years, he was an alcoholic and a womanizer. He left the survival of our family to my mom.

Before I reached the age of two, Mom had given birth to her third son and was holding down three jobs just to make ends meet. Dad's alcoholic ambition made it difficult for Mom's incomes to sustain us, so she was forced to hire cheap daycare for me and my brothers. Our sixteen-year-old neighbor girl agreed to watch us for a meager sum. Her name was Willie.

While supposedly caring for us, Willie was spending very intimate time with our father. Mom arrived home from work one day to find Dad, Willie, and Willie's parents.

Willie brought her parents (or perhaps they brought her) into our home to confront my dad about the child Willie was carrying. Willie had conceived a child by my father. Willie's announcement brought down the gavel, ending the marital saga of my parents. They divorced, and Dad left to marry Willie. When Dad left us, my older brother was three. I was not yet two, and we had an infant brother.

When the divorce was final, Mom was only nineteen, trying to feed three boys. With the birth of another son, Mom continued to dedicate herself to as much work as she could handle.

A young, ex-military man named Ben came into her life and swept her off her feet. Mom describes Ben as the perfect gentleman to a young mother looking for stability and a future for her boys. During the courtship, he was all a dashing young suitor could be. But as soon as the vows were spoken, that dashing young gentleman became the raging tyrant who terrorized our home.

It wasn't but a short time into the marriage that Mom gave birth to her fourth son, my half-brother.

This lays the groundwork for the story that follows—my story. Because Ben was the only dad I can remember, I will refer to him as Dad rather than Ben or my stepfather. To me, he was the earliest father figure I can recall.

> Beware, that you don't despise a single one of these little ones. For I tell you that in heaven their angels are always in the presence of my heavenly Father.
>
> Matthew 18:10 (NLT)

Looking back, I felt from day one that I was to blame for being conceived. I was to blame for surviving my birth. I was to blame if the sun didn't shine, and I was to blame if it did.

When I reflect back on the earliest years, I recall my waking hours as a child who was always under the cloud of fear. The man we knew as Dad didn't need a reason to shove us out of the way, slap us, or backhand us across the room. Just the fact that we were in the room was reason enough. At the time, our home was nothing more than a rebuilt chicken coop, so it was hard to stay out of the way.

My mother was seldom around during the day. She was the breadwinner in our home. My dad was a dedicated alcoholic; so looking back, I feel certain Mom's job served a dual purpose. Her dedication to her employers fed us and kept the bills paid, but it also was her sanctuary away from an abusive, angry, and hateful husband.

I remember daily waking with the fear that Mom's absence would mean another day of his reigning terror. As soon as her car would disappear down that old dirt road, the verbal and physical abuse would begin. I wished I could disappear like the cloud of dust behind the car. That old car would take Mom away for hours at a time. Oh, how I wanted it to take me away.

My memories of Mom arriving home held my sliver of hope for the day. She, like me, would keep a low profile, enter in by the back door, careful never to let it slam. Her main focus was on the little brown bottle of blue pills she immediately fished from deep inside her purse. She poured herself a beverage and tried to relax. It was her way of dealing with the evening ahead.

In retrospect, I know Mom's medications helped her deal with life in our home. I can't fault her for it. Most of the time, it was probably what kept her sane enough to function.

I have no clue what went on between the two of them when I wasn't around. It repulses me now to think of the kind of life Mom must have endured. Though there were countless times I felt abandoned by her, I have no idea how many times she might have intervened on my behalf. I can only thank her for times she may have stood between me and the back of my father's hand.

> Through the Lord's mercies we are not consumed because His compassions fail not. It is good for a man to bear the yoke of his youth.
>
> Lamentations 3:22, 26 (NKJV)

My earliest recollection of Dad's rage goes back to my very young years.

I remember smelling the country dust kicked up by the wheels as I heard our old car driving Mom away. In the past, my bedcovers would serve as my hiding place, but today I could not hide. I pulled the covers away from my face and saw the intimidating figure of Dad standing in the doorway of my room. He didn't have to speak. I knew it was time for me to get out of bed. Trying to do what I had to without being told, I threw one leg out from under the covers, and he grabbed it. His grip was stinging around my weak and skinny ankles. He jerked me free from the bedclothes and slammed me up against the headboard of the bed.

I remember an unfamiliar taste in my mouth as I screamed in pain and without control. His effort to straighten me up brought vomit of bile to my throat. He threw me back down on top of the covers. Blood from somewhere dripped on the nicotine-stained pillowcase, and my arm felt weak with pain. His cursing voice stabbed through my head like poisoned darts in my ears. He continued to strike with his open hand. Every blow smelled like stale hatred. It hurt to cry. He grabbed the hand that felt crippled across the bed. I screamed until my throat had no more voice.

"Well, I'll be! Look at that, boy! Did you bust that arm?"

He grabbed me by my good arm and jerked me to my feet.

"Now I gotta haul you to the doctor, you worthless little twit! Where's that money gonna come from, huh, boy? You better hope it's only bruised and not broke! I ain't got time to mess with no handicapped kid. Now, you listen to me, boy! When that doctor asks you how you did this, you make sure you tell 'im you fell. You, got that, boy? You fell!"

I don't remember the ride into town. I don't remember the doctor's face. I do remember the kindness of his voice.

"Well, son, let's have a look. We'll have to take some pictures to see if that arm is broken or not. Now, what in the world did you do to cut your lip and hurt your arm so bad?"

I swallowed and said, "I fell."

I was not yet four.

Memories just kind of hang
above the balance of forgetfulness;
There are some you would like to forget...
Those will never be forgotten.
There are those too precious to forget...
Those will never be forgotten.
And then there are those
That leave a brand upon the psyche
like the scar of a sizzling iron.

AVS 10/28/07

It was summer. It was hot. Dad's anger heated with the rising California temperature.

He never needed a reason to threaten me with the most horrendous scenarios he could muster up in his demonic mind.

In his twisted world, I was a menace just because I drew my breath from the same open sky as he. He was repulsed by my very presence. Many were the nights it was easier to go to bed hungry than to share a space at this man's table. I can recall to my senses the nasal annoyance of stale booze, manure, and cigar smoke in his pickup.

We always had a few chickens scratching out an existence in the yard. They provided eggs, and from time to time, one of them would serve as our means of existence at the next meal.

I remember an afternoon when Dad had been sitting outside most of the day drinking one beer after another.

My brother and I had been playing nearby, throwing rocks at the tree in the chicken yard. My rock throwing didn't have an aim; it just had a destination. One went a little astray and hit a windowpane on the chicken house. I didn't have enough punch in my throw to break it. It just knocked some dust from the frame, but it startled Dad and got his attention.

"Hey, you worthless idiot! I ain't got money to fix no broken window. Ain't you got any better sense than to throw rocks?"

And with that, he picked one up and hurled it at me. I dodged, but I felt it whiz past my face. "You little heathen! I'll teach you a lesson you ain't ever gonna forget!"

He grabbed me under his arm, and we halfway fell over the dilapidated wood fence that was meant to contain the chickens. He grabbed my older brother by the arm and ordered, "Get out there and catch me one o' them hens, boy!"

Even my brother didn't question the man when he spoke.

Turning to me, he bellowed, "Boy, wait'll you see what I got planned for you! What you're about to see is exactly what I'll do to you if you don't change your idiot ways!"

My idiot ways? That was one of his favorite phrases for intimidation, but he never bothered to explain to me exactly what *my idiot ways* were.

Having cornered a nice fat specimen, my brother grabbed the hen by the leg and carried it over to the man who, by this time, was wiping the blade of the knife he wore on his belt. That knife did everything from pick his teeth to clean his fingernails to serve as a baton when he was making a point to me.

"Now, you watch this, boy! Unless you do as I say, you're gonna be next!"

He held the frightened hen upside down by one leg while he glared at me, shaking the hen in my face.

"Don't you turn your head, boy! You watch this! This is you, boy! This is you!"

Squawking and squealing, the hen surrendered to his hand in execution. He made me watch while he lowered the hen to the ground and stepped on its head. He severed the head and neck just above the wishbone. My screams drowned out the hysterical laughter coming from his twisted psyche. He threw the carcass at me while I ran.

I doubt the sacrificial bird fed us that night. He considered the bird's reason for living and dying complete once he made his point with me.

After every terrorizing incident that gave Dad his thrill of victory, the common thread of recovery that launched itself in me was to hide. I always just wanted to hide.

No matter how I tried, I could never be invisible enough. Looking back, Dad must have been obsessed with the agony associated with death. I doubt that it was the actual dying that intrigued him. I think it was more the process of getting there, the examples of which he used to terrorize me.

Dad never ceased to find new fantasies of terror. Fear was the only honest emotion I knew. Then there was the day that, looking within our own sufficiency to survive, was another great object lesson to turn me from *my idiot ways*.

As well as that small handful of chickens, we had an old cow out back. Mom called her Bess. At one time, it was my brother's job to milk her so we had milk in the cooler. I'm not sure what led to the decision of this dreadful day.

It had been a long while since she provided milk for us. Perhaps we could no longer feed her, or perhaps Mom could no longer feed us and the old cow was there to be had.

But I remember the little band of men who came right at sunrise. There were three of them. The rumble of their old truck on the gravel road stirred me from sleep.

I heard their voices and smelled their cheap cigars through the humidity of the morning. Low and muffled was their conversation.

One was big with a dirty-looking mustache. He had a red farmer's hanky tied around his head knotted on the side.

One was skinny with tattoos covering both arms. He wore a dirty, stained ball cap.

The other one was short and skinny and bald. He never said much. He didn't smoke a cigar like the other two, but, as a lad, I knew he had something in his mouth because he kept spitting in the dirt. Every time he spit, the dry dusty dirt shivered. It was like big raindrops hitting the ground, and the dirt would flutter until it got too wet.

I could hear Dad grunting and snorting his way to the front yard. I closed my eyes, and I could smell him and see him saunter out the front door, his shirt half buttoned and smelling stale, suspenders hanging to his knees and stretched to the point of useless gartering. If these men had come for the day, there was a good chance he would avoid me. I eased out of bed and peered through the threadbare curtains that covered the one and only window in my room.

There was the slightest breeze. The four of them stood around and smoked their cigars and talked quietly until the sun's first light broke past the horizon. Two of the three walked to the barn with my dad and came back carrying sawhorses and wood to make a table. They lined buckets and dishpans across the wooden slab and then began to fill containers with water. My curiosity was focused on the skinny man's tattoos.

Dad walked to the near side of the barn and began calling old Bess, just like he taught my brother to call her. "Heh! Heh, Bess!" Bess took her time coming to the gate. There was no reason to hurry.

Once inside the barn lot, gates were all closed to contain her. She didn't mind. This was home, and these were her surroundings. She sniffed the empty feed trough. Convinced this was not feeding time, she sauntered to the corner of the lot where a huge black oak tree towered over the fence. There, she scratched herself on a board.

Dad walked back to the house and said, "Pull up a stump there, boys. Don't know 'bout you, but I need a little something to start the day. I'll get us a little refreshment, and then we'll get started."

He headed for the back door. I could hear him rummaging in the kitchen, drawers opening and closing, muttering to himself. Soon, he appeared back into my view from my window. He was carrying several bottles of beer in both hands. Clenched in his teeth was Mom's long-handled knife that she used for cutting up chickens. He passed out three bottles of beer to his friends and opened one for himself. He dropped the rest of the beers into a bucket filled with cold water. He took the knife from his teeth, jabbing it into the makeshift table on the sawhorses. I fought the urge to throw up. He was going to make me watch another massacre of a chicken.

I sneaked across the floor and slithered back into bed and pulled the covers tight over my head. "I can't...oh, please, no. I can't."

I began dry heaves with every breath. Nothing came up that I couldn't hide in my nightshirt.

Our old screen door had a squeak that once you heard it you'd never forget it. At least I never did. I heard the familiar squeak— *step, step, step...squeak...slam.*

"Don't you come out here, ya hear?"

I hoped he was talking to me, but then I heard Mom answer, "I won't."

"Send that boy out here though. He needs to see this!"

"Please, Ben. He's asleep. Let him sleep."

"I said, send 'im out here."

This command was followed by silence. I heard nothing, so I slithered out from under the covers.

"May, is that boy up? Don't make me come in there and get 'im myself. You tell that sorry little mongrel to get his lazy self out here."

By that time, I had tiptoed to the kitchen, trying to hide the slight vomit soaked up in my shirt.

"Your dad wants you," was all she said.

"Can I have something to eat?"

She opened a bag of shortbread cookies and handed me one.

When I stepped to the door, I could see what Dad had come back into the house for. He was seated on an old tree stump, humped over, smoking with one hand, and holding a beer with the other. Leaning up against the backside of the stump was a shotgun he kept in the pantry in the kitchen. I was told never to touch it. I walked way out around the stump and came to him from the front, so as not to even get close to the gun.

"Sit down, boy."

We had no grass. The yard was bare California soil. I sat down right where I stopped at his orders. I kept watching his face for some clue. My brother hadn't been called to appear, so why was I called to be part of this manly gathering? I tried to take a bite of the cookie, but every time I got it to my mouth, my stomach would act like it was going to throw up, so I just sat there.

I noticed the empty beer bottles all around the tree stumps that served as seats for the hardcore frames of the three strangers. I figured most of the beer he threw in the bucket was gone. Sometimes that was good, sometimes that was bad.

"Well..." said the tall skinny one. "Soon as I finish this here beer, I'm ready to get started." There was some grunting and groaning and attempts at agreement.

As the last bottle was thrown to the ground, Dad looked me square in the eye, "Come on, boy. You're gonna see somethin' real special t'day."

He left the knife stuck in the wood but reached out and grabbed the gun. I tagged along a few steps behind, hoping no one would notice I was lagging. We walked to the lot where old Bess stood content.

Every man had his job. Two of the three men walked to their old pickup, dropped the tailgate, and from somewhere in the back, they pulled out brown-stained aprons and tied them around their bellies. The biggest, burliest guy went to the cab and pulled out something wrapped in a towel and laid it down along the fence. The towel, like the aprons, was covered with those same brown stains. It was hard to tell what color the towel really was.

The tall, skinny one crawled into the driver's seat and started the truck. He backed around, stopping close to the fence that was closest to Bess's tree. Twisted and coiled in the back of the truck was a pile of rope. The skinny man with the tattoos and the one who never said much grabbed the rope and climbed over the fence. Dad was standing next to the fence tying our barn rope around old Bess's neck.

"Get over here, boy."

My bare little feet seemed so heavy. I knew better than to refuse.

Something inside my stomach started to shake. I wanted to cry. I wanted to run. I wanted to throw up, but I took my place by the tree.

"Now, boy, I want you to stand here and think about all those times you've been bad and no good. And when you've remembered how no good you are, I want you to watch what's gonna happen to old Bess here because, boy, unless you change your ways, I can see to it that all this happens to you. You understand? Look at me, boy! You understand?"

I lifted my eyes to look at his face and saw eyes of steel. Ashes fell from the cigar when he smiled down at me and shifted it to the other side of his mouth. I knew he could see the shaking going on inside my stomach. My legs wanted to run so bad I thought they would fall away from my body and leave me lying on the ground. But I stood there. I looked at old Bess's kind eyes and wondered if she was shaking. She didn't look like it. She lowered her head and put her nose against the fence and looked right at me and snorted a little. She turned her head to see what was going on behind her while Dad jerked the rope to keep her head secure.

The skinny one and the short one walked toward her hind side. Each had a rope in his hand, tying some sort of knot as they walked. Silently, they lifted one hind foot and then the other, slipping her hoof through the knot and then jerking it tight.

"You watchin,' boy?"

"Yes, sir, I'm watching."

They tossed the bundled ends of their ropes up and over a big limb of the black oak. I didn't know if I should keep my eye on Bess or if I could turn my head. I was curious to see where the ropes would land. The big guy in the farmer's hanky caught them and started tying them together in another fancy knot as he walked toward the truck. With another kind of knot, he tied the rope to a big piece that stuck out under the bumper. I looked back at old Bess. Her big brown eyes were sparkly, and she gave me another gentle snort. I didn't know what would happen next, and I knew she didn't either. We just looked at each other.

A sudden piercing command from the skinny one broke that one brief moment of repose for Bess.

"Hoist her up!"

The big guy was in the truck with the door open. He had one foot on the accelerator and the other on the running board so he could look back at the ghastly sight that I was supposed to see. Dad let go of the rope around Bess's neck, and her hind feet were jerked up, lifting her heavy body. Her legs were being spread as the ropes pulled her higher and higher into the air. I dropped my shortbread cookie. All I could do was wrap my tiny fingers around the thin wire of the fence and scream.

"Nooooo!"

Bess was making sounds I never knew a cow could make. Her bellowing was piercing my ears, and her eyes looked like the terror that was eating my flesh.

"Stop it! Stop it!" I screamed. Dad handed the gun to the skinny one and grabbed me by the chin and said, "That ain't all, boy. Now, watch this."

The gun exploded, and the air was silent. I felt a warm, wet flow of urine running down my leg that I could not stop. My head felt like an open can of spiders quickly covering my flesh. I couldn't run. I couldn't breathe. I couldn't scream. I couldn't cry. I couldn't find her eyes. Her face was gone. Bess hung silent, turning, swinging slightly over the pool of blood on the ground. Blood was everywhere.

"How 'bout that, boy? D'ja ever see anything like that? Makes ya wanna sit up and pay attention, huh? Bring that knife over here, Pete."

The big guy picked up the towel with the brown stains and drew from inside the folds a knife with a long blade. Dad shook the blade at me and with a stub of a cigar still between his teeth, he said, "Yeah! One more thing we gotta do to them that disobey. You watchin,' boy?" I don't know if I answered or not. Everything was a blur. In a foggy haze, I saw Dad climb over the fence. Bess's blown up face swung in front of the black oak. Dad drew the long blade straight and deep across her throat. Blood spilled from her like a fountain.

I was still preschool age.

"For he shall give his angels charge over you, to keep you in all your ways."

Psalm 91:11 (NKJV)

I knew the best way to avoid the wrath of my intoxicated father was to simply stay out of sight. But how many places were there for a young lad to hide? I was yet too young for school. Mom left every morning with a lunch pail in her hand for her job. My older brother was back in school, the babysitter would come to pick up my younger brother, and I was always alone with a man who detested the very sight of me.

One morning in the quiet of dawn, I figured out a way that I could disappear all day. Seldom did Dad rise in the early hours of morning. Often I would hear Mom as she readied herself for work. This day, I listened particularly close to the sounds. I heard running water in the bathroom, boiling water whistling in the tea-pot, and then the fragrance of fresh coffee. I could stir that into my senses with the aroma of slightly burned toast in the pop-up toaster. Once in a while, the scent of oatmeal filtered through the door to my room.

If there was oatmeal, Mom would leave enough for me when I woke. Never to wake the man of the house, I would tiptoe with the stealth of a kitten on the attack, taking just enough steps to carry the pot from the stove to the chair. There was always a big spoon left in the pasty cereal, and I ate it cold.

On this, *my day,* it was a warm Friday morning. Something inside of me released a driving force to do one of the most daring things imaginable to a boy my age. Not yet old enough for school, I got myself up and pulled on a pair of summer shorts and tugged my red and yellow knit shirt over my head. The windows had been opened all night, and the soft air of morning had a gentle and pleasant sweetness, as if to say, "Donnie, this is your day!"

The curtains barely moved as the new breeze of daylight floated through the doors and corridors of our house. I had a goal. My goal was to disappear.

I could hear Mom readying herself in the bathroom, so I tip-toed through the kitchen and ever so quietly opened the old screen door. I pushed it open just far enough so I could slither my skinny little body through without so much as one of those annoying squeaks from its rusty old hinges.

Once through the old screen door, I ran to Mom's car. I jerked open the back door and crawled in, keeping low on the floor. Mom always had clothes, sweaters, blankets, and light jackets cluttered in the backseat. I laid down right behind the driver's seat and covered up with her old, navy blue sweater with the red cuffs and collar. *Hmmm!* It smelled like oranges. I found a handful of orange peelings stuffed in the pocket and left them there. It was the most pleasant aroma I enjoyed in quite some time.

Ah, yes. This was going to be a good day. I lay there, getting hotter by the minute. She always rolled the windows up at night, so I dare not roll them down now. The heat under that orange peel sweater was making me itch, but I stayed put until I heard the screen door squeak and heard her footsteps outside my hiding place.

She opened the driver's door and threw her purse and lunch bag across the wide front seat and then got in. She rolled both front windows down before starting the engine; so far, so good.

I felt her lean against the back of her seat and listened as she rummaged through her things in the back. *Oh, please, don't be looking for your navy blue sweater!* I think she found a silk scarf because when I peaked out, I could see her tie it around her neck and fashion it in a dainty knot. Checking it out in the mirror, she turned the key, ground the gears into reverse, and began to back out of the driveway. I was on my way to freedom!

As soon as she pulled out onto the dirt road, she turned on the radio. It was a cheery early morning program where requests were phoned in from listeners. The man and woman talking kept calling it the radio station of California coast love songs. I could even hear my mom quietly sing along to tunes she knew the words to. When she didn't know the words, she hummed. It was a voice I never heard before. A soft, sweet, gentle voice she kept hidden at home. I wanted to ride under the heat of that itchy old sweater all day just to hear her softly sing.

I got lost somewhere in the pleasantness of the ride. Suddenly, she was parking the old car and gathering her things together. She checked her lipstick in the mirror once more before snapping the closure of her purse and then got out.

The deadly silence was so loud to my ears that I began to panic. Now what was I going to do? My plans had gone no further than to not be home today, and so far my plan was on schedule.

Under the cover of the blue sweater, I could hear cars coming in, parking, doors slamming, and voices chatter. The sun continued to warm my hiding place as I waited I know not for what! Finally, I shed the cover of my blue sweater and crawled up on the seat, staying low. There was little activity in the parking lot now, and the morning grew very quiet. From time to time, I rolled down the back window for a little relief from the heat.

I have no idea how long I waited. I played make-believe games in my head. I drew imaginary pictures in the air and flew make-believe planes off the back of my hand. I was enjoying the backseat of my freedom. My stomach was letting me know I had neglected an even further area of my great plan. The orange peel in the pocket of the sweater smelled fresher by the minute. I hoped I might find a piece of candy or something left in a pocket of clothing cluttered on the seat. Digging through pockets, I found a half piece of Juicy Fruit gum. The wrapper was stuck and the gum was hard, but it tasted good. I also found a cherry-flavored Vicks cough drop with lint and dirt stuck to it. I put it in my pocket for later.

Voices began to creep louder and louder around the shelter I was enjoying. Several people were coming in my direction. Panicking, I lowered myself back to the floor and quickly pulled the navy blue sweater over myself. I heard a voice that sounded like my mother's talking with three or four people walking with her. They approached the car and opened the front door on the driver's side.

"I can't imagine that boy would have done a thing like that," Mom commented with an edge of irritation in her voice. "I certainly would have known if he crawled in this car!"

34

Never in my wildest nightmare did I expect the element of fear I was experiencing when I devised this great plan of mine. My half piece of Juicy Fruit gum was somewhere between my tonsils and my stomach. Someone opened the back door on the other side from where I was hiding. I tried my best to hold so still. They had to hear me breathing. Then the other back door opened on the side where I lay trembling. A big gnarly hand pulled off the sweater, and there I was—as exposed as if I had sprayed myself with fluorescent paint and glitter, shaking in violent uncontrollable fear.

"Well, lookie what we have here." These words came from the most threatening voice I had ever heard from a man I did not know.

"Donnie! What on earth are you doing in this car?" Mom stepped around the open door. For the moment, all she could say was, "How long…when did you…Donnie Foster! Do you know there are people at home looking everywhere for you? Do you realize the trouble you have caused? Do you know there are police out looking for you?"

Doom had infiltrated my perfect day! Now what was I to do? I swallowed my gum.

After several minutes of confused discussion, the element of surprise settled down. Mom asked the man with the threatening voice if he would please call her husband and tell him I had been found. He assured her he would take care of it and suggested she take the remainder of the day off. She pulled me to her side and asked if she could take me with her to go inside and gather her things.

"Well, under the circumstances, take him with you, but see to it this doesn't happen again. We're a place of business and not a babysitting or rescue facility."

She stopped at a water fountain to swallow a little blue pill. It was going to be a long ride home.

Strangely enough, very little was said as we drove back to the house. I rode in the backseat, and there was no radio music. There was no humming of gentle tunes. Mom's face had the same look of fear I was feeling.

Finally, after we had traveled a fair distance, the silence was broken.

"Donnie, do you have any idea what your father is going to do about this?"

Well, no, I hadn't, but now that the subject came up, I thought to myself, *What? A beating maybe?* That was a pretty normal occurrence. If that's what Dad was going to do, it didn't seem to make the day much different than any other day, except this time, I guess a beating seemed to be in order. That was the difference. Even at five years of age, I figured I had one coming. The good thing about the frequency of them was pretty simple. When I thought I had one coming, it didn't seem like such a terrifying thing. Maybe even earned!

"Yes, ma'am," I said. "Dad will beat me good when I get home."

I could smell the lunch in Mom's bag, but I was too afraid to ask for something to eat. I still had the Vicks cherry cough drop in my pocket, so I put it in my mouth … dirt, lint, and all.

We turned down our graveled lane. Police cars were still parked along the side of the house. Dad stood among them, shirtless and suspenders hanging below his waist.

I held on to the navy blue sweater when Mom grabbed me out of the backseat and pulled me in the house. She never stopped to discuss the ordeal with anyone. The air was hard to breathe.

She escorted me directly to my room. I knew what was coming. She grabbed the sweater from my hands and walked out. If she spoke to me, I don't remember. But I remember thinking I wish the men outside would stay for a long, long time.

I heard the screen door open and close, and Mom walked around the corner of the house. Purse in hand, she seated herself behind the steering wheel. She laid her head on the steering wheel and, for a long time, just sat there. Once or twice she pounded her fists against the steering wheel. She never looked up. I couldn't tell if she was crying or just angry. Soon she checked herself in the mirror that hung from the window, ran her fingers through her hair, and started the car. She spoke to no one. Dad pretended he didn't see.

I watched the men as they talked and moved about a little while longer. One of the smaller of the policemen handed my dad a clipboard with paper on it and a pen.

"Just sign here, sir, and we'll be on our way. I'm glad we found your boy. These things don't always have a happy ending."

A happy ending? I knew for me the end had not yet come. One by one, they returned to their cars, and one by one they drove away. Dad shook the hand of the last one to leave, and I heard him say, "I can't thank you enough for your help. It's a father's worst nightmare to get up and discover one of your children is missing. All I could think of was the worst that could be happening to him. Thanks again."

The worst that could be happening hadn't happened yet. The worst was still to come.

I hid under the covers. I heard him walk through the kitchen and guessed he was opening a bottle of anger management to support the wrath that was seething inside him. If it weren't for the growling of my empty stomach, there would not have been a sound in the house. I was hungry, but I knew better than to stir his wrath just now. Besides, as soon as the beating was over, I would probably throw up. I stayed under the covers until...

"Boy! Get out here!"

I was right not to eat. The beating was severe, and I ran outside. I threw up red stuff that tasted like cherry Vicks.

It was getting dark, and Mom still wasn't home. While Dad wasted himself on the sofa, I fixed myself a sandwich and found some stale chips on the counter. I dared not create a stir, so I ate my bologna sandwich dry without ketchup. The ketchup was on the top shelf and out of reach. I had welts across my back and legs that stung when I tried to sit and bruises on my arms that ached. The salt from the stale potato chips burned the open wound on my upper lip. My face hurt, but I was relieved the day was over—or so I thought.

I ate my sandwich and went back to my room. I could hear my brother's radio behind an adjoining wall. I wished I could go to him. I doubted that he even knew what all happened today. Mom hadn't come back yet, and I knew that was adding to Dad's anger.

I was beginning to finally feel relief that the day was over when my door opened and Dad's frame shadowed against the light behind him.

"Get up, boy! We're goin' for a ride."

"Where're we goin'?"

"Just get up."

"But—"

"Did you hear me, boy? I said get up!"

I was still wearing my summer shorts and the red and yellow knit shirt. I was barefoot, and the welts on my legs and back were sore.

"Go get in the truck."

Were we going to go look for Mom? We never did before, but then I didn't remember any time when she was gone so long or so late. At least it seemed late. The early morning excitement of my great escape seemed like forever ago.

Dad crawled in and started the engine. The familiar smell of stale booze, sweat, cigars, and exhaust made me feel sick.

We pulled out on the road in front of our house and turned to the left.

"So, you want to run away from home, huh, boy? Well, seein' as how you're my boy now and I'm your dad, I think it's my responsibility to help you out with big jobs like that. You just ride along here, boy, and I'm goin' to help your little dream come true."

Was he taking me back to the place where Mom worked? Why? Where was he helping me run away to?

We drove down county roads, made a few turns, and soon we

were on a deserted dirt road. There were no city lights in the distance, no house lights anywhere, nothing but dust and dark and Dad.

"Get out, boy."

"Huh?"

"I said get out!"

"Right now?"

"Yeah, now! You wanna run away, get out and run!" He reached across me and lifted the door handle and pushed the door open. "Get out!"

I was stunned. Was he serious?

"Boy! I said get out!"

His big foot pushed me over the edge of the seat. I tripped over the running board and fell to the gravel on the edge of the dirt road. Now, my knees stung as well as my back and legs. All I could think was that I didn't have the navy blue sweater with the red cuffs and collar that smelled like oranges.

I got to my feet, and the last thing I heard was his laughter over the rattling sound of the old pickup as he took off down the dirt road. I could see the passenger door still open, and the exhaust smell made me sick. The last thing I saw was the lights go out. There was nothing but total blackness that was moving in to crush me under the breath of my fear.

I couldn't see the path of the dirt road. I didn't know if I was on flat ground or if there were slight or steep embankments beside me. I didn't know if I was in open field country or if there was the mystery of forests and their eerie sounds around me. I was a little child, and I was alone in the darkest dark I ever knew existed.

I will never forget the lights of that old pickup truck that simply went out in front of the dust that smothered the last light of hope I could see. Where was the small policeman with the clipboard now?

My memory fails me concerning the next few minutes or hours. In searching for the answer to my rescue, Mom recalls arriving home terror stricken at what had been done. She drove with my

Dad to where he had dropped me off. My memory, however, has closed the door on the rescue.

You will find, as my story unfolds, why there were memories wiped from my mind, but somehow, at some point, I got home.

But I do remember reaching out to hold the smell of Mom's navy blue sweater.

Looking back, I have no doubt that angels had been summoned to watch over me, but then, being preschool age, I had no knowledge of angels.

There is surely a future hope for you and that hope *will not* be cut off.

Proverbs 23:18 (NIV)

These were young and tender years when a child should know what it meant to be loved and cared for. I did not know what love was, that it had feelings, that people offered it, gave it away, and embraced it in return. All I knew of life and its day-to-day activities was a fight to survive

I was somewhere between the ages of five or six when the monster we knew as Dad simply disappeared. As far as I knew, he merely left one day and, for weeks, never returned. I never asked where he was, nor did I wonder why he was gone. He simply was no longer there, and I was glad.

Mom fared well financially for herself and her boys without him. The longer he remained absent, the more my daily confidence improved. That knot in my gut slowly disappeared. Seldom did I have to swallow to keep my stomach from heaving itself from that pit of terror I could not control.

Though my life was improving, Mom seemed always uptight and nervous. She became edgy and overly cautious about everything.

She arrived home after work one night, fed the four of us boys, and put the two youngest to bed. I was probably five, my older brother was somewhere between six and seven, my younger

40

brother was four, and our half brother was somewhere around a year old.

My older sibling and I had our baths and were in our pajamas when he asked Mom if we could sleep in her bed that night.

She said, "Of course. Now go brush your teeth, and I'll come and tuck you in."

It was always a treat to sleep in Mom's big bed. I was never brave enough to ask, but I was always brave enough to include myself when given the slightest opportunity.

We ran to the bathroom and gave our teeth a flying effort at brushing and ran to be the first in Mom's bed. We were still awake when she herself came in to retire. Our two younger brothers had been asleep for some time.

We laid there and giggled, begging Mom to tell us a story.

"All riiiight." She finally decided it would take less time to tell us a story than to get us to quit begging. She began some aging tale when she suddenly sat straight up in bed. My older brother also sat up to attention.

"Mama, did you hear that? What was that noise?"

"I didn't hear nuthin,'" I said, wanting the story to continue.

Mom flipped on a small lamp next to the bed. I could see my brother's eyes were as big as saucers. He pulled the sheet up under his chin, and I could feel him shake. As I sat there, I heard a noise that sounded like it came from the kitchen. It sounded like someone dropped a spoon or fork into the sink.

"I heard something," I said. I was caught up in the excitement around me, but I really wasn't afraid.

"What was that?"

"You boys stay here. Don't you dare step out of this room, do you hear me?" We both shook our heads indicating we heard, but as soon as Mom stepped through the door, we were out of the bed and right behind her.

She gingerly crept down the hall and stepped into the front room. We were right at her heels. She could see the kitchen from where we hid in the darkness. As she stepped forward, the kitchen light came on, and there stood Ben. We could only see his silhouette, but we knew it was him. He raised his right arm, and I heard a click. He had a gun in his right hand, and we were in his sights.

"Evenin,' May."

"What are you doing here?"

"I came for my boy."

"What are you talking about?"

"My son, May. I came for my son."

"Ben, you can't do that. He's my son too, and you can't just walk in here and take him."

"Go git 'im, May."

"No, I'm not going to go get him. You get out of here or I'll call the police!"

With that, she stepped closer to the kitchen where we had our one and only phone. Ben saw the two of us huddled behind her, and before we knew what was happening, he stepped around Mom and grabbed me and my brother in a tight grip and put the gun in his hand to our heads.

"Now, go get the boy, May."

Mom stood there dumbfounded. She couldn't move, and she couldn't speak.

"I mean it, May. You go get my boy, or I blow their brains out right here and then yours."

"Ben, what is wrong with you? Please—"

"Go get him, May."

Mom started to move toward the back of the house where the two younger boys were asleep. Ben kept his arm around us and shoved us ahead of him into the hallway. Mom stopped and turned to say something when Ben shoved us to the floor and grabbed Mom and drew the gun to her temple.

"Now, are you gonna get my boy?"

"I'll get him." She stepped into the bedroom where their only son lay sleeping. Ben grabbed me and held the gun to my head while she scrambled to pack what few belongings he had. She had no luggage, so she stuffed all of his clothes, a few toys, and diapers into a pillow cover and picked up the sleeping baby.

"All right. Now we're all walking to the door together." He shoved the pillowcase full of baby things in my brother's hand and took the baby from Mom. Mom stepped up between Ben and the two of us, and we walked to the door, keeping an eye on Ben and the sleepy-eyed baby.

"Don't try anything stupid, May. It will only get somebody hurt. You so much as call the cops or do anything to get this boy back, and I'll come back! When I do, I'll kill you and your sorry kids. You got that, May? I said you got that, May?"

"Yes, Ben. I understand."

With that, he walked side-angled steps to his truck, never taking his eyes from Mom. He opened the driver's door and all but threw the baby across the front seat to the passenger's side. My brother walked up and handed him the stuffed pillow cover. He grabbed it and threw the baby's belongings under the dash. That was the last we saw of Ben.

For months and months, that last night of reigning terror hung over our home like a plague. More than ever, Mom depended on medications to relieve the memory, the fear, the hurt, and the horror of that night. To my knowledge, she did not see her youngest son for years to come. She continued to work to keep us fed and the bills paid. My brother and I returned to school in the fall, so Mom's babysitting expenses lightened to provide daycare for only one child. We coasted. We didn't go hungry, but Mom knew she needed help.

Mom was a beautiful young woman. Gentleman callers came to our door from time to time, but with three boys in the shadow, most guys weren't willing to pick up the baggage we brought to the relationship. Then she met Frank.

Frank was a schoolteacher. He called on her every now and then, but there was never any interest shown in me or my brothers. He didn't seem to care if we were there or not. I was just relieved to be able to walk freely through my own home, sit where I wanted, watch TV if I chose, help myself to a snack as I passed through the kitchen, and play as I desired. I still had no idea that anyone loved me. My joy in life was simply cradled in the euphoria of being unafraid.

THE AGE OF INFLUENCE
THE CATALYST: **FEAR**

Fathers, do not embitter your children or they will become discouraged.

Colossians 3:21(NIV)

By the time I was seven, Mom married Frank, the schoolteacher. He started out to be a financial help to Mom. He taught the fall and spring semesters and was home during the summer when school was out.

My euphoria of being fear free was short lived. As hopeful as my life seemed when Ben left home, Frank's presence restored everything I thought disappeared with Ben's absence. Frank and Ben were bred from the same stock of angry, hateful men. Frank returned all the hatefulness to our home that I had grown accustomed to from the man I knew as my father. And once again, I faced anger directed at me.

Somewhere along the way, I acquired a BB gun. I don't remember if I received one as a gift or if it belonged to one of my brothers and got passed on to me, but I remember the last day I captured outlaws with it.

Soon after summer vacation started, I was allowed to have a friend over for a sleepover. It might have been a cousin, a neighbor; I don't really remember. But he had a BB gun too. We had occupied the backyard playing cowboys and ranchers with BB guns full of shot.

We weren't idiots. We set some ground rules before we played—no aiming above the shoulders. Besides, neither of us were a good enough shot to hit something as small as the other guy's head. For some reason, we thought our skinny little bodies would be easier targets.

We had quite a shootout going on at the old waterin' hole in our backyard. He was a cattleman shooting for the rights of his heifers, and I was the sheriff trying to run him and his cattle out of Dodge. I was hiding behind a turned over lawn chair, and he was shooting from behind a tree.

Down behind my lawn chair, I crawled on my belly, shoving the chair ahead of me where I could get a good aim at him behind the tree. I fired a few good rounds from that position, but when I had the chance, I rolled out from behind my cover and slipped in behind the corner of the house. I had a good open view and had him in my sights. I pumped the lever on my Daisy BB gun and pulled the trigger.

"*Ow! Ow, ow, ow, ow!*" The worst crying, screaming, and carrying on I ever heard was coming from behind the tree. Mom came running out and nearly ran me over trying to see what the commotion was about. The hombre I was after threw his gun on the ground and grabbed his nose. I didn't know whether to run or go see what the problem was. I knew I aimed low enough. Maybe a bee stung him.

When Mom finally got him calmed down enough to see what all the yelling and screaming was about, there it was. Stuck right in the side of his nose—my BB!

Up until now, we'd been having a good time. I looked toward the house in time to see Frank step through the back door. The breath I was taking got stuck in my chest. Mom was taking my wounded rancher to the house to call his mom. Frank was coming after me.

I knew better than to run or even open my mouth. Frank never said a word. His piercing eyes never left mine. He simply reached out and grabbed my BB gun and swung it against the tree and busted it. BBs rolled everywhere. That was the least of my worries. He slapped at my legs with the splintered piece he still held in his hand and bloodied them. Then he took off his belt and gave me the licking of my life. It didn't matter which way I turned. He cursed at me with every swing of the belt. He thrashed me with his belt repeatedly, creating welts wherever they hit. I had slashes across my chest and my back. Then when he'd done enough with the belt, he backhanded me across the yard, and I fell over the lawn chair that had been my cover. When Frank was angry, there was no hiding behind cover. Frank went back in the house, and I stayed outside. Outside of the cursing, he never said another word.

Mom immediately put my wounded friend in the car and took him to the doctor. I learned later she had called home to tell Frank they were sending her with the boy on to the hospital. They had to surgically remove the shot from his nose. The miracle of this story? The kid had a deviated septum, which acted as a cushion and stopped the BB from entering any further inside his head. Had I hit a fraction of an inch in any direction, the results might have been much, much worse. Yes, I admit, it was all fun and games and it was an accident. We should *never* have been allowed to have BBs in the guns in the backyard. For that, I deserved to be disciplined, but with Frank, it was not discipline; it was pure hatred unleashed at any opportunity that came along.

I stayed outside long after dark until Mom returned from the hospital. Several hours had passed, and I was hungry and hurting. By the time she returned, Frank was wiped out on the couch from highballs. Mom fed us and put us boys to bed. The busted BB gun lay under the tree in the backyard until it rusted and rotted. It was always a dark reminder of a good day gone bad.

Frank had several children from a previous marriage, and in time, two of his boys came to live with us. My memories of Frank and his boys in our home left deep scars burned onto the pages of my childhood reverie.

With his kids came toys we could never afford. Both of his boys had a bicycle, and within a short period of time, my brother also somehow acquired one.

Frank's boys soon joined forces with my brother, and in time, it became them against me. Having allies under our own roof encouraged him to focus his rage and terror at me, just like Ben used to do. The three of them quickly became a constant threat to me.

All my life I wondered what made me so different from other boys. I would be the first to admit I was no angel. I was a typical adolescent boy whose disrupted life became a battleground for survival and favor from someone. Looking back, I know now, love was the missing ingredient. I had no other father figure to run to or call on when I needed the positive voice of a true man. I ran from them, yet I was destined to become just like the men that terrorized my life as a lad. I had none other with which to compare the ways or the spirit of a man.

This particular day, I had been taunting Frank's two boys and my older brother. I pestered them, begging to have a turn riding down the street and back, just one time, on one of their bikes. Instead of simply telling me no, it was a bigger challenge for them to use me as a target. On their speeding rides, it was a challenging attempt to knock me down or make me run.

Survival was teaching me to be aggressive, so I poised myself, ready to grab my oldest stepbrother taking aim at me as he peddled across the yard. I reached out to pull and jerk on the handlebars, but as he approached me, he got just close enough to take a swing at me with a stick. I saw the stick a little too late, and as I turned, he struck me behind my knees and bloodied my leg. By now I had a very high tolerance for pain, and the sting it left was nothing more than a vengeful fit of aggravation. I swore a few threatening words at him, only to turn and see my brother barreling down the sidewalk headed straight for me, his head low, pedaling for all he had. Already on the ground, I rolled to try and dodge the speeding maniac on the bike. The bike pedal slightly nicked my skinny shin as he coasted full speed and bumped across the yard on his moving bullet. He slammed on the brakes and spun the bike around. I knew he wasn't giving up. When he stopped long enough to pick up a stick for himself, I jumped up and hit the ground running. I headed around the corner of the house just as the younger stepbrother came out of nowhere with a rock the size of a baseball and hurled it in my direction. He missed my running figure, so I picked up my strides and continued around the house.

I now had all three of them chasing me with sticks and taking swings at me as they sped by me on their bicycles. I ran through our yard and the yard next door. My only reprieve was to make sudden turns, causing them to slow enough to skid or slide and pick up their chase. I looked back to see just where they were when I ran full speed into the street and directly into the path of a car.

The impact knocked me a hundred plus feet in the air. I came down on the concrete face first and tumbled several yards. My leg was broken, and the bone was protruding through the flesh. I remember smelling that funny smell I experienced whenever there was a severe blow to the head or face or especially on the bridge of the nose. It was like no other odor. I vaguely recall the driver running to pick me up. He ran with me to a house, not knowing where I lived. Somehow he found the house that was ours. My brother and stepbrothers disappeared on impact, I'm sure.

I remember Frank grabbing me from the driver's arms without caution of care or concern that the femur of my leg was poking through my flesh. He laid me on the sofa where I floated in and out in agonizing pain while the driver of the car and Frank exchanged conversation. I could hear the conversation as though I were in another dimension.

I heard the driver leave once he felt secure that the accident was not his fault. I heard Frank assure him he would not be called upon to fund any of the medical expenses that I was going to hear about for months to come.

My head swam with the rhythm of Frank's voice in my semiconscious state, cussing and cursing at my stupidity—what idiot kid would do what I had done; didn't I have any better sense than to get hit by a car? Not once did Frank ask me about the pain or show any compassion for what had happened, not to mention any concern over the fact I might have been killed. His only words of solace were to make sure I knew I was an idiot and this was going to cost him a bundle.

The arrival of the paramedics and the ambulance quieted Frank's ranting and raving. Once in the care of emergency personnel, the cold sheets of a sterile-smelling gurney became very comforting to me. In the haze of drugs and the consolation of caring people, I heard the sweetest voice that I'll never forget. "Hey there, big man." She brushed the hair that lay tousled against my forehead. I could feel the sting of open scrapes and scratches on my face.

"Hi. My name is Susie, and I'll be taking care of you. What on earth happened?"

I had no words. I forfeited the funny smell of injury inside my head to the sweet fragrance of Susie's soft and gentle perfume.

She took my hand and assured me I would be okay and that I soon would drift off to sleep and the pain would quickly go away.

I faded off an angry hurting child.

When I awoke, it was Susie standing beside my bed. From my waist down, I was confined in a hard plaster cast. I saw my leg hoisted up in the air in a sling-type contraption and remember thinking of old Bess when she was hoisted up by her back legs. A shudder of panic tried to penetrate the haze I was under, and I closed my eyes. I dozed in and out, always waking to see if Susie was there. Several times I heard her talking to someone with her head down and eyes closed, and I heard her say my name, but I didn't know who she was talking to. Neither Frank nor Mom was anywhere around.

I remember waking one morning, and she was holding my hand. I heard her asking someone named Jesus to please heal my wounds and heal my spirit. Was she talking to a doctor? What was wrong with my spirit? I didn't know I had one. I didn't remember wounding it. Different times I thought, *Why would you talk to someone and keep your eyes shut?* Both Frank and Ben would yell at me, "Look at me, boy, when I'm talking to you!"

Once, I asked her, "Who are you talking to?"

She pulled the blanket up under my chin and cupped my face in her hands and said, "I'm talking to someone who loves you very, very much. He's my best friend, and I hope he can be yours too."

As a lad, I needed a friend.

Mom would drop in from time to time just to say hi and then quickly be gone. She was still holding down a very hectic work schedule, and her time was limited. Looking back, I know now how restricted visiting hours were for patients in the intensive care unit. At the time, the only thing I could think of was that the shortness of Mom's visit was at Frank's orders. He had no time for me, and he tried to control her time and dedication to me.

The radio and television in the room were options for those wealthy enough to afford it. To this adolescent child, twenty-four hours, seven days a week on my back in a lower body cast became an eternity. I had nothing to do but think. I kept telling myself this was better than being exposed to Frank and my brothers at home. Susie's company was the one thing I looked forward to every day. When she had a day off, it was as if the door had been slammed on my hope. I became familiar with a new emotion called depression when she was not there. Whenever she was near, I felt the unfamiliar tranquility of peace.

As the weeks passed, the lower body cast was removed and replaced with a hip-to-toe cast. Finally, the day arrived. I was going home!

Mom and Frank came to pick me up. Mom opened the front passenger door for me to get in. She adjusted the seat as far back as it would go, but it was still a good trick to get my long cast in the front. She crawled in the backseat behind Frank. As soon as the car door slammed shut, Frank started in.

"Now, Donnie! I hope you know this inconsiderate little prank of yours is costing us money we don't have. Every day you laid up there doin' nuthin,' you cost me a bundle so I hope you came up with a good idea for paying for your stupid little prank! You get this one thing straight, and you get it now: don't you even *think* about anything that will ever cost me another dime. Do you understand me, boy?"

I said I did. I was just glad to be outside, traveling, seeing something, anything, besides white, chalky walls, white bed sheets, white coats, white uniforms, and white caps—except for Susie's. Susie's wasn't white but a radiant shade of joy and warmth, probably the closest thing I ever felt to love. I didn't know I loved Susie, but I knew she made me feel like somebody special, and I liked it. I always meant to ask her more about who she was talking to when her head was down and there was no one in the room. That was one thing I didn't understand about her.

Once home, the terror of hell started all over again. Frank never missed an opportunity to terrorize me by attacking me physically or verbally. I was now, more than ever before, a bother to him. It was summer, and school was out. Frank was home every day, and Mom was never home. My stepbrothers and brother were also gone every day hanging out with friends. Frank took care of Frank, and I was on my own, so again I did without decent meals just for the lack of being immobile for the first couple weeks. Frank was not about to offer any aide in dealing with the necessities of day-to-day living.

The cast encased my leg up to my hip. I could maneuver myself around but with great difficulty. Frank delighted in jabbing me on my mending leg. Several times a day, I would see him coming in my direction, and I couldn't move fast enough to avoid the pounding he would inflict on my leg. I would scream out in pain while he sneered and walked away. Even before the cast came off, he would kick my wounded leg or he would hit it with his fist when I had it elevated.

I remember one day in particular. I was struggling to walk with the cast and crutches. I was only allowed to be on my feet for no more than the bare necessities of a day. I could walk to the bathroom, walk to the table and back to my chair, and walk to my room at night. Frank repeatedly found reason (or perhaps no reason at all) to pass by me and strike my leg. I was still recovering from one outburst of inflicted pain when stomach cramps gripped my belly and the urge to quickly make my way to the bathroom hit me. I started to get to my feet when Frank came around the corner and paused long enough to line me up like a punter and then kicked my mending leg from behind. I hit the floor in excruciating pain to my hips, and the back of my head struck something nearby. I remember my sight going black as I grappled to protect myself. Before I regained control of my senses, the very worst happened. I lost control, and I soiled myself.

Frank went ballistic! For a few seconds, he was without words, but that was short lived. Several verbal outbursts of cursing and screaming followed before he turned and left the house.

Looking back, that was a trophy day! I do believe that was the first time I ever held the upper hand with Frank. The unexpected happened, and he didn't know what to say. Satisfying as that seemed for a moment, I was left to clean up myself and the mess I left on the floor. I was alone in the house, but I managed. I wrapped my soiled clothes in layers of newspaper to hide the odor and threw them in the garbage can out back. The can was nearly full, so I rummaged through the trash and garbage debris to place the telltale bundle near the bottom of the can.

Once back in the house and able to relax, all I could think of was Susie. How I missed her sweet smile and tender hands of healing. She had a way of helping me care for my personal needs that didn't make me feel like a bother. For several moments, I truly wished to return to the white chalky walls, white sheets, white coats, white dresses, and hats. White had no shadow of darkness, and darkness had again become a plague in my world of survival.

It is good that one should hope and wait quietly for the salvation of the Lord.

Lamentations 3:26 (NKJV)

Because I was never told I might not walk normal again, I was soon carrying on as any young boy would. I naturally had a limp, which became my dreaded curse. I was teased unmercifully and called names by my brothers. Frank took every opportunity to shove me and knock me off balance whenever I walked close to him. I would walk out of my way to avoid him, and he would walk out of his way to shove me. His delight in pushing and calling me his little crippled kid kept me off balance physically and emotionally. I was becoming a very bitter and angry young man.

I had been out of my cast for a while when I was called back to the attending physician for a checkup to see how I was doing. The doctor was surprised at the progress I made. I wanted to tell him that when running was required as a tool for survival, a kid my age mended and restored needful agility pretty fast.

He manually moved my leg to check for strength and a range of motion, and for the most part, he was satisfied. He turned to Frank and said, "It would be good if the boy could just do more walking and not so much running, at least for the next few months. He's healing really well, but I don't want to see him over stressing the healing of the fracture."

"Sure, doc, we'll see to it he gets in a good walk every day."

Frank shook the doctor's hand, asked the office girl to please send us the bill, and as we walked to the truck, he shoved me off the curb. He walked on into the parking area behind the office while I stumbled but stayed on my feet. I looked toward the building to see if anyone might have witnessed that little moment, but I could see the blinds were pulled, so I got in the truck. We pulled out onto the street in the opposite direction of home.

"Where're we going?"

"You'll see."

I wasn't familiar with the area we were driving in, but Frank soon pulled up in front of a junk shop. At least that's what it appeared to be. Outside the dilapidated old building, a wringer washer and some tubs gathered California dust in the hot sun. Old garden tools leaned against the building and a couple of old bicycles were propped up in front. The front door was open, and it appeared quite dark inside. There was one lone light bulb hanging from a cord in the middle of the room. The sun that filtered through the dingy windows lit up the dust that filled the air.

"Wait here, boy. I'm gonna buy you a gift."

"Yeah, right," I muttered to myself.

He stepped up on the broken down stoop and peered in. I could hear him and another man talking. They came out together and walked around to the side of building. I heard Frank say, "Now, I ain't spendin' over a couple bucks for one."

"Yeah, I think I got one back here I can let you have for, oh, say three dollars. Ya might hav'ta sharpen the blades, but it rolls good."

My body was feeling the heat as I waited in the car. My anger was rising as well.

I remember having a feeling about me that I would describe as *dark*. Looking back, I believe it to be the spirit of revenge welling up inside of me. I couldn't have recognized it as revenge; I just knew my feelings of hatred were evolving into darker and deeper enmity toward Frank. My bitterness toward him was becoming so vile I was repulsed by the man's very appearance. I had lost myself deep in these thoughts when I heard him open the tailgate of his old truck. I turned to look out the back window, and he was picking up my gift—a push reel lawn mower. Frank and the man walked around to the driver's door, and Frank handed the man a few bills. He pointed to me and said, "Right there's the boy that's gonna be pushin' that fine piece of equipment."

"Tell your dad to get those blades sharpened for you, son. That's a good old mower. You ought to be able to make lots of money mowing yards with that." So that was it.

Frank climbed in, and all the way home, he made cracks about his poor, little crippled kid mowing yards to earn a few pennies for bread.

Within a few days, he had several neighborhood lawns lined up for me to mow, and it was he that set my price. He was pleased with himself that he got me out from under foot and, in so doing, he was quite satisfied I had to struggle to exercise my leg as the doctor requested. It was hard on my leg, but for every yard I mowed and got paid, the more excited I got about mowing the next one. Within a few weeks, I had earned enough money to buy myself an old beat up gas-powered mower from one my customers. The old gentlemen who sold it to me helped me get it running and offered it to me for just a few dollars if I would mow his yard for free for the next two months. That was my first experience tinkering at mechanics, and it felt good.

I should have known better than to let any enthusiasm for a good thing show. My accomplishments and my happiness about my purchase were like an acid burn to Frank. When he saw I had actually endured and excelled at something, he intended to be an infliction of pain on me; his anger overruled his common sense. He sabotaged my mower so that I had to continue to mow with the old push reel mower.

That did it! Every time I walked through the garage and saw my mower sitting there, anger burned through me like the fire behind a Roman candle. Frank even talked about selling *my mower* as though it were his own. I grew to despise the very sight of it. I hated Frank, and I hated that mower. I wanted them both out of my sight and out of my life.

Why couldn't Frank just die or at least leave like Ben did?

I walked by that old mower one day, and the hate in my gut threw my brain into overload. I knew Frank was in the back of the house with at least one of my stepbrothers. My brother was in the front room watching television, and Mom wasn't home from work yet. I picked up a box of things belonging to my aunt and uncle. I really didn't pay any attention to the contents, I just saw their name on the lid, and it was a good size box for what I had in mind.

In my mind, today was the day Frank was going to die.

For several weeks prior to this special day, I had developed a fetish for fire. One day, I set the field on fire out behind our housing addition. Wow! What a rush! It was a great feeling to have the power to control a whole community and watch as they turned their attention to something as exciting as flames fighting to survive.

I knew how they felt. I was like those flames, fighting to survive while being stoked by the fury of hate, anger, and abuse. The fire trucks arrived, and the flames lost. I knew how it felt to lose and have hope extinguished.

Today was the culmination of too many days of fear and abuse. When I walked by my lawn mower, my anger overcame my fear, and I was compelled to come out of pyromania retirement. Today was the day things were going to be different. I paused long enough in front of that old lawn mower to make the decision to do what I had to do.

I set the box of my uncle's belongings right beside my mower. I even opened the lid and added some things to the box—some old newspapers, some old, dried-out paintbrushes and wood sticks for stirring the paint, and some oily rags Frank used for wiping up when he worked on the car.

I didn't want anyone else in the house to die—just Frank. But anger doesn't always allow for wise thinking, or even thinking at all.

I walked to the coat hooks beside the door leading into the kitchen. There, Frank hung his old work shirts, and I knew he always had a book of matches in his shirt pocket. I fished them out and lit one. Then I lit the rest of the matches in the book and dropped them into my uncle's box of things. I immediately went into the house through the kitchen and into the front room where my brother was watching a rerun of *Get Smart.*

"Where's Frank?" I asked in my most controlled voice.

"I don't know. In the bathroom, I think."

Within a matter of what seemed like an eternity, the box of my uncle's things burned down to ignite the gas mower, and the garage exploded. My brother jumped to his feet, and I followed. He ran to the kitchen door and jerked it open and the flames from the garage engulfed the kitchen within seconds. He started to scream, "Fire! Fire! Get out! The house is on fire!"

I said nothing. I went outside. I wanted Frank to die. I wanted Frank to die. I wanted, more than anything, for Frank to die in the fire.

Someone called the fire department, and the fire was extinguished. The house was a total loss. Frank survived. We all survived, and we moved into a small apartment someone provided for us. We lost the house and all we had, except Frank.

I was a fearful and angry, out-of-control young man with ideals developed from hate bent on destruction, and now I had the desire to kill.

After the house fire, my rage for vengeance quieted down. Even Frank never accused me of starting the fire. If the cause was investigated, I don't remember. Life simply went on.

But something inside of me was happening. After several weeks, I emerged from that incident with a tremendous guilt complex. I couldn't eat, I couldn't sleep, and I couldn't face anyone. I now had a new emotion to further complicate fear, hate, and anger in my life—a guilt complex.

Due to the location and small size of the apartment we were in, there was literally nothing for me to do during any free time but think, and all I could think about was what I had done.

One day I told my mom about the fire. She was washing dishes at the sink, and I bravely stepped up and said, "Mom, I started that fire in our house."

"What did you say?"

"The fire, Mom; I started it."

"What on earth are you saying, Donnie?"

"I did, Mom. I started the fire."

She dried her hands on her apron and sat down next to me at the table. She pulled me to her and said, "Donnie, look at me. Are you telling me the truth?"

"Yes, Mom. I lit a book of matches and dropped them in a box, and the fire started."

For a few moments, she was speechless, and I just stood there waiting for the worst. Finally, she spoke.

"Donnie, you have to tell Frank."

"Mom, I can't. I can't tell Frank. He'll beat me, Mom. He'll beat me bad." I started to shake. "Please, Mom, don't make me tell Frank. I had to tell you, but I know what Frank will do, Mom. Please. Don't make me tell Frank."

Why did I tell her? I tried to pull away from her, but she pulled me even tighter to herself, and then she cupped my face in her hands.

"You listen to me. It's the right thing to do. Now, Donnie, I know I don't always do the right thing, but this time we have to. You were very brave and did the right thing to tell me, but now we have to tell Frank. I'll go with you, and we'll tell him together, but, Donnie, we have to tell him."

I felt like I was choking on my own tongue. I was shaking so bad I didn't know if I could even walk into the bedroom where Frank was watching television.

"Okay, Donnie. Let's go do it now, and then it will be over." She took my hand and put her arm around my shoulders. She held me close to her, and together we approached the man I tried to kill.

"Yeah? Whaddya want?" was his response when we stepped into the bedroom.

"Frank, Donnie has something he wants to tell you."

"Not now. I'm watchin' TV."

Well, that was a relief. Out of conditioning from this man, I turned to go. If Frank didn't want to mess with me, I learned I'd better leave. Mom's grip on my hand tightened.

"No, Frank. Donnie needs to tell you something *now*."

Those hateful burning eyes stung my face.

"Yeah, whaddya wanna tell me? Make it snappy. I'm busy."

"I started the fire."

He sat up a little straighter on the bed and took those hateful eyes from me and looked at Mom.

"You what?"

My whole body was shaking so bad that I could hardly talk. My jaws wouldn't move, and my voice was squeaky.

"I did it, Frank. I started the fire in our house." This time it got him to his feet.

I stood there and put my hands to my face and closed my eyes. I waited for the first blow that I knew was coming. Then Mom spoke.

"I don't know, Frank. He says he started the fire."

I couldn't look at either one of them. I didn't want to see what was going to happen. Please, just get it over with.

There was no blow. There was no cursing. It was silent. Then Frank grabbed me by the shoulders.

"Now you listen to me, boy! You don't tell nobody this, ya hear? Nobody!"

I don't remember what I did after that. I just remember going to bed that night thinking sometime during the night he would come to my room and deliver the beating his anger was working up to. I must have slept because the next morning when I awoke, Frank had not shown himself. There had been no yelling or cursing. I was afraid to leave my room, but I had to go to the bathroom, so I ventured out my door. Frank was sitting at the kitchen table, and Mom was gone.

"Hey, boy. Do you remember what I told you last night about telling nobody 'bout that fire?"

I shook my head.

"All right then. I don't ever want to hear you *ever* talk 'bout that fire. Never! You hear me, boy? If I ever hear you say one word about that fire, I'll beat you within an inch of your life. You got that?" I shook my head.

I remember the day the check from the insurance company arrived. There was celebration.

> Be merciful to me, O God, for man would swallow me up; fighting all day he oppresses me; my enemies would hound me all day for there are many who fight against me, O Most High.
>
> Psalms 56:1–2 (NKJV)

After we moved into our new house the insurance money built, Mom and Frank became the parents of *their* child. Mom gave birth to my half brother. At first, I figured he would be just an annoyance that kept Mom even less interested in anything else going on in the house. Looking back, I wonder if yet another child didn't push her past the edge of her weakest fortitude. Did she ever have aspirations that our home would function like a well-oiled machine? I can't speak for her, and yet, in the midst of all the turmoil within the framework we called home, that tiny infant touched a chord in my heart. It was foreign to anything I had ever felt. I truly cared for that little baby. I found great pleasure in tending to him, watching him, talking to him, feeling so very special every time he cocked that little head and smiled at me. I felt special when he would take my finger in his tiny hand while I talked and he would listen and laugh. He was the one reason I had for returning home at the end of the day.

Frank resented anything that gave me pleasure or satisfaction. When he began to notice the attention I was giving the baby, he tried to put a stop to it. As my little half brother grew from an infant to a toddler, I so badly wanted to hold him, sit on the floor with him and play, bounce him on my knee, and hear him giggle, but anytime Frank saw the child respond to me, I was slapped or kicked and told, "Get away from that kid, and go mind your own business!"

One evening, I witnessed Frank slapping the child for reaching for a delicate figurine. I slipped back into my room and closed the door behind me, wondering what I could do to prevent this sweet baby from knowing the fear I knew. There had to be a better life.

Later that night, the scenario picked up where it left off. My baby brother's eye again was drawn to the shiny glass figurine, and his tiny hands reached for it. Frank's yell startled the baby, and he began to cry. I had to intervene. Off the top of my head, I blurted out a most asinine offer.

"Don't, Frank! Hit me! Hit me!"

"What?"

"Please, Frank, don't hit the baby. Hit me."

"That's the stupidest thing to ever come out of your mouth,

but if that's the way you want it..." He backhanded me across the face. He busted my lip, but I knew it gave him satisfaction.

I wiped the blood on my sleeve while Frank said, "Boy, you're a bigger fool than I thought you were. Are you nuts?"

Maybe I was, but I believe what I felt for that innocent child was the closest thing to love I'd ever experienced. I looked down at that little face that looked back at me and smiled. I just knew I didn't ever want him to experience the life I knew at his innocent age.

"Just beat me, Frank, but please don't do that to the baby."

"Well, I'll be. How stupid can one idiot kid be? I believe a beatin' *is* the best thing for a fool."

And so it was. Any discipline he felt needed to be administered to my infant half brother, Frank was more than happy to inflict on me. For several weeks from that day on, when the toddler misbehaved or disobeyed, I was summoned to receive chastisement. I placed myself at his mercy, but it was either me or an innocent babe.

That little child created feelings I'd never experienced before. Looking back, I think my behavior baffled Frank. He would call me to appear with his diabolical smile and chide me about being a fool.

"Best thing for a fool is a beatin'! Come here, fool boy! It's time for the court idiot to entertain the king." The thrashings he gave me served him as sick entertainment.

After a couple of months, for some reason, Frank became less eager to jump at the opportunity to attack me. At the time, I didn't understand. Thinking back, I'm not sure he knew how to handle my courage. I wasn't sure I knew how to handle it either. At the time, I guess I didn't attribute it to courage. I simply saw it as running interference for an innocent child, and I was not going to allow him to become another victim of Frank's rage. As I grew out of childhood, courage was in my corner. This experience was simply a symbol of things to come. I was growing up to know pain, to accept it, to not back away from it or fear it. Within a few short years, the day would arrive when I would have no fear—no fear!

I guess it's possible for love to take on a variety of faces. I experienced it with a face of compassion for the infant in our home. Because I stepped into that realm, it set the destructive groundwork for never again caring for anyone or anything. I had allowed myself to be abused for the sake of another, and I would never let that happen again. Caring for another, in this case, required pain on my behalf. Was it worth it? It was the driving force that governed the multitude of errors in my thinking for years to come.

The first stage of my life was plummeting me into a spinning well of hate and anger. My character was scorched and raw, like an open blister fighting desperately to be healed. I felt the onset of the hurt-them-before-they-hurt-you mentality. I thought it was the only way to be accepted and respected. I just wanted somebody to accept me; they didn't have to love me, just accept me and show me a little respect.

At the time, I had no idea about love, but I guess every individual is created with a capacity for it. When love is absent, a substitute will arise to fill that void, and I believe when love is absent, hatred and anger flourish.

Anger saturated in my own fear was becoming the catalyst that was to make me who I would become. The rebellious dimension into which I was spiraling would be my demise in the following decades. But I also learned that caring comes with a price.

> Let them turn the other cheek to those who strike them. Let them accept the insults of their enemies. For the Lord does not abandon anyone forever.
>
> Lamentations 3:30–31 (NLT)

I was becoming that adolescent every parent warns his child to stay away from. Every beating inflicted on me for the next three years twisted me tighter and tighter into juvenile destruction. Friends became my escape. They were a reason not to go home. They were also the fuel I created to prove myself toughest of the tough.

Somehow, Mom continued to stay afloat. Later in life, I learned her escape was a very common drug prescription for the treatment of anxiety. They became her sanctuary just to maintain her sanity in an environment of a reigning tyrant. I asked her on several occasions why she took those pills. Was she sick? Did they make her feel better?

Yes, that was it. They made her feel better. Even I could see her mellow out a short time after pulling one from the bottle that never left her purse.

I didn't have any idea what they were for, but if they made her feel better, maybe they would make me feel better, so one day, I decided to try one.

I waited until she had finished her after work chores, put my toddler brother to bed, and retired to her room for the evening. In the aftermath of bourbon, Frank had passed out on the couch, and my brothers were out somewhere on the streets of our city.

I sneaked out of my room and found Mom's purse on a bench in the foyer. The flap was open, and there it was. That little pill bottle right on top. I removed the lid and stuck my finger in and pulled one out. I was afraid to run water for fear of waking Frank, so I tried to swallow it dry. It stuck in the roof of my mouth, and I started gagging. I grabbed a cup sitting on the table with just a swallow or two of cold coffee. The cold coffee alone was enough to make me gag, but the little blue pill slipped right down.

I wondered how long it would be until I would feel better. So far, everything seemed good. I went back to my room and lay down on my bed. On my back, knees bent with one foot cocked up on the other knee and my hands behind my head, I started counting lines in the ceiling.

When I awoke, the sun was already bright. I was still on my back, one foot still cocked up on the opposite knee, but I couldn't feel my hands. When I finally stirred, my hands tingled. I evidently drifted off in that position and remained there all night. I sat up afraid to make any movement. My hands were asleep and tingled so bad that they hurt.

Although I didn't remember dozing off, I did remember taking the little blue pill. Mom was right. They do make you feel better.

But now, a good nine hours later, the knot in my gut returned; the uneasy trickle of fear on the back of my neck returned, and I felt the cloak of terror wrapping itself around me once again. I refused to forget the experience of the night before. I found hope by embracing the memory of the freedom being found in that little bottle.

I returned there again and again. I was still in elementary school, and drugs were now my escape. Alcohol was soon to become the next element to my self-destruction. Like quicksand, I was being sucked down into a world of drugs and alcohol that would enslave me deeper than I ever could have imagined.

One evening, as Frank slept sprawled on the couch, in the depth of a bourbon binge, I helped myself to my first ever *big swig* from his brown bottle on the floor. I guzzled several swallows as though it were a cola. *Whoa!* I never tasted anything so nasty and strong. It took my breath, and I nearly suffocated to keep from coughing until I could get out of hearing range, bottle still in hand. I ran to the bathroom to regain my composure. While in privacy, I opted for a few more sips, rather enjoying the burn as it went down. Within a very brief time, I wasn't feeling too bad. As a matter of fact, I felt a little goofy, and that felt a little good.

The message going through my head was, *Get back to your room before you get caught.* I slipped across the floor and paused to find Mom's little bottle of miracle blues in her purse. I was feeling very secure and overly courageous, so I took out three. Tomorrow night I might not be so lucky. If Mom ever missed the pills, and I'm sure she did, she must have thought Frank was taking them, because I was never questioned. I tiptoed past Frank on the sofa and sat his brown bottle on the floor where I found it.

I went to my room, closed the door, and sat down on the floor. The only light came through the window from the light across the street. I had a partial bottle of stale flat cola left from a day or two ago, and I swallowed the little miracle pill. I found my niche.

Nearly every night I waited for my opportunities to steal a little bourbon to wash down the little pill. Whenever I had a chance, I would sneak bourbon into my room for consumption at my own good pleasure. Frank would have long visits to the bathroom, which was always a good time to intercept a little from his open bottle. So that Frank wouldn't notice the missing contents in the vodka or bourbon bottles, I would add sufficient water to make sure they appeared untouched. From time to time, I would refill bourbon with bourbon from another bottle, but I always was careful to cover my tracks. I thought I had outfoxed him. Even when an undeserved beating occurred, it was easier to take. I played this little game every night and added to my own private stash by confiscating near-empty bottles and hiding them in my room, knowing he would never know whether he emptied one or not.

I was still an elementary student, and I was setting in motion the vicious cycle of booze and drugs that would become my mental and emotional death trap. I wasn't old enough to have my own locker in school, but I had my own stash of hard liquor and drugs.

> They will be entangled among thorns and drunk from their wine; they will be consumed like dry stubble.
>
> Nahum 1:10 (NIV)

Middle school finally came through the barrage of ongoing beatings and verbal abuse. I had become a walking-running miracle since the fracture of my leg a few years before. With sheer grit and determination, I gained complete and full use of my leg to do whatever I wanted, and the limp disappeared.

Junior high became a battlefield of wits. Racial conflicts exploded over nothing. Frank filled my head with derogatory information regarding the African American population in our school. I used that misguided information to exploit riots and disturbances in school. I would call out the African American students, taunting them with the same hateful anger I had been taunted with since a very young child. I'd been trained by the best, and I had no fear. Fighting was a near daily occurrence, and eventually, I was kicked out.

I was not allowed by the courts to be home every day without some sort of program of education. The home schooling program was a total disaster, so I was ordered to have a job. Someone got me a babysitting job watching two small children a few hours every day. I hated that job. I terrorized those little kids, as I had been terrorized. It wasn't long before the mother realized I was not doing the job I was hired to do. One evening, she approached Frank and my mother and told them I was abusing and molesting her kids. Although I had never laid a hand on either one, I did emotionally terrorize them. I verbally threatened them with barbaric threats. It was the only way I knew to make them less of a nuisance.

With Frank involved in the school system, he knew enough strings to pull and insisted that I be admitted to a mental institution near Pomona, California. So, as a twelve-year-old middle school student, I became a psychiatric patient at Sycamore Psychiatric Hospital in southwest California.

Upon admittance, there was the normal routine of questionnaires and verbal therapy. Repeatedly, I was asked to describe the molesting and/or abusive incidents, to which I replied there were none. The goal there was twofold: I either had to admit to the charges that landed me in that place or there had to be significant changes in my behavior. I was never sure what constituted significant behavior changes. I was preteen. I acted like a preteen. I thought like one. I responded like an adolescent, and I was not going to admit to something I did not do.

Several weeks passed and the day-in day-out routine continued: rise early, medicate, eat, counsel, medicate, eat, counsel, eat,
talk, medicate, and retire. The drugs (though not as effective as
street drugs or Mom's and Frank's bourbon), made the stay toler-
able, until one morning when I was aroused before the sun.

Taken from drug-induced sleep, I was moved from my bed to a
hard steel gurney and wheeled to a cold room of suspicious odors and
dank atmosphere. I tried to sit up to observe my whereabouts. One
burly orderly in white pants and shirt with a full beard and ponytail
pressed my shoulders down against the cold gurney while two others
slapped leather straps across my forehead, chest, and torso, pulling
them tight into the stainless steel buckles on the edge of the gurney.
I couldn't see the rest of the team, but I knew two more were binding
my knees and my ankles, and I could feel the leather straps tighten
across my thighs and my shins. They were shaving my temples, and
I could feel cool gel being spread across the shaved areas. Electrodes
were then stuck to the temple areas, and I was being injected with a
drug that totally paralyzed my muscles. I was full of questions and
fight but never received a verbal response from anyone.

Suddenly, a force of electric voltage forged its way, stabbing
through my skull. I could feel my body begin the convulsing
response under the voltage of electrical currents. I remember hoping that this was the end. I wanted more than anything to die. This
had become the most horrendous abuse I had known. I would have
endured a beating any day as opposed to the horror of being help-
lessly strapped down to a cold, steel gurney and convulsed into a
state of torment.

This became the first of six identical treatments administered to me over the next two weeks. During each and every treatment, my immediate hope was that I could die before I recovered
from this horrible thrashing. My hope was that I was being put to
death. How much longer until death would finally come?

*Somebody, please help me. If I am forced to live like this, please ... I
do not choose to live!*

The workers called the big burly brute with the full beard and ponytail Fish. I asked him one day how he got that name.

"My mama gave it to me."

Okay. The look on his face said, *Don't ask nuthin' else, boy.*

Fish quickly became the strong arm of terror I despised. Daily, I was at his mercy. I couldn't run from him. I couldn't make a move without his eye of intimidation following my every move. I hated that man. But just as quickly as I was driven to hate Fish, I was being drawn to care for a young lady at Sycamore named Terri. She was sweet and quickly became my sounding board, and I was falling in love!

Between the shock treatment and the injections administered to paralyze the muscles, I remained pretty wiped out for a good part of the day. The muscles were paralyzed to prevent the patient from fracturing any bones during the convulsing and violent thrashing from the shock. The injections were a bit like Novocain from the dentist; it took some time for the effect to wear off.

I was an already angry and socially dysfunctional lad when I was admitted as a psychiatric patient. The shock therapy only added to my already debilitated character, and by now, I was hiding under a cloak of hate. Hate became my weapon of attack, as well as my offense. Living for me was pain; my pain was the product of anger, and I made sure my anger bred itself back into my social circles.

My name was called at dinner one night as the recipient of a day pass to participate in activities away from the psychiatric center. These passes had to be earned. I don't really know how I earned it except that I was too emotionally slaughtered from the shock treatments and medications to create too much of a disturbance at any time.

It was to be a fun day away from the center with a sack lunch and bus ride to our destination. I could look forward to this on Friday of that week. Usually a couple orderlies and nursing aides acted as chaperones for the outing, and basically they babysat the half dozen of us for the day.

Friday morning after breakfast, those of us privileged to make this a special day were boarded on the hospital bus. I had one goal. I was not coming back on that bus. I didn't care where I slept that night, but I was not going back to Fish and his chamber of horror.

I took a seat next to a window near the back. I spread my skinny self out the best I could to take up the seat so no one would sit with me. Names were called before departure. I listened for mine and responded, "Here." That was the last thing I heard anyone on the bus say. In my head, I was making my plans.

During my stay at the center, I had befriended an African American boy named Jerome. We were close to the same age, both adolescents. Long before my admittance, Jerome had been a patient there due to an attempted suicide. He had been released only a few days prior to the day of this little excursion. Jerome and I exchanged phone numbers and addresses, not that I expected him to ever call me. We talked, as boys do, about our dreams and what we'd do if we had a chance. Well, this was my chance, and what I told Jerome was going to happen *was* going to happen, and it was going to happen today.

Our destination was a city park. I remember there were hills for climbing, sandpits for digging and building, and activity centers of equipment for climbing, soaring, swinging, etc. Around the perimeter of the park was an asphalt track for joggers and bikers.

I kept to myself most of the day. At noon, we gathered in

the picnic area and ate our sack lunches. After eating, I told the orderly I wanted to jog around the track. He looked at me with slight skepticism, as if to say, "Boy! Don't even think about getting off the track or leaving this park." I told him I'd jog around once and report back to him. He told me to go, but I knew he was watching my every move.

I trotted across the grass and then, in my best effort to look aloof, I jogged down the track. I could feel his suspicious stare burning on my back. I ran part way and then turned around. I had time. I ran back and sat down on the park bench beside him.

"It's too hot to run," I said. "Wanna toss a football?"

"Yeah, I'll toss the football with you awhile."

We stepped out on the grass, and for the next fifteen or twenty minutes, we threw passes. After a while, I began to get a little careless with my pass so that he would have to run a few steps to catch them. It wasn't long until sweat was pouring from his face and he suggested we take a break. He walked over to the picnic table where we'd left the cooler with sodas and got a cool drink. The afternoon sun was struggling to stay high, but rain clouds were moving in, and the wind was picking up.

"I'm going out on the track again till you're ready to throw the football some more," I said in my most casual voice.

"Yeah, go ahead. I need to catch my breath. Looks like it might rain. Let me drink this soda, and I'll be ready to toss some more passes with you before we have to go."

I sauntered back out onto the track and started to jog away from the playing field. I rounded the first turn and stayed on the track. I rounded the second turn, the third, and then I was on the homestretch to where I started. *Yup!* There he was, still sitting on the bench talking with the other orderly in our group. I yelled at him, "Hey! You ready?"

"Naw! I've had enough." He waved me on. I trotted over to the bench and sat down, resting my elbows on my knees. "I think I need a cool drink too," I said as I got up and started toward the cooler. I could feel them watching every step as I walked to the cooler about thirty yards away, but I never looked back. I walked to the opposite side of the picnic table where I could take a quick look in their direction from time to time without them knowing I was observing them. They were deep in conversation, so I took my time drinking my soda. My heart was pounding in my throat. I was becoming a master in the art of deceit. This was my biggest challenge yet.

I sat down on the corner of the park bench, drank the last make-believe soda from an already empty can and then twisted it and crushed it flat under my foot.

"Don't leave that there. Pick it up and put it in the trash receptacle," said the other orderly. I picked it up and tried my best basket shot, aiming for a trash barrel only a few feet from the running track. I missed, so I said, as I started toward the barrel, "I'm going to jog again before we leave."

The clouds were getting thicker and darker, and the wind was picking up. I knew our day's outing would be cut short if the rain started.

I began my track run with all the ease of innocence I could muster. I rounded the first turn and then the second. Then without looking back or in either direction, I broke loose in a full sprint across the backside of the park, across the parking lot, and I kept on running. I crossed a street through another parking lot, my eyes focused only on what was ahead. I ran through yards and empty lots until I thought I couldn't run another step.

I found myself in the heart of a community of poverty. Only then did I begin to scout the areas around me. My legs wouldn't stop running, and my fear kept me propelled to flee from nowhere to anywhere. Finally, my body had accepted all the strain it was going to take, and I fell behind an abandoned garage. Only then did I realize the darkness of the sky and the pelting rain. I don't know how long I ran or how far my skinny legs carried me. I was soaked, and my tennis shoes sloshed from having run through puddles. Looking around, I saw no one except a wet, stray cat huddled under a broken down awning, questioning my presence in his alley. I sat with my back against the dilapidated structure, rain pouring from the sky. It felt good against my heaving chest and terrified, exhausted body. For the first time in months, I wanted to cry. I was trembling, and I was scared. Now what? I knew a white boy had no business in this part of the city alone, so I eased into the old garage and wept.

I don't have any idea how long I sat in the abandoned building. Fortunately for me, it was a quiet neighborhood. I never heard a voice, nor did I ever see anyone. I was glad for the torrential rain.

When it was finally dark enough for me to move on, I eased back into the alley. The pouring rain tapered off to become a gentle shower. I walked out to the street and began to move in the direction of what looked like a business district. I had gone only a few blocks when there on the corner in the light of the street I saw a phone booth. I fished in my pocket for a dime and Jerome's phone number. One of the secrets we shared was our desire to run away from the psychiatric facility. The day before his release, he gave me the phone number of his sister's house because he preferred to stay there than at home with his parents. I only had a few coins. I hoped this was a night he chose to be there.

My hands were shaking. The rain soaked through my jeans and saturated the near disintegrated piece of paper that held the number of my freedom. It was written in pencil and was barely legible, but I held it up to the light and dropped my dime in the slot. I dialed the number.

"Hello?"

"Is Jerome there?"

"Yeah, just a minute. Jerome! Phone!"

"H-lo?"

"Jerome, this is Donnie."

"Donnie? Hey, man, where are ya?"

"I don't know."

What kind of idiot was I? I had no idea where I was or even where Jerome lived in conjunction to my location. I just knew right now he was my only help and my final hope.

"Whaddya mean ya don't know?"

"Jerome, I ran away. Just like I said I would. Can you help me?"

"I don't know, man. What if you get caught?"

"I don't know. I just know I need some help. We were at the park on Simon Street, and I ran."

Looking in both directions from the phone booth, I saw at one end of the block a stop-and-go mini mart, and beside the mini mart was a drugstore. On another corner was a fast food restaurant, and next to it, a parking lot belonging to a rather large church with a huge cross in the front. I told Jerome what I could see, hoping he might recognize the only landmarks I had.

"Oh, yeah! I know where you are. Hang on a minute."

"Hurry, man. I haven't got much money, and my minutes are going fast."

I could hear Jerome talking with someone in the background that I supposed to be his sister. Finally he said, "You're only about five miles from here, so go to the church parking lot, and we'll come get you."

Then, before I could answer, a monotone voice came on the line saying, "Please deposit twenty-five cents for another three minutes."

I slammed the receiver into the cradle and took off running in the direction of the church. My only hope was that Jerome knew I didn't hang up until I received his instruction.

Once in the church parking lot, I realized it was a much bigger building than I thought. For the most part, the parking lot was deserted. There were a few lights on throughout the building, and the foyer door was slightly ajar. The cross directly in front of the church was surrounded with flowering bushes. I crouched down behind the bushes and tried to roll as far under the branches as I could to hide myself.

There, behind the blossoms and the cross, I cowered. Through the foliage, I could see the entrance to the parking lot. My body was shaking violently under my skin. What had I done? Maybe I was the idiot Frank always said I was. I covered my face with my trembling hands, and it was all I could do not to cry out in absolute terror at what I was doing. *Was I nuts?* I knew the orderlies in the park had taken steps to find me by now. How many were out looking for me? I tried to tell myself the rain was my friend because it washed out any tracks or scents just in case dogs were on my trail.

Where is my pickup? It can't take this long to cover five miles. Maybe they weren't coming. Okay. So what if they don't? Then what? I never took my eyes from the street entrance.

Finally, the rain stopped, and it was dark. I had no idea what time of day it was. I saw first one light and then another go out in the church, and then someone came to close the foyer door.

The night air seemed gentle. The atmosphere had a sweet fragrance, as though it had been washed and hung to dry. My body was beginning to relax as I thought about all this. For the first time since I boarded the bus that morning, I wasn't afraid. I rolled over on my back and lay quietly, looking at the clouds pass across the moon. The rain clouds had moved out, and the night was clean. What would it be like if I could feel like this forever? There, as I lay hiding behind blossoms of rain-washed purity and in the shadow of the cross, I felt a sense of peace.

As I lay there soaking in the peace of my short-lived freedom, headlights turned into the parking lot. I was afraid to rise up. The vehicle moved into the lot slowly. Was it Jerome? I had no way of knowing.

The car passed by the front of the church and the cross, but I couldn't tell anything about the passengers. It was an older model Chevrolet. The tailpipe was hanging low underneath, and the fender on the driver's side had been crunched. I could hear music playing from the radio. "Oh, please don't leave," I whispered to myself. "Please drive around one more time."

The old car rounded the corner of the church and was out of sight. Soon I heard it coming around the far side of the building. "Oh, please, don't leave."

I had to make myself visible, so I hustled to get to the steps in front of the foyer.

"I'll sit here, and maybe they'll come around one more time."

Sure enough, the car made the far corner, and instead of exiting the parking lot, it was coming around again, this time even slower.

My attention was focused to my right, watching the car, when a voice to my left said, "Donnie, is that you?" I nearly jumped out of my skin as I turned to see Jerome's big, toothy grin.

"Oh, man, am I glad to see you! Where'd you come from? I thought you were in that car."

"I was, but we weren't sure you were here, so Chantal told me to get out and walk around the church while she drove around. That's her in the car. Come on; get in the car. Let's get outta here."

The old Chevy pulled up next to where we were standing, and Jerome's sister was behind the wheel. She said, "You Donnie?" I just shook my head.

"Hi. I'm Chantal, Jerome's sister. You boys get in."

I crawled in the back, soaked clothes and all. I collapsed in the big, old backseat. It was hot and sticky in the car, but I felt safe.

"Have you eaten lately?" asked Chantal.

"I had lunch at the park."

We pulled out into traffic, and I felt relieved. I really didn't care whether I ate anything or not.

"Man, how'd you get away?" Jerome asked me.

I told the details of my day in scant terms and thanked him and Chantal for coming to get me. They really had no idea how grateful I was. I'm not sure I even knew just how thankful I was.

The five-mile ride back to Chantal's house seemed a lot shorter than the time it took them to come to the church. We pulled up in front of her house and got out. I followed Chantal, and she opened the front door for me. I stepped inside.

Playing on the floor was a young child. I couldn't tell if it was a boy or a girl, so I just ignored it. It looked at me with very questioning eyes. I was probably the only white person ever to cross the threshold. Above the television was a cross with a man hanging on it. It reminded me of the cross I hid behind. I didn't know who the man was on the cross or why he was there. It just caught my eye.

There was an older black lady sitting on the sofa watching *MASH*. Chantal spoke first, "Donnie, this is my mama. You can call her Granny like we do."

I looked at her without speaking.

"Lawd have mercy, son! What happened to you? What were you doing out in that terrible storm? You come on in here and get dry. Jerome, go to your room and get this boy some dry clothes. Chantal, go fix this boy a sandwich."

I didn't know how to respond to this kind of hospitality, so I did as she said. I kept thinking of all the derogatory things Frank told me about black people, and for the first time, I began to doubt that what he said was true. Granny seemed like a kind old soul, and Chantal was just as kind.

I stepped around the corner and changed into the dry jeans and T-shirt, and Granny took my wet clothes and hung them up in the bathroom to dry. Instead of a sandwich, Chantal fixed me a couple of eggs, ham, and toast, and I made my own sandwich. I still hadn't spoken a word to Granny or Chantal since we came into the house. I tried to be quiet and not disturb their evening anymore than I already had. I noticed another cross with the man hanging on it above the kitchen table. Why would you have two of the same decorations in the same house? Maybe they bought them as a set.

I finished the food and followed Jerome to his room. There we talked about my escape from the psychiatric hospital and what I could do to stay away from there. I knew Jerome and his family would help me for a while, but I couldn't stay there forever. Besides, Mom and Frank had probably already been called about my escape, and I'd better have a plan.

As we talked, I could hear Chantal and Granny having their own discussion in the next room. From time to time their voices would raise and then get quiet again. Something inside told me I was the topic of discussion. I didn't know if that was good or bad.

"You like comic books?"

"Yeah, sure."

"Here's a stack. These are three new ones I got." Jerome threw several in my direction. We propped ourselves up on pillows, and I started to leaf through the pages. I wasn't much for reading, but comic book pictures were always interesting. I could hear muted conversations from place to place throughout the house and finally resigned myself to the fact that I was safe for the night. I looked across his room, and there, above the closet door, was another cross with a man on it.

I asked to use the bathroom. Jerome took me down a narrow hall to the bathroom and turned on the light above the sink. I noticed the floors and the facilities in the house were clean, but the sink, toilet, and tub were all stained with rust. As I stood in front of the commode, I saw another of those crosses hanging by the door. What was that all about? What sick individual in that house found beauty in some man hanging on a cross? And why would they hang one in every room? That whole idea seemed very strange to me.

I washed and dried my hands and went back to Jerome's room. He was engrossed in a superhero comic book, so I just lay down on the bed. I tried to recreate the feeling of peace I felt as I laid on the ground at the church, hiding in the shadow of the cross. My mind recalled something that didn't really register while I hid there. I recalled a fragrance in the air of sweetest scent. I closed my eyes, and I could see the beauty of the rose pink blossoms on the bushes surrounding the cross. In my mind's eye, I could see the delicate formation of every petal. Funny, it seemed that my mind captured the beauty of the blossoms. Beauty was not something my life was full of.

I was beginning to really feel at ease when I heard two car doors slam, followed by footsteps on the front porch. My heart leaped to my throat. I grabbed Jerome's arm. Neither of us said a word. I heard someone answer the knock on the door. The voices in the front room belonged to Granny and at least two men. I remembered seeing a high window in the bathroom, so I eased down the narrow hall and, without turning on a light, stepped up on the toilet so I could look out the window. There was a black and white police car pulled up to the curb with the lights on. Behind the black and white was an ambulance.

I started to shake. I was not going back. Granny or Chantal had called the cops on me. Was it too late to run? Quietly stepping down off the toilet, I grabbed my drying clothes from the bathroom racks and stepped back out in the hall. I hadn't been in any other rooms of the house except the front room, kitchen, and Jerome's bedroom, but I knew there had to be a back door. I could hear the officers coming toward the hall, and I knew there was no way out. I stepped back into the bathroom, but it was over.

"Young man, we know you're hiding. Come on out. We're here to help you."

My breaths were coming in short shallow gasps. Tears welled up in my eyes, and my fight was gone.

"Are you Donnie Foster?" one officer asked. I shook my head. "Son, you'll have to come with us. You've been reported as missing, and there are a lot of people worried about you right now."

Yeah, right, I thought. *Who? Frank? Fish? Mom?*

I looked one of the officers straight in the eye. "Please, take me home. I don't want to go back to the hospital. Please."

"Son, we can't do that. You'll have to go back, and when the doctors think you're ready, they will send you home, but tonight, we have to take you back to Sycamore."

One officer stepped ahead, and I followed him with the second officer behind me. As I passed by Granny, she stepped up and took me by the shoulders. "I'm sorry, son, but I had to do what I knew was right and what was best for you and best for my family."

We walked to the front door where two EMTs were waiting to see if I was going to need to be sedated. The only sedation I wanted was a permanent fix. I remember thinking Jerome had the right idea when he tried to commit suicide. I understood why he would do a thing like that, and I knew the feeling of not wanting to live to breathe another breath. I knew things would pick right up where they left off, only a little bit harder and a little bit worse. I felt my stomach rebel, and when I stepped through the door and onto the front porch, I heaved until I regurgitated my eggs and ham sandwich.

The officers pulled up to the back entrance to the hospital. Both men walked me through the double doors. There sat Mom and Frank. Mom got up and came to me saying very little. She asked me why I ran away. Didn't I know I was there for my own good? Yadda, yadda, yadda. I looked in Frank's direction, and he just sneered at me. Not one word came from his smug expression. I really didn't care what he was thinking.

Fish appeared from somewhere in the back. Did this guy live here? He was here night and day. He came forward and spoke to Mom and Frank with words of comfort that they would do all they could for me and see to it that I had a good night's rest and that tomorrow I would be eligible for a re-evaluation. It all sounded good, but I knew Fish. After several moments of discussion, Mom asked if she could walk me back to my room.

"I'm sorry, ma'am, but I'll be taking Donnie back. I think we'll be moving him to a different wing where we can keep a closer eye on him. You know, for his own safety."

He took me by the arm and escorted me away from everyone.

81

The farther our steps took us, the tighter the grip he had on my arm.

We walked to a different wing all right, a different wing and one floor down. There, I was shoved into my new room. My new quarters just became lockdown in solitary confinement. I'd heard about it, and now I knew it.

To elaborate on the details of the next several weeks would be redundant. Fish continued to terrorize me with whatever was available to him. I cooperated and listened to what they told me, knowing the better I behaved, the quicker I would be released.

It is better to trust in the Lord than to put confidence in man.

Psalms 118:8 (KJV)

For several weeks after my release, my fight for survival at home was no less traumatic than it was before. I returned to drugs on the street, Mom's drugs, and Frank's alcohol. Frank's reign of terror continued. This time the severing act between me and him was over a wrench.

Frank was working in the garage one Saturday. I was on my way to meet some friends, and I stepped into the garage from the kitchen to hear, "Bring me that Allen wrench!" In my own reckless thinking, I thought, *Get your own*, but I grabbed the first heavy-looking tool I saw in the toolbox and handed it to him as I walked past. I didn't get two steps past Frank until, "You idiot! That's not an Allen wrench."

I thought I kept on walking, but when the daze passed and I could focus my eyes, it was Mom cleaning the open wound in the back of my head. As was his way, Frank threw the tool at me as I passed and busted my head open. My head felt like it weighed a ton, and the pounding in my skull was making me nauseous, but I left the house anyway. I found my friends and didn't go home until the next day.

The only thoughts that consumed me were *get away*. I had to get away. Quite often, I found myself reminiscing about Terri, and since my release from Sycamore, I wondered if I would ever see her again. Her gentle face and crooked smile returned to me now. I missed her.

I left our front yard on foot late one afternoon, walking nowhere in particular. I had very little money, no food, and nothing but the clothes on my back.

I started walking in a westward direction when the drive to escape Frank overcame all common sense. I decided I was going to hitchhike to West Covina and find Terri. I figured it to be about thirty-five miles, and I was in no hurry. I knew from past experience Frank denied Mom the right to act on her maternal instincts, so nobody at home was going to look for me or question my absence.

By hanging around gas stations and asking drivers where they were headed, I got a couple short rides on trucks. This tactic got me to Pomona, where Sycamore Psychiatric Hospital was. I was not anxious to stop there for any amount of time. I walked for several hours and then caught a ride on the tailgate of an old pickup carrying fruits and vegetables to West Covina. Taking my time and hanging out here and there, it took me less than twenty-four hours to arrive at my destination. The old guy driving the pickup stopped at a service station. I stuck a couple pieces of his fruit in my shirt and bounced off the tailgate. I waved and thanked the driver.

"Thanks, buddy! I can make it from here!"

I went in and asked the mechanic on duty to use the phone for a local call. After a couple tries, I reached Terri.

"Hello." It was Terri's voice.

"Terri! Hey, it's Donnie."

"Hey, Donnie. What's going on? I heard you were released. How are things at home?"

"I'm not at home. I'm in West Covina."

"What? How'd you get here?"

"I hitchhiked. Can I see you?"

"Uh … well … sure. Tell me where I can reach you, and I'll call you back."

I turned to the mechanic in the shop, "Hey! What's the phone number here?"

"This ain't no public phone, kid."

"I know, but my Mom's going to call me back, and she needs the number."

He gave me one of those you-think-I'm-going-to-fall-for-that looks. Rushing him gave him less time to think, so I said. "Hurry up. She's got to get off the phone." He gave me the number followed with, "You can wait on her to call you back, then you git."

I gave Terri the number. While I waited for her to call me back, I bought a bottle of pop. I had nothing to eat but a piece of fruit since I left home. When the mechanic turned his back, I stuck a couple bags of potato chips in my shirt. Those would come in handy later. I then ate my other piece of fruit and drank my pop.

Within a couple minutes, the phone on the counter rang. I hoped it was for me. "I think that's my Mom!" I yelled to the mechanic. He didn't take any chances but came in to answer it himself. It was a customer, and they talked for what seemed like forever. He finally closed the conversation and went back to work. Within a few minutes, it rang again. He returned to answer and then handed the phone to me.

"Donnie. Listen, my folks are leaving soon. I told them I was going to a friend's house while they're gone. Can you find your way to West Hilton Drive? There's a hamburger place at the corner of West Hilton and Genevieve Boulevard."

"Yeah, I'll find it."

"How soon can you be there?"

"I don't know. Hang on a minute." I turned to the mechanic who was watching me closely. "Hey, buddy! Where's West Hilton Drive?"

"Up that way a coupla miles."

"What's the quickest way to get there?"

"Bus."

"Where's the bus stop?'

"'Round the corner and 'bout a block up."

I turned my conversation back to Terri. "Hey, Mom, I don't think I have enough money for the bus, but I'll take it as far as I can and walk the rest of the way."

That baffled Terri, "Mom? Since when am I your mom?"

"Okay, I'm leaving now. Tell Dad I love him, and I'll call you when I get there. Bye, Mom."

I was feeling rather confident. Terri's voice gave me courage to be a little bold. I hoped the mechanic fell for the tell-Dad-I-love-him line.

I started to walk out of the station. "Hey, kid!" It was the mechanic. "Where you headed?"

"I'm s'posed ta meet my mom at a hamburger place on Genevieve Boulevard."

"Well, just hang on there a minute."

He stepped behind the counter and handed me something. "Here, give this to the bus driver. It'll take you as far as you need to go." It was a bus pass. I looked at the name on his greasy shirt and took the pass from his grease stained fingers. His name was Joe. My arrogance suddenly turned to humility. I wanted to cry.

"Thanks, Joe." He reached out to shake my hand. "Just hand that to the driver."

I rounded the corner, trying to figure out what just happened. I had the man's potato chips in my shirt, and he was handing me something I did not deserve. I was used to receiving what I often felt I didn't deserve, but never from a stranger and never in an effort to help me.

I was not used to using public transportation, so I told the driver I wanted to get off at the corner of Genevieve Boulevard and Hilton Drive. He shook his head and said we would stop near there. I was just to watch his face in the mirror and he would tell me when to get off. We made several stops, and people got on and people got off. Each time I watched for his instruction in the mirror. As we pulled up to another stop, I saw the street sign West Hilton Drive. He motioned for me to come up front. I made my way to the front of the bus and sat on the edge of the seat right behind the driver until he opened the door.

"Where you wanna go is just two blocks up that way, son. Take care now."

I sprinted the two blocks to the hamburger place, and Terri was there waiting on me, drinking a Coke. I sat down across from her. I felt like a new person being with her. We talked and talked, and I told her all that had taken place after my great escape from Sycamore. I told her how I missed her. I thought she was going to cry, so I quickly changed the subject. Then I told her how much I hated Fish.

"Yeah, we all did. I tried to tell my parents what he was like, and they told me I didn't know what I was talking about. Where are you staying, Donnie?"

"I don't have a place. You're the only person I know here. I guess I was hoping you could help me. Do you think I could stay with your family for just a couple days?"

Who was I kidding? I didn't have any more plans for after a couple days than I had today.

"Donnie, I know better than to even ask them. I'm kind of, like, on probation since I came home from Sycamore. They have to know where I am every minute and who I'm with. They would probably send me back to Sycamore if they knew I was here with you now."

"Yeah, well, okay. I'll find a place. Will I get to see you while I'm here?"

I knew we were going to have to be very deceitful. She gave me the phone number of her best friend, and we communicated through her. She told me under *no* circumstances to call her at home.

I figured I came too far to give up too soon on Terri. The last thing I wanted to do was get Terri in trouble, so I dropped the expectation of her parents helping me.

A couple hours had passed. I didn't realize how much I missed her. I was now officially a teenager, and she was fifteen, but she seemed to have a handle on life. I never did figure out, nor would she ever tell me, why she had been committed to Sycamore. We parted company and planned to meet back at the hamburger stand the next afternoon.

I wondered around West Covina late into the evening. I found a couple housing projects going on not too far from where Terri lived. For several nights to come, I found shelter there. I had nothing. The clothes on my back were filthy, and most of the time my stomach was empty. The weather was rainy, and the nights were cool. At one point, I used scrap lumber to cover me for warmth. I ate whatever I could find that workers on the projects had left behind in trashcans. When I found something I could use, I stole it. A couple things I stole were shirts the project workers would shed midmorning as the California mornings got warmer. I was not a novice thief.

For a couple weeks, I did what I had to in order to survive. I decided there was no way I was going home. Frank had his last shot at me. I would survive any way I could and by any means necessary.

The hamburger stand became our hangout when Terri could get away. Some days I would see her, and some days I would not, but I always hung around outside until I was sure she wouldn't show.

One Saturday, she showed up just as I was ready to give up and leave. She was as giddy as a little girl.

"Donnie! How would you like to go to a movie tonight?"

"Yeah? How can we do that?"

"My sister and her boyfriend said they would take us. They offered to buy dinner and pay for the movie. How 'bout that?"

"Wow! Your sister knows about me?"

"I told her. She's cool about me seeing you. She won't tell any-one. She was even the one who asked Dad if it was okay for me to go to the movies with them tonight. She promised Dad they'd have me home as soon as the movie was over. Wanna go?"

"Sure." I hadn't seen a movie in ages.

"Do you want us to pick you up here?"

"Wherever you say. I got no plans. I'll be wherever you tell me."

"There's a pizza place about a block from the theater. It's about five blocks in that direction. Can you meet us there at six?"

I shrugged my shoulders and said, "Sure."

"You'll like my sister. She's older than me, and I think she's thinking about getting married. How exciting is that?"

Before I could answer, she gave me a peck on the cheek and took off across the street.

Hmmm. That was a nice surprise. I asked an elderly lady walk-ing by to give me the time. It was a little after four. I had just a couple hours to wait. I hung around the area, going nowhere in particular, just killing time. Eventually I headed in the direction Terri pointed and set out to find the pizza place.

It was right where she said. There were a couple outdoor tables in the front and a small bench near the street. I sat on the bench next to some big flowerpots and watched traffic. I tried to guess what her sister's boyfriend would be driving.

Finally, I saw a 1969, four-door Chevelle pull into a paral-lel parking place several yards from where I sat. There they were. Terri jumped out of the backseat and started across the street wav-ing as she ran.

My eyes froze when I realized what was about to happen. My head went numb, my lungs locked tight, and my throat tried to suffocate the sound I was trying to make.

I watched as Terri ran directly into the path of an oncoming car. I saw her helpless body tossed into the air. She went limp upon impact, and her delicate form came to a deafening thud on the street. Cars in both directions screeched to halts; those in her path locked up their brakes to avoid running over her lifeless form. Blood immediately began to pool around her face. I felt my gut rise to my throat. People ran to her. Voices were shouting things that did not register in my head. Her sister was frozen in place. Her hands covered her face, and pathetic screams lurched from somewhere deep inside.

The driver of the car stopped. People got out of their cars. Those on the street gathered around him trying to calm him down and to protect whatever they suspected might have happened next.

Finally, my feet started to carry me in the direction where Terri's body lay in the street. Everything I saw, every move I made, was in slow motion. I heard sirens coming and people yelling. I wanted to run. I wanted to step up to her bleeding body and hold her next to me. Surely if I talked to her she would open her eyes. I pushed my way to the front of the crowd when the West Covina Ambulance made its way through the onlookers to my left. Terri's sister was at her side, and she was hysterical. Her boyfriend tried to pull her away from her dying sister. Emergency personnel bailed out of the vehicle. Some ran to Terri's side, and some opened the back doors, pulling out a long gurney.

I heard somebody say to Terri's sister, "I'm sorry, miss. Your little sister's gone."

I ran. I ran and I ran. I finally collapsed somewhere.

When I thought how to understand this, it was too painful for me until I went into the sanctuary of God, then I understood.

Psalms 73:16–17 (NKJV)

Every day my anger soared, and my hate burned deeper.

I slept wherever I happened to be. I ate whatever I could find. Every time I closed my eyes, I saw Terri run across the street waving at me.

I had no one.

After several days, my instinct to survive kicked in, and I began to scout out the city. I had to do something to keep myself alive. Not far from the projects where I found shelter was a high school I passed from time to time since my arrival in West Covina. I did my best to spruce up my dirty clothes and started to hang around the school early in the mornings, trying to look like I belonged there. When classes started, I would enter the building like all the other kids and filter around the halls looking for easy targets. My survival was to steal anything I could find of value or to eat. Once classes commenced, I would hang out in a restroom until I thought the halls would be empty. I then went from locker to locker looking for an easy break-in. I took anything I could find. Finding money was the real excitement. I found out the easiest steals were to be found in the sports locker room. There, clothes were left on the floor, and locker doors were not always locked. I pilfered a couple of nice jackets and a couple pairs of shoes, not to mention radios and the latest electronic craze—handheld calculators. Food was easy to find but difficult to collect. There was always plenty in the trash barrels outside the lunchroom, but some kid digging through a trash receptacle looked pretty suspicious.

I really don't remember how long I hung out around the school. My guess would be a couple of weeks. I was usually there in the mornings before the doors were open. Apparently, someone had been keeping an eye on me. Soon after my arrival one morning, I spotted a West Covina police car cruising around the block. I wasn't sure if I should run or act like I belonged there. To run would have given away my predicament, so I picked up my pace a bit and tried to disappear around a far corner of the building. On that side of the building was another black and white. I started to turn, and that was my giveaway. Officers bailed out of both squad cars and ordered me to stop in my tracks.

Again, it was over. They arrested me and held me until a brief investigation could be done of my past, and that was all the court needed to rule for placement in a boy's home. Going home was not an option even discussed. My mom was called to tell her of my situation, but apparently no one reported me missing during my stay in West Covina. If I wasn't home, I just wasn't home. That's just the way it was. The investigation (and probably Frank's input) was enough to determine my destiny for the next few months. I was sent to McGinnis Home for troubled youth in the Los Angeles area. There, I turned into one of society's most despicable creatures. Not only did I show up laden with all my hate and anger, but every boy in that place carried his own baggage of evil ideas. I became one of Los Angeles's juvenile terrors. There was nothing I wouldn't do to prove myself to be the toughest of the tough. Not only did I arrive with rebellious hostility and rage, I learned how to let it burn like a flame of venom. I arrived with a no-fear attitude, and that attitude escalated every day I was there.

I refused to do anything expected of me. It was as normal for me to steal, cheat, or lie as it was to blow my nose when necessary. I was becoming the terror Ben, Frank, and Fish had been to me, and after a few months, I was kicked out. I was told I was a worthless failure and that there was no hope that I would ever fit into society. If I couldn't be helped by a structured discipline of a boys' home, no one at that level of rehab could help me.

I was told Mom and Frank were called, and they refused to take me back into their home. I think Mom knew what terror I would face to be forced to return and live with Frank, so she held back her maternal desires. There was no place to go but to send me to a juvenile facility for trouble-making boys. Because Rialto technically was my home, Rialto authorities were called. Two officers showed up. They were used to handling juvenile punks like me. The younger of the two officers gave me a sneer as he grabbed one arm. He spun me around, slapping the cuffs around my skinny wrists, and then shoved me in the backseat of his patrol car. Before he slammed the door, I spit at his feet. He shook his head and said, "It's gonna be a long ride, boy!"

They drove me directly to a correctional facility in San Bernardino. This was now to be my home.

> He who ignores discipline despises himself but whoever heeds correction gains understanding.
>
> Proverbs 15:32 (NIV)

I'll never forget the ride to San Bernardino. We left McGinnis Boys' Home in the middle of a sultry afternoon. We traveled east, passing through West Covina where Terri lived and I was arrested at the school. We continued east through Pomona, where I ran away from the psychiatric hospital and where Jerome's grandmother turned me over to the authorities. From there, we passed through Rialto, where somewhere Mom, Frank, and my little half brother were living. After roughly an hour's travel, we arrived in San Bernardino. The first years of my life lay open within that sixty-mile strip of California highway.

I rode in the backseat of the police car and refused to speak. I was so angry I felt crazed. It's one thing to be angry and be able to display hostility, but it's quite another to be confined in body, voice, and spirit with anger's seething gall burning inside you like a volcanic boil with no place to erupt.

Once we arrived at the correctional facility in San Bernardino and all the preliminary admission chores were done, I was shown to my quarters. The place was cold, gray, and unfeeling of anything pleasant or comely. I entered with absolutely no respect for anyone or anything.

There were boys there of every nationality and culture. I took all my prejudice and hostility in with me. Fistfights were an everyday occurrence. I wasn't afraid to swing the first lick over everything or nothing. Fighting came with a price. I spent a good deal of my time in solitary lockdown. I would be there for weeks, only to come out, pick a fight, and go right back in. Lockdown gave me plenty of time to think. What I thought about was nothing short of getting even. I would see to it that paybacks would be hell, and Frank was at the top of the list. Vengeance became my obsession. I wasn't afraid of being hurt. I could take a beating or I could give one.

Anyone who tried to come close to me changed his mind in a matter of seconds. I was not about to make friends. I tried that at the psychiatric facility, and I remembered where that got me.

When I wasn't enjoying the solitary loneliness of lockdown, I was allowed to take part in outdoor activities with the rest of the juvenile residents. My favorite outdoor activity was basketball. I enjoyed the roughness of the sport. Fouling was my game skill and when I fouled, I fouled hard.

There was a chain-link fence around the court on three sides, and the brick wall of the building served as the fourth line of fence. For security, the top of the fence was edged with heavy, barbed-wire rings.

For several days, I eyed the corner of the lot where the fence and the building joined. Could I make it? I debated that question every night when the lights went out. I would drift off to sleep, watching myself climb the fence, run across the roof, and jump off the far side into a parking lot and be gone.

I didn't weigh much, and I was quite athletic. To make my little dream come true, all I had to do was be ready when the opportunity presented itself.

I found my darkest T-shirt and jeans. At night, I would throw clean clothes in the laundry, and nobody noticed that for the next few days I wore the same dark clothes.

We were always under supervision, so I knew once I made the move, I had to climb and climb fast. The building was a single-story structure, and I had a determined spirit. I also had the confidence of a junkyard dog.

The night of the great escape, I worked myself up into a sweat, giving the illusion that I was out there to make it a game. In the heat of the game, I told my teammates I was going to sit out a while to catch my breath. With the ease of a gazelle, I walked over to where the fence and building met.

Our supervisor had been reading the evening news, paying little attention, so I did not consider him much of a threat.

It was now or never. I turned and started to climb, one sneaker clinging to the links on the fence and the sole of my other sneaker gripping the bricks. I didn't dare look back. I made it to the top even quicker than I had rehearsed it in my head. When I got to the top of the chain links, I had the barbed wire to deal with, but a few quick moves and I was past the barbs. By now, I had a very high tolerance for pain and discomfort. The nicks, cuts, and scrapes I got were nothing compared to the strappings I received from Frank.

Although the sun was slipping down behind the horizon, I didn't think about it still casting its evening glow on the top of the flat roof. As I eased over the edge, I tried to stay low and roll my skinny body onto the warm asphalt surface of the roof. I listened for clues. The basketball continued to bounce, and play was still in progress. I stayed flat on my back for a few moments and then began to roll across the rooftop. My plan was to get to the other side of the building and jump. Then I would be within a few short running strides of a huge parking lot.

Just as my confidence was at its peak, I heard the call for outdoor evening activity to end, and all residents were to prepare to return to the building. Supervisors organized their groups, and then my absence was discovered. Naturally, it didn't take the supervisor long to make a quick assessment of the number of boys on the court, and he knew immediately which one was missing.

I heard, "Hey! Where's Foster? Anybody seen Foster? Foster! Where in tarnation is that boy?"

The next sound I heard was the shrill cry of the whistle he wore around his neck.

"Any of you guys seen Foster? When did you guys see him last? Dobbersett, wasn't he playing with your group?"

"The last time I saw him he was sitting over there in the corner," replied the voice of one of the boys I'd beat up a couple times since my arrival.

"That idiot kid! I'll bet he climbed the fence to the roof! He had to! There's no other place he could be!"

By this time, I heard other voices coming from the building. Now what? When I played this scene over and over in my head, I didn't include this part. Well, there wasn't but one thing to do if I was going to have any kind of a chance to escape. I ran to the far edge of the roof and bailed off. When I hit the ground, there to pick me up was the superintendent of the center and two of his men on security staff.

It took them a good two weeks before they let me out of solitary lockdown this time.

After a couple weeks in solitary, I was allowed to return to my normal quarters when Mom surprised me with an afternoon visit.

"Donnie, I came by to tell you Frank and I are going on a family vacation. Donnie, did you hear me? We're going on a family vacation. Well, can't you say something?"

"Uh...yeah...where're ya going?"

"We're going to fly back east to Indiana. I wish you could..."

I quit listening. I was hurt. *I was so hurt!*

"Okay," I managed to say. "Uh...I gotta go to the bathroom. You might as well leave." I turned and walked away.

"Go to Indiana! Go anywhere you want! Just get out of here."

That night I couldn't sleep. I was so angry, and I hurt! I made a pact with myself—it was going to be me against the world. I knew I was going to be alone the rest of my life, and somehow I had to be okay with that.

Yeah, I cried that night. I was a tough kid, but at night when it was dark, the hurt would hurt so deep I would cry. I didn't cry because I was lonely. I cried because I hurt! Oh, God, how I hurt!

When the family vacation was over, Mom and Frank were able to get me released and take me home. Nothing at home changed. I decided I had listened to the last voice of authority I was going to listen to. I decided I would not back down from anyone. I was not going to even try to be a student. I would take the beatings, I would take the abuse, and I would drink my anger away with Frank's own bourbon and whatever drugs I could find, buy, or steal. I determined my day would come. Someday, Frank would beat me for the last time. Someday, I would have my chance, and payback was going to be hell.

THE AGE OF REBELLION

THE CATALYST: **INFLUENCE**

O Lord, my God ... save me from all those who persecute me
and deliver me, lest they tear me like a lion, rending me in pieces
while there is none to deliver me.

Psalm 7:1–2 (NKJV)

Don't be misled. Remember that you can't ignore God and get
away with it; you will always reap what you sow! Those who
live only to satisfy their own sinful desires will harvest the con-
sequences of decay and death. But those who live to please the
Spirit will harvest everlasting life from the spirit.

Galatians 6:7 (NLT)

We still lived in the house the insurance money built almost
directly across from the middle school where I was expected to
complete my junior high education. Every year I entered school
kicking and fighting all the way.

The early seventies were years of racial violence in schools and neighborhoods. I was fourteen, and fighting was a near daily occurrence for me.

What was going on in the nation was a wider scale of what was going on in my head. In my head, it was strictly on a personal level. School counselors and social workers were always looking for ways to keep me out of trouble and keep me out of fights. If they had only realized they were fighting a losing battle because I didn't want to stay out of trouble. Trouble was my middle name, and fighting was definitely my game.

Also, I was becoming a bigger challenge for Frank. I could outrun him now, and I had grown so accustomed to the pain he inflicted on me over the years, there were times I almost dared him to lay a hand on me. Not that my dares stopped him. They didn't. But my attitude was simply this: I'll do what I want when I want, and I don't care how bad you beat me. I'll outlive you, and some-day, Frank, I'll have my chance. Payback will be hell.

One morning, Frank went to leave for work in the family station wagon, and all it would do was growl when he turned the key. I remember hearing him curse as I passed him in the driveway on my way to school. Once I got past him, I chuckled to myself at his misfortune. Someone picked him up and gave him a lift to work.

At noon, I walked home to grab a bite of lunch, intending to head back to the school in time to participate in a little basketball before afternoon classes started. The old station wagon was sitting right where Frank left it in the morning. The windows were down, and when I looked in, I saw the keys in the ignition. I went on in the house and made myself a sandwich and spied a note Frank left for his son: Jimmy, see if you can get the station wagon started when you get home.

Well, I thought, *I'll just save Jimmy the trouble. I'll just see if I can start it.*

I crawled in behind the wheel, turned the key, and the old gal started right up. She coughed and sputtered a couple of times but then smoothed right out and purred like a kitten.

This was one of those days when my brain was not engaged before I shifted her down into reverse. She started her slow backward roll out of the drive, and I let her keep right on rolling. She almost backed herself into the street. I cranked left to straighten her out, and I gave her all the gas she could burn all the way to the corner. At the corner, I slammed on the brakes and made a right. Halfway down the block, I pulled into the parking lot behind the gymnasium, where I knew a couple of my buddies would be hanging around to flirt with the girls.

I pulled up beside them and said, "Get in!" The guys jumped in, and we were gone! *She's running okay now,* I thought to myself.

"What're you doin,' man?" asked my buddy. "Ain't this your dad's car?"

"Yup, just thought we'd have a little fun before the principal misses us. Where you guys wanna go?" I asked

My friend said, "Hey! Let's go down to the motocross track."

What my driving lacked in skill, I made up for in determination. We snuck around by back streets to get to the main road, and then I pulled out all the stops. The motocross track was about four miles from the school.

In the middle of the day, the track was without activity, so we had it all to ourselves.

There was no discussion about whether or not we were going to jump the hills; we just did it. We were pumped up, and I was free styling over one jump and bouncing to the music to the next. Coming off a jump, I threw my hands in the air yelling, "Look, Ma! No hands!" We laughed and whooped and hollered through every jump. Every landing jarred the shocks of the old wagon into spasms. Frank would be proud of his car. I'll bet he had no idea it could do all that stuff. When she'd hit the pits between the jumps, it would nearly knock us off the seat. Frank's wagon would never be the same after the beating we were giving it

As you know, all good things come to an end, and we decided we better get back to school. We pooled our money and had enough to put some gas back in the tank. I pulled onto our street feeling really great. Now every time I looked at Frank's old car, I had a secret he'd never know about.

We got back to the house and pulled into the drive just as the mailman was making his deliveries on our block. He stooped down and said, "Did you just put gas in that?

"Yeah."

"Well, you must have overfilled it. It's spilling out."

I got down to look under the car, and gas was pouring from a hole in the gas tank and eating the asphalt as it ran. My buddies already took off across the street, and I knew I was in big trouble.

"I guess Frank will have to take a look at that," I said in my most innocent voice, and I went on back to school.

I spent the next three hours in class trying to decide what I was going to do. One thing was for sure: I wasn't going home. My mom was in the hospital at the time, suffering from a nervous breakdown, and it was going to be just me, Frank, and his boys at home. I wasn't about to show my face.

Between classes, I talked my buddy Jeremy into letting me go home with him that night. His mom didn't like me and refused to let her son be my friend because of my reputation as a trouble-maker. I promised him that if he'd let me stay there I would stay out of sight and she would never know I was there. He finally agreed, so I walked home with him after school.

His mom was in the kitchen, so Jeremy suggested I hide in their garden shed until it was safe to sneak me into the house. While his mom took a shower, he would return and take me in. I'd been smelling a tomato and garlic creation and couldn't wait for a serving, but when he was finally able to sneak me in, he brought a peanut butter and jelly sandwich. No one knew I was there for three nights and four days. I couldn't go back to school because I knew Frank would have the word out that I had run away again.

As only kids can spread rumors, word got out in school that I was living in Jeremy's closet. So after about four days, my junior high hiatus came to an end. It was Friday afternoon, and the superintendent and the principal came to my friend's home with the intention of taking me back to my house. I got scared. I tried to tell them, "Please, don't take me home. Frank's gonna kill me!"

"Oh, come on now, son, it will be okay. We'll talk to Frank, and he'll understand this was just a little prank. I'm sure you'll be fine."

"Look, man. You don't know him. Frank hates my guts. He beats me all the time!"

"Now, son, we know Frank. He is an excellent teacher, and I'm sure he'll be upset, but you have to go home."

No, I thought to myself, *You don't know Frank.*

They put me in the car and drove me home. Frank's boys were outside and sneered at me as I made my way to the door. Frank immediately sent me to my room and then invited the men in to talk. I was wishing I had never told them of the beatings. They said they would talk to Frank about my discipline, and I knew they would question him about what I had told them. If they told Frank what I said, I knew Frank would give me a lashing like I'd never had.

I left my door open a crack so I could hear the conversation.

"I really appreciate you gentlemen bringing my boy home. This has been a father's worst nightmare."

"Frank, the boy is worried about the discipline he might receive for this little prank, but we tried to assure him the repercussions would not be as severe as he fears."

"Of course there will have to be some discipline. I can't let this go for fear of it happening again. You know how young boys are. They act before they think. I'll take care of it, gentlemen, and again, I can't thank you enough for bringing Donnie home."

Wake up, guys! Don't you think if he was concerned he would have called the school at least once to see if I was there?

I turned to open the window and was ready to bail and run again when the door opened and there he stood. I had seen Frank mad more than I ever care to remember but I never saw him with this evil hatred he had in his eyes nor felt the daggers of his despicable terror as when he crossed the threshold to my room.

"Come here, boy."

I turned to face him but stood where I was. He was going to have to come to me.

"I said come here."

I took about three steps toward him, and he dealt a blow to the left side of my head that knocked me to the floor. As I fell, my chin struck the corner of the bureau, and I could taste blood. I was too dazed to respond, and he started to kick me. He was good. He was smart enough to kick me where bruises would not show but where pain was excruciating. I remember him grabbing me up and knocking me to the floor again. He never gave me body jabs, but the blows continued about the back of the head, where bruises were less likely to show.

When the beating started, the cursing from his mouth was all about me telling the school authorities that he was a maniac. As the blows and kicking continued, it turned to how stupid I was because I ruined his station wagon and his driveway. I don't remember the beating coming to a halt. I just remember remembering it the next day.

I woke up on the floor hurting everywhere. He had kicked me so often I could hardly walk. My head felt like it was ready to split open, and my vision was a little fuzzy.

When I finally had the courage to leave my room to go to the bathroom, Frank was ready and waiting. I had to walk within sight of the kitchen, and there he sat at the table peeling an apple with his pocketknife.

"I been waitin' on you," he said.

I just stood there.

"I got another little surprise for you, boy. This ain't gonna be over 'til I say it's over. You ain't ever gonna wanna tell nobody nothin' else 'bout me, ain't that right, boy?"

I nodded my head, but it hurt just to hold my head erect.

Frank got up, and the apple peel fell to the floor where he left it. He walked to the pantry and pulled out a box of long grain rice. He never took his hateful eyes off me while he opened the box with the same pocketknife.

I had no clue to what he was thinking. He walked to the door in the kitchen that led to the garage. He motioned for me to follow. Apparently he had made his preparation for what was to take place because I could tell he had cleaned out a spot in one corner just big enough for me to occupy. He walked over and dumped the long grain rice on the cement floor. I had on a pair of shorts and no shirt.

"That's for you, boy."

I didn't know what he meant, so I just stood there.

"Get over there."

I stepped toward the rice.

"Get on your knees, boy." I did as he said. The pain was intense.

"Now, boy. We'll just see how tough you think you are. You stay there on your knees on that rice 'til I tell you to get up. You got that, boy?"

I nodded again. After just two minutes of kneeling on the long grains of rice, I was experiencing excruciating pain. It felt like my entire kneecap had been punctured with nails. How long was I going to have to be there, I wondered. I tried to relieve some of the pressure on my knees by shifting my weight and using my hands, but everything hurt, and nothing gave relief.

I don't know how long I was there on the rice on my knees. By the time Frank lifted my sentence on the rice, my mind was nearly insane from the pain throughout my body and from what felt like spikes driven in my knees.

I never again told anyone about Frank's abuse.

When you are in distress and all these things come upon you in the latter days; When you turn to the Lord your God and obey His voice … He will *not* forsake you nor destroy you.

Deuteronomy 4:30–31 (NKJV)

I came to the point in my life where I could not stand to be in the same house with Frank. I had a life on the streets and became very street smart. I could manipulate him and outlie him. I was filling out and becoming a strong, young man. All the fighting I encountered in school helped to build my body and I could take pain most boys my age would have buckled under.

Frank wasn't sure how to handle me now that I could outwit him so he resorted to punishing me through my emotions. He decided to adopt my two brothers but not me. Everyone in the house had his last name, Carpenter, but me. I think that was his way of showing his authority over me. What he didn't know was I didn't care.

At the age of fifteen, I became acquainted with an Asian kid who lived down the block. We were hanging out around the neighborhood one night when he offered me a cigarette. When he pulled it from a small plastic bag, I knew we had something a little more special than just a Lucky Strike or Camel. This was my first taste of marijuana.

"Yeah, I'll have one."

This began another negative aversion embarking on my already troubled life. I started hanging out with these guys and was introduced to peyote buttons and psychedelic mushrooms, two hallucinogens readily found in California. Peyote buttons were collected from the peyote cactus, and you could chew them, drink a tea made from them, or dry them and grind them into a powder for smoking.

Psychedelic mushrooms also grew wild in the California sun, and to consume their powers was like a short LSD trip. They were easy to come by and a cheap trip. I felt as though I had finally found my niche. I could smoke, chew, or drink away my anger and the hate I carried.

> For the enemy has persecuted my soul; He has crushed my life to the ground; He has made me dwell in darkness, like those who have long been dead.
>
> Psalms 143:3 (NKJV)

As far back as I could remember, I looked forward to the day I could leave home; to be more specific, the day I could get away from Frank. But here I was, seventeen and without a high school diploma, no skills, and no positive references. I was scratching the bottom of the barrel for a livelihood. I stole what I could and sold what I stole. It kept me in drug money and sometimes even kept me fed.

It dawned on me one day that I could join the military and have everything I wanted. I would have a roof over my head, food in my mouth, I could get an education, and—the best part—Frank couldn't touch me. Although I was in no condition to be picky, I wanted to enlist in the air force. It didn't take me long to find out I had to have a high school diploma or at least my GED. Well, what did I have to lose? I made some calls and made arrangements to take my tests for a GED. Believe it or not, I was excited.

I showed up at my appointed time ready to achieve. I was one of several to appear that day. We all signed in at a long table in the hall and were given a number two lead pencil.

We were told to find a seat in a large room of individual desks widely spaced so there could be no cheating.

The first test they gave us was on history. *History?* I don't even remember being in a history class. I was sure I must have sat in one at some point, but I sure didn't remember ever owning a book on history. Once Mom registered me for school and my schoolbooks were paid for, I seldom saw them, so I suppose there could have been a history book among them.

The tests were handed out, and I was relieved to see they were multiple choice. At least I had a twenty-five percent chance on each question. We were to read the question and choose the correct answer from A, B, C, or D choices and then fill in the little corresponding circle on the answer sheet. That didn't seem too difficult. There was no time limit. I wasn't the first one done, but then, I wasn't the last one done, so I figured I finished in average time. I walked to the back of the room and handed the lady my answer sheet. I stood quietly by while she graded my sheet of little black circles. She had nothing there to compare my answer sheet to except a plastic overlay full of little holes that she placed over the top of my test answers. Then all she had to do was see how many of my little black circles showed up in the holes on her answer sheet and when one did, it meant I got it right. Well, there just weren't enough of my little black circles that matched up with the holes on her sheet, and I failed.

When I saw her procedure for grading, a light bulb went on in my head, and my mind clicked right into gear. The test was designed to take about a week, so when I went back the next day, I had a plan with a lot better odds. I took my time to make it look like I was thinking, but as I went down the sheet, I filled in three of the four circles for every question. Then I handed her my answer sheet. She never looked at my answers, she just laid her little grading overlay on top of it, and my score was in the nineties. I did the same thing for the remaining tests and came away smelling like a genius. All of my scores were in the eighty and ninety percentile. I got my GED, and I was on my way to the United States Air Force.

I enlisted and in a matter of days was told to be ready to leave for boot camp at Lackland Air Force Base, San Antonia, Texas. I believe for the first time in my life I had hope. I had a positive attitude and an encouraged outlook. I climbed aboard that bus that took us to the airport with a spring in my step and hope in my heart.

We landed in San Antonio and boarded a bus with a sour-faced driver in fatigues. He delivered us inside a gate. I had arrived at boot camp.

As soon as we set foot on Uncle Sam's training soil, some dude in a Smokey Bear hat started yelling at us. We were immediately whipped into a line, our bags at our feet, and told how to assume the position of attention. Nose to nose he yelled at me, "What's your name, missy?"

"Donnie Foster."

"Donnie Foster what!"

"That's all, just Donnie Foster."

I heard a few snickers in our pitiful line. "Every time you open your mouth, Foster, you will address me as sir. Do you understand? Now, what's your name?"

Oh, yeah, I'd heard about this. "Foster, sir! Donnie Foster!"

"Foster, you *will* stand with your heels together! Your toes *will* be slightly out! Your back *will* be straight! Your shoulders *will* be back! Your thumb and forefinger *will* touch the seam of those girly pants you're wearing! Your eyes *will* be straight ahead! You *will* not move! You *will* make no sound! You *will* stare a hole in that sorry ugly head in front of you! Do you hear me, Foster?

"Yes, sir."

"*What did you say?*"

"Yes, sir."

"*I can't hear youuu!*"

"*Yes, sir!*"

Oh, brother! What had I done?

"Now! If any of you miserable prissy little girl scouts think you're tough enough to take me on, you just step forward and let's get it on right now because from here on out, I am the master of you pitiful little worms!"

I was tempted, oh, was I tempted, but I saw no other movement in our pathetic line of cadets, so I stayed put.

The yelling finally stopped sometime after midnight.

I had a bottom bunk and was sleeping sound when I heard, "Get up, you bunch of sorry wimps! Whaddya think this is, a brownie festival?"

I looked at my watch. It was ten minutes till five. In California, it was only three in the morning. Most nights I would just be coming home from hanging with my buddies all night—if I went home.

I was just shaking my head when someone grabbed me by the legs and jerked me straight off my bunk. I got to my feet, and there was that Smokey Bear hat. I tried my best to get my heels together, my toes out, my back straight, my shoulders back, and my thumb and forefinger on the seam of my boxer shorts.

Well, there was more yelling and pushing and shoving and belittling as we fumbled our way through dressing.

Every day that followed was no better than the day before. My anger deepened, and my need for vengeance exhilarated. I saw Frank's face every time the training instructor opened his mouth, and I left California to get away from that.

At the end of the third week, they told us we could smoke if we wanted. That was the first good word I heard since I crawled off the bus.

I met a guy named Joe who hated boot camp as much as me. He told me one night while we were out smoking, "Man, I'm getting outta this place. I hate this!"

Someone back home told him how he could get out and still receive an honorable discharge. He had done his homework, which was more than I could say. I listened to his suggestions, and the next day I put them into action.

I went immediately to the health center and asked for medication. I told them I needed something for my nerves and my headaches.

"What makes you think you can just waltz in here and ask for medication?"

"Well, sir, I have a problem."

"What kind of problem? You don't look sick."

"No, sir, I'm not sick. I am addicted to drugs, and these last three weeks I've been having flashbacks from too many LSD trips. I can't deal with them. I'm just telling you, hoping you can give me something to calm me down before I hurt somebody."

"We don't do drug detox here. You need to go talk to your commanding officer—the sooner the better."

That was all it took. Within a short period of time, I received papers stating I was hereby granted an honorable discharge and released from my obligation to serve in the United States Air Force due to my incapability to perform my duties.

I found the nearest phone and called Mom and said, "I'm coming home!"

Hear my voice, O God … preserve my life from fear of the enemy; Hide me from the secret counsel of the wicked.

Psalms 64:1–2 (KJV)

From those who were around to welcome me home, I had a near hero's welcome. For a while, I was the man of the hour. I took up residence with my brother and new sister-in-law. Within a few days, I landed a job nearby in Palm Springs working in a quaint little plant boutique run by Ross Paulus. Ross's boutique was a front for his real job—dealing drugs. He trusted me almost immediately and gave me keys to the shop and his apartment.

Ross asked me to spend Christmas with him and a friend in Los Angeles. Upon our arrival, he dropped me off with our host and said he'd return in about an hour. I knew he was going to go make a drug buy.

I made myself at home with his friends and even took the liberty to steal a nice Polaroid camera I thought would make a great gift for someone. His buddy would never miss it. I hid it in my jacket until I could hide it under the seat of Ross's car.

With Christmas over, we returned to Palm Springs. Ross soon discovered I had burglarized his friend's home and fired me on the spot. I didn't want to stay with my brother that night just in case someone might be looking for me for the camera theft. I had enough cash, so I stayed in a cheap motel making plans.

The next morning, I waited until I knew Ross would be at the boutique. When Ross fired me, he was so angry he neglected to ask for his keys back, so I returned to his apartment and let myself in. In addition to finding some cash, I also found the plastic bag of drugs he picked up in Los Angeles. He had about five thousand black beauties rolled up in a sleeping bag in the closet. I stuffed them in my shirt and left.

I went back to the motel to collect what few things I had and called Pete, a bar friend of mine. I knew Pete and his girlfriend, Connie, had plans of moving to Oregon; I just didn't know when. I did most of the talking, and we decided there was nothing keeping us in Palm Springs, so why not strike out first thing the next morning?

I knew Ross would be looking for me as soon as he saw his apartment ransacked and the drugs gone, so I called a girl I had dated and asked if I could spend the night at her place. I called Pete back and told him where to pick me up the following morning. I paid my bill and checked out.

Pete and Connie picked me up at five o'clock the next morning. From the money I stole in Ross's apartment, we had just a little more than enough money between us to purchase three bus tickets, and within an hour we were on our way to Roseburg, Oregon, on a Greyhound bus full of hippies!

Meanwhile, Ross arrived home and found his apartment trashed and his black beauties gone! What I did not know was whom he was doing drug business with. He had been purchasing drugs from the Angels of the Abyss motorcycle gang. He'd been a good customer, so this time they fronted him the drugs. When they found out he had no drugs and no money to pay for them, they went out for blood. Somebody was going to pay! To this day, I don't know Ross's fate. I just know somebody paid for five thousand black beauties one way or another.

Pete, Connie, and I arrived in Roseburg, Oregon, in the middle of the afternoon the next day.

We had several layovers, during which time we made the most of our resources. About one third of the bus passengers were of the hippy persuasion, and I had a pocketful of black beauties, so during our layovers, I peddled the pills. That gave us enough money to buy a little food and a night's lodging once we arrived in Roseburg. The climate was nothing like California. The air was clean and fresh. It felt good.

We got a room in a cheap motel the first night and started looking for jobs early the next morning. The year was 1977. Back then, unless you were at least twenty-one, jobs that paid anything at all were almost nonexistent, and I was only nineteen.

Somehow I had to convince prospective employers that I was at least twenty-one. I pulled out my driver's license and studied it for quite a while, wondering what I could do.

Back then, a driver's license was printed on paper about the thickness of card stock. It was the only identification I had. I flipped it back and forth between my fingers thinking, *In order to be twenty-one, my birth year would have to be at least 1956, and I was born in '58.*

Bingo! I had it! I pulled my fingernail clippers out of my pocket and oh so carefully and ever so lightly scratched away the left side of the eight to make it look like a three. Then I rubbed a little soapy water over the license to make it look worn. I towel dried it and left it on the nightstand to dry, and by the time I was ready to walk out the door the next morning, it was dry and voila! I was twenty-four!

My first goal was to find the nearest DMV and get an Oregon

driver's license. By noon, I had a job. I was hired as a bartender in Sutherlin at the Hiker's Haven Bar and Grille. I didn't know one mixed drink from another. I could drink about anyone under the table but didn't know the first thing about the finer details of bartending.

After several weeks at Hiker's, I bought myself a motorcycle. Speed was still my passion, and everywhere I went on the bike, I rode wide open.

From day one, I buttered up to one of the waitresses whose name was Paula. She was twenty-seven and thought I was twenty-four. She knew I needed a little help with specialty orders of mixed drinks, so she took me under her wing and taught me the skills I needed behind the bar.

Paula had been around the block and back again with a lifestyle of promiscuity. She also had a couple kids of her own, and despite her habits of ill repute, I cared for her and wanted her to meet my mom. I kept in contact with Mom since coming to Oregon.

I called Mom early one Saturday from the bar to tell her I was coming home. She was so excited. The mysterious brother I vaguely remembered was also coming home to see her. She started to tell me more when, out of nowhere, I experienced a very frightening flashback—a strong arm and a cocked pistol with a steel barrel at my temple while Mom fought to keep her baby. I dropped the phone.

"Donnie? Helllooo? Donnie, are you there?"

I picked up the receiver. "Yeah, Mom. I'm here.

"Are you okay?"

"Yeah, Mom. I'm okay. I just had a bit of a scare."

"Is everything all right?"

"Yes, Mom, everything is fine."

"Do you remember your brother, Donnie?"

"I do now. What you just said stopped me in my tracks."

For the first time in years, I remembered the night Ben held the gun to our heads and demanded our little brother. As Mom continued to share her enthusiasm of his coming, I knew it was out of fear she chose not to pursue or investigate that horrible night, but now he was coming back to see her. I let her talk and tell me whatever she wanted about Rick. Believe it or not, I was excited as well. I would get to meet a brother I never knew, and I had a girl I wanted Mom to meet.

We left Sutherlin late one night after we closed the bar. It was about an eighteen-hour drive, so we drove all night. I still had a nice stash of black beauties to keep me alert so we could keep driving without making any stops to rest. Paula and I talked the entire trip. I tried to prepare her for Frank without going into any detail. Then we began to discuss the possibility of marriage.

"Donnie, why don't we stop at Las Vegas on the way back and do it?" She was ecstatic at the idea. It seemed like she had lost the true eight years difference in our age and become the young girl nearer my true nineteen years of age.

"Yeah?"

"Yeah, Donnie. Why not? You love me, don't you? I know I love you. What are we waiting on?"

"I s'pose we could do that. We'll go see my mom and meet my brother and then head back through Vegas and make you Mrs. Donnie Foster."

We were both so excited that we could hardly wait to tell my mom. I knew Frank would have some demeaning comment, but I really didn't care. Frank was no longer a physical threat to me. At this point in my life, he was just an object of tremendous hate and anger. For one brief moment, I thought to myself, *I dare that cursed old buzzard to belittle me anymore.*

We pulled up in the drive at my mom's house around ten that night. Frank was having his last rounds of bourbon and Coke. He came to the door red eyed and lethargic. Mom gave me a hug, and I did the introductions. "Mom, I want you to meet my fiancé, Paula. Paula, this is my mom." Mom even gave Paula a hug.

"Did you say your fiancé? Donnie, you didn't tell me this. Paula, it is so nice to meet you. This is a pleasant surprise."

"Well, Mom, we thought it would be fun to surprise you. Paula, this is Frank." He stuck out his hand, and Paula took it and then he dropped his arm, never bothering to even shake her hand. I didn't even bother acknowledging his presence for myself.

"Come in, come in. Are you two hungry? I've got some leftover macaroni and cheese and some sausages."

I could always eat, but I looked at Paula, and she said, "No, thank you. I'm fine," so I declined too.

"Mom, is Rick here?"

"He'll be back, Donnie. He's out with some guys tonight. I told him you were coming home, so you can meet him in the morning. So tell me, Paula, do you have a date set for the wedding? Will you be getting married here in Palm Springs or Oregon? Tell me about your family." She went on and on.

Mom seemed different. She was more talkative than I ever remembered her to be. She had a calmness about her I never saw before. I didn't know if her serenity was drug induced or if she was just relieved to have me out of the house and on my own where she didn't have to worry about Frank and me butting heads.

My mind drifted away from the conversation between Mom and Paula. I found myself psyched out, remembering my life in the same house with Frank. There he sat, staring at the television, nursing a fresh bourbon highball. The thoughts going through my mind would have blown him into a thousand pieces if thoughts could kill. I remembered the beating I got for telling the school principal and superintendent what the man was like. I caught myself rubbing my knees to extinguish the phantom pain, reliving the afternoon after the beating when he made me kneel on rice for hours. I could feel my pulse pounding in my chest, and my breaths were labored and deep. There was a pounding in my head agitating my whole body.

Somewhere in the deep crevices of my mind, I heard, "Donnie…Donnie…Donnie. Are you okay?" I looked up and saw Paula looking at me. "Donnie, I thought maybe you would like to tell your mom what our plans are."

"What plans?"

"The plans we made for our return to Oregon, silly."

"Oh, those plans. Uh…yeah, we thought we'd go home by way of Vegas and get married."

I was wishing Rick would show up. I was suffocating in memories of the monster that sat across the room thinking himself to be a man.

All of a sudden, Frank came alive. "Hey! That's great. You know, that's only about a four-hour drive from here. Why don't the four of us drive up there tomorrow? You guys can tie the knot, and then we can gamble a little while and come on back home? Make a day of it!"

Everyone but me quickly agreed that was a fabulous idea. I knew Frank's only interest was in the blackjack tables and slots. Truthfully, it didn't matter to me when we got married, so I didn't argue with the idea.

It was after one in the morning when Mom finally announced she was going to bed. With the aide of the black beauties I'd been taking, I had been up about forty hours, and the effects of them were wearing down but had not totally subsided. Paula was ready to retire, so Mom showed her to her quarters. Frank and Mom went to bed, and I walked out on the front porch and sat down on the steps.

What went through my mind the next couple of hours was a reliving of every horrible hour I spent in the presence of Frank, and I even recalled the more terrifying events with Ben. The drugs were wearing off, and my emotions were surfacing. I started to weep. At times, I wept so hard I shook. It was an uncontrollable weeping, as though my whole being were crying out for someone to come and clean it all up and make it all go away.

I don't know how long I sat there. When the grief and lamenting had cleansed itself as best it could from my mind, I realized I was tired, more tired than I ever remembered being. A near debilitating exhaustion wrapped itself around me like an iron vest, weighting me down while stirring up the past and all its bitterness and hate. I had not shed a tear for years, and it felt good.

I stood to my feet to go back in the house when I saw a figure coming up the walk. I wondered if it was Rick, so I lit another cigarette and sat back down to wait. The figure approached the house and turned in. I stood to my feet. A nice-looking young man stepped up to the porch. He stopped abruptly when he saw me.

"Rick?"

"Yeah."

"Hi. I'm Donnie."

We shook hands, and I was glad it was still dark enough he couldn't get a good look at my face. I knew I still had puffy red eyes and swollen features from the weeping I had done.

"Were you sitting out here waiting on me?"

"Naw. I don't need much sleep, and I guess I'm still a little wired from the trip down here."

We sat down on the steps and talked until the sun came up and I could smell the coffee brewing. I knew Mom was up, so we went in. The three of us sat at the table and talked until Paula came out about three hours later. I introduced her to Rick and then went to take a shower. I had to get some sleep, and I knew Rick had been up all night, so we decided to wait and drive to Vegas the following day. I told Paula to wake me in a couple hours.

The next morning, Mom was up at daybreak again and ready to go. So was Frank, but for a different reason. I could tell his palms were itching and his gambling fever was wearing him down.

Paula pulled me aside and said, "Donnie, are you sure you want to do this?"

"Heck yeah! Why not?" After all, we practically lived together, so what was the big deal? If she wanted to share my name, I was okay with that.

We were ready to leave by 8:00 a.m. Rick was staying home. Mom had an elderly lady living next door whose granddaughter was staying with her for the summer, and Rick found her to be good company.

We arrived in Las Vegas a little after noon. Mom, Paula, and I went directly to find a chapel. The ceremony was just like the thousands before ours, but the license was signed, and legally we were man and wife.

We found Frank right where we left him, drinking and throwing money on the table like he was a high roller. I couldn't help but wonder where he got the cash he had to throw away. I didn't even care enough to pursue an answer to the question. I was better off not knowing. I doubted that the bulk of it was respectfully earned anyway. After losing a few bucks of my own, I drove us back to Palm Springs, and Frank passed out in the back. We pulled in the driveway a little before 3:00 a.m.

We decided on the ride home from Las Vegas to go to the coast the next day. Paula had never been on the southern Pacific coastline and was eager to get her feet in the warmer oceanic water. The coastal waters in Oregon were seldom warm enough to enjoy much more than getting your feet wet.

Mom packed us a lunch and collected towels, blankets, sunscreen, and all the needful things for the day. Rick and I went to the corner station and got a bag of ice for the cooler for pop and beer. I was hoping Frank would be too wiped out to go, but there he was in his Bermuda shorts and a flowered shirt and flip-flops.

The car was packed, and we were all seated at the kitchen table waiting on Rick to get back. He had gone next door to see if the little gal he'd been spending his time with wanted to go with us. He returned with her, but she was concerned about going without letting her grandmother know, and Grandma wasn't home.

Anxious to get on our way, I suggested, "Why don't you just leave her a note?"

"That's the most stupid thing I ever heard of," were the thorn-covered words that came from Frank's mouth.

"Stupid? Did you say that was *stupid?*" I stood up. "No, Frank. That's not stupid. If there's any stupidity going on around here, it's coming from you!"

He had called me stupid in front of my wife and my brother, whom I had just met. Something snapped.

Frank stood up. He took a couple steps in my direction, and I met him in full stride.

Twelve years of beatings, belittling, and traumatizing terror and abuse surfaced. I hit him with my right and knocked him backward over the chair he just got out of. Before he could get to his feet, I grabbed him by the shirt and stood him upright, landing three or four good blows to the gut. Then for good measure, I kneed him in the chin, which lined him up for another blow that broke his nose. Blood was splattering from his nose, and I continued to pummel him. Finally, I got him in a headlock and rammed his sorry head into the corner of the doorframe over and over, busting his head open, throwing more blood around the appliances, walls, and floors.

By now, he was helpless. Mom was screaming, and Paula was crying. Rick just stood there with his chin hanging to his chest and his eyes ablaze with horror. In one last effort, I threw Frank across the kitchen, and he hit the door to the garage. The door popped open, and he fell onto the garage floor. I walked to the door and picked up one of his flip-flops that fell from his feet. I stepped up to him, wanting to slap him across the face with the rubber sole, but he wasn't worth bending over for. I threw the flip-flop at his face instead, and all I could say was, "Payback is hell, Frank. Payback is hell."

I walked to the bathroom, and it wasn't until I looked in the mirror at myself that it totally registered what I had done. My day had come. I started to run water over my hands. I grabbed the bar of soap and started to rub, working up a lather to wash away every moment of dirt, grime, and filth that man ever inflicted on me. I couldn't rub hard enough or work up enough lather. I started to sweat and then realized I was going to throw up.

After purging my hands and my stomach, I walked back out to the kitchen. Mom had helped Frank in to the table. He was a mess. I just stood in the door and waited for him to speak. He never lifted his head.

"Get out."

I just stood there.

"I said get out!"

Mom looked at me. Her eyes filling with tears, and her chin began to quiver.

Finally, she said, "You better go, Donnie."

I took Paula by the arm, and we walked out the door. Rick followed us out, still trying to figure out what went wrong.

"Hey, man, I'm sorry," I said. "I'll tell you the story someday."

He shook my hand and gave me a hug.

And then I heard that diabolic voice from the man I'd just thrashed, "Hey, boy!"

I turned back to the house, and Frank stood in the doorway covered with blood, his face already beginning to swell. His eyes were cold as steel between the puffy lids, and his voice was almost demonic when he said, "I'm only gonna say this once, boy. Don't you *ever* come back. *Never!* You hear me, boy?"

I didn't even bother to acknowledge his words. He need not worry. I wouldn't be back. Mom stepped to the edge of the porch and gave me a timid wave.

"I'll see ya, Mom."

It was a long ride back to Roseburg, Oregon.

I spent the entire eighteen hours telling Paula about Ben and then about Frank. When the story was over, she said, "I'm proud of you, Donnie. Frank had that coming."

Answer me speedily, O Lord; my spirit fails! Do not hide Your face from me lest I be like those who go down into the pit.

Psalms 143:7–8 (NKJV)

Several nights after we returned to Oregon and were back in our normal routine, a group of men came into the bar on a little R & R from work. They were members of the first team to implement an exploration drilling rig in an Oregon oilfield. I served them drinks at the bar and listened as they talked about their work. I was fascinated. They gave me names, numbers, and addresses I would need if I were interested in applying for a job. I was more excited about the prospect of working the oil fields than I'd ever been about anything, so that very night, I closed the bar at 2:00 a.m., drove home, got a bite to eat, and Paula and I were at the oil field job site by seven o'clock the next morning. We left her children with her mother.

They hired me on the spot as part of the oil rigging team and told me I could start work immediately. We went back home, packed what few things we would need to get by, and I began a whole new career as an oil rigger.

The job didn't last long, because there was only one oil rig there, and when it left, we decided we could go back and tend the bar or we could follow the job and move on to the next location. We opted to move on, and the next stop was the oil fields in Texas.

Knowing we were leaving Oregon, we made the most of the nights we had left with our friends at Hiker's Bar. We spent our evenings there drinking and raising cane. Just a few nights before we were to leave for Texas, I had been out on a drinking binge alone. My money was gone, and it was time to go home.

As I left the parking lot at Hiker's, I pulled out onto the street, barely missing an oncoming car. Drunk or sober, speed was my game, and I left the poor startled driver in my dust.

I hadn't gone but a block or two when I saw the lights of a patrol car in my mirror. I immediately turned into a trailer park, hoping to lose him, but by then he had me. He asked to see my license and then ordered me out of the car for a sobriety test. I failed it big time. He told me he was going to have to take me in, to which I immediately responded, "I don't think so," and I tried to take a swing at him. I was in no condition mentally or physically to make such a dumb move. In about three easy moves, he thoroughly manhandled me to the ground. As I was trying to make sense of what was happening, he cuffed my wrists and threw me in the backseat of the cruiser, and I was on my way to jail. For the duration of the ride, my inebriated mind wouldn't shut off and my loose tongue wouldn't shut up. I sat upright in the backseat of his black and white and called him every name in the book. I threatened to beat his face in the sand. I used every phrase I could think of to intimidate him and bulldoze my way past his tolerance. He never said a word and just let me run my mouth.

We pulled up behind the jail, and as I got out, he started to undo the handcuffs. I'd been arrested enough; I knew this was not protocol. Cuffs weren't undone until you were stripped down ready for the drunk tank.

I asked him repeatedly, "What are you doin,' man? Hey! What's goin' on?" He never said a word all the while he took off his belt and revolver and laid his hat on the front seat of the car. He unbuttoned and rolled up the long sleeves on his shirt.

"Now, you sorry punk. Let's just see what you're made of. You've been running your loud mouth for the last fifteen minutes about whipping my tail. Let's see you put some muscle behind your mouth."

All right! I thought. I looked him up and down and decided I had youth and my skinny, agile frame on my side, so I danced around his huge frame for a few seconds and then threw my best shot at his face. He blocked the jab and landed one of his own, right across the nose that stunned me as I hit the ground. I got to my feet, and he lit into me like a junkyard dog on a biscuit. That big bull moose turned me every which way but loose. My nose and my lips were bleeding, and my rib cage felt busted with every breath I tried to take.

I shut my mouth and did as I was told.

Once booked and stripped down, he threw me in the drunk tank with my own kind. One smart aleck looked me over and said, "Looks like you messed with the Bull." I found out later, that's what everyone called him. Nobody messed with the Bull and won. That's just the way it was.

The next morning, I was released. I called Paula to come pick me up. A court date was set for my hearing. But I had other plans.

Court date or no court date, I was leaving for Texas. We spent the day packing our Caprice Classic and then went by Hiker's for one last hoorah with the gang. I didn't remember telling anyone we were leaving that night for Texas, but someone knew. Our car was spied in the parking lot packed, loaded, and ready to haul. Whoever it was assumed it to be his civic duty to alert the authorities that I might be running. I'd had a few beers when the Bull and two other local deputies showed up at the bar. There was little conversation while they arrested me again. This time it was for intent to skip bail.

They cuffed me, and we headed back to jail. This time, I kept my mouth shut. The guys at Hiker's took up money among them and again paid my bail. This time, Paula and her fugitive husband headed straight for Texas, leaving the charges pending.

Paula had family living in McAllen, Texas. It was a 2,400-mile trip from Roseburg, Oregon, hidden away in the southern most tip of the Lone Star State, about 240 miles south of San Antonio.

It was hot! Southern Texas was nothing like Oregon! The air was sticky, sultry, and clammy. Paula got sick soon after we arrived at her relatives' home. I didn't know if it was the heat or what, but she couldn't get a grip on our new location. She was always exhausted and sick to her stomach. It took a couple of months before she began to adjust to our new location. She was relieved to be staying with folks she knew because her health was not improving and she truly needed someone with a more caring spirit than I was willing to give. Several times I told her, "Suck it up, girl. We're here, and we're stayin.'"

I went to work in the oil fields for a prominent oil company. My job was to drive a cement truck. Cement was used to stabilize casings when drilling a well. It was a hot job and a dirty job. By evening, I would take my frustration from the heat and irritation of the day out on Paula while I was losing myself in booze or drugs, whichever happened to be in greatest supply, sometimes both.

It wasn't long until I was able to get a place of our own for Paula and me. We rented a trailer right on the edge of the Rio Grande River. It was in a large mobile home park, and the majority of the residents were Hispanic.

I immediately nosed around until I found a source for marijuana. The Mexicans on the border were also looking for a dealer to sell their goods. I struck a deal with Consuelo, a dealer in Reynosa. On a regular basis, his boys would literally swim across the Rio Grande at night right to my back door with bags of marijuana. I, in turn, sold it on the job to men working the oil fields. So I drove a cement truck by day and dealt with Mexican drug rings by night.

You've probably guessed Paula's secret by now. Yes, the nausea and vomiting was part of her being pregnant.

Even in her delicate condition, I had no concern or respect for her or the precious life she carried. Night after night, I would come home and take my frustrations out on her. Many were the nights she went to bed with a busted lip or a black eye or bruises on her arms and body.

When Paula couldn't tolerate my behavior or my attitude any longer, she met me at the door one night with her bags packed and announced she was moving back to Roseburg, Oregon. Was I surprised? Not really. As a matter of fact, it was a bit of a relief. She was one less person I had to contend with. I had no tolerance for her complaining about the heat and being pregnant. When she left, my drinking and dealing increased.

She called me at work the day she went into labor to deliver our child. The whole idea of parenting began to set in and played havoc with my psyche. In some strange, bizarre sort of way, I wanted to be with her. Since that was impossible, I went to the bar like always and consumed my depression with the bottle. I was pulled over that night for DUI, and my license was suspended. I was allowed to keep it in my possession for work only. While I was behaving like a fool, Paula was giving birth to our son.

> The fear of the Lord is the instruction of wisdom, and before honor, is humility!"
>
> Proverbs 15:33 (NKJV)

I called Paula one night, playing on her sympathies. I used our baby as a tool to get her to allow me to go back to her in Oregon. I stayed on the job in McAllen long enough to make traveling money for returning to the northwest. Before I left, I collected fifteen pounds of marijuana from Consuelo's men. He agreed to front me the weed, but I burned Consuelo by leaving in the middle of the night, not paying one dime for the weed under the seat of my car.

I drove back to Paula and my son in Roseburg. The charges against me were still pending, so I stayed away from Hiker's bar. I did contact some of my old friends and let them know I was back in town.

Computerized technology and the information highway were still several years away, so I had no trouble getting a license or finding a job as a driver.

Using my suspended Texas license, I got an Oregon license

and landed a job driving a gas truck for Texaco. I also bought Paula and me a brand-new Toyota station wagon.

Little did I realize it would be the insurance investigation that would reveal the suspension of my license, and when my boss received that word, I was fired on the spot.

With word out in the Roseburg/Sutherlin area of my DUI in Texas, I thought it was risky to stay there. The last thing I needed was to run into the Bull again and be thrown back in jail.

Once again, Paula and I were on the run.

Several of my old buddies from Hiker's were impressed with the job I had in Texas. Four of them decided if they went with me, we could follow the work force to Utah, and my oil field experience could get us jobs rigging oil wells. Paula and I made arrangements to leave the kids with her mother in Oregon until we could get established in a new area. Three of the four left early, heading east as far as Utah. Branson (who we called Dutch), the fourth, Paula, and I met up with them a few days later.

Paula and I shared an efficiency apartment with Dutch. It was small for the three of us, but Dutch took the sofa, and Paula and I had the tiny bedroom. Little time was actually spent there. When we weren't working, we were out drinking and snorting cocaine, so basically we slept there. The three of us decided to stay in Vernal, Utah, and the other three eager beavers moved on to Colorado to apply for jobs working the oil fields.

Dutch and I decided to try our skills at something different. We applied for mining positions in northeast Utah. Mining was the scariest thing I encountered since my departure from Frank. We hired on with a crew mining Gilsonite.

Hear me, O God, as I voice my complaint;
Protect my life from the threat of the enemy;
Hide me from the conspiracy of the wicked,
From the noisy crowd of evildoers.
But God will shoot them with arrows;

Suddenly they will be struck down;
He will turn their own tongues against them
And bring them to ruin ...

Psalm 64:1, 2, 7, 8 (NIV)

Eventually we found a larger apartment and sent for Paula's kids. My lifestyle created one chaotic event after another. One night, in a foolish rage, I totaled my car and lost my job. I sold a little marijuana now and then, which kept me in enough cash to get by and keep up my alcohol consumption, so for the next couple of weeks, I coasted. I couldn't get to Rangley to party with my friends there, so I hung out in a local bar in Vernal. Dutch had enough of me and moved on.

It was a cool autumn evening in Vernal, and I was drinking my way into oblivion at my new favorite hangout. There were always roughnecks around, and my experience in the oil fields allowed me to fit in with them. Beside me was a man who I'd seen there on numerous occasions but never formally met. This particular night, we found ourselves next to each other at the bar. Between drinks, he introduced himself as Slate.

I stuck out my hand. "Hi, Slate. My name's Donnie."

"Whaddya do, Donnie?"

"Right now, nothin.' Had a job mining Gilsonite till I totaled my car. Lookin' for somethin' close by. How 'bout you?"

"Aw, I'm just a roughneck on a drillin' rig. Hope ya' find what yer' lookin' for."

"Thanks."

Slate ordered another drink and then got up, and I watched him go into the restroom. Maybe he was the source I needed to get hired on an oil rigging crew. I got up and followed him to the restroom. When I opened the door and stepped inside, I saw him bent over the filthy wash sink counter snorting cocaine. I knew we could be friends. We went back to the bar, found a corner table, and shared stories until almost closing time. I told him about my oil field experience in Texas, and Slate said he would see what he could do to get me hired as a roughneck working alongside him. We became immediate friends and working buddies. We snorted cocaine together and drank the nights away. Not a day went by that I was not high on cocaine on the job. I was a danger to myself and to everyone who worked around me.

Slate was buying his drugs from a man called the Butcher. I finally learned his name was Todd Easterman. Todd was an enforcer for the drug cartels around the northeast area of Utah. He excelled in money laundering, he bought and sold drugs, and he embezzled when he could. He was a ruthless and vicious man who thought nothing of killing when necessary. He was an expert in the art of swordsmanship and could handle a pair of nunchucks like they were part of his own body.

Slate became a right-hand man for Easterman. Easterman was buying kilos of cocaine in Salt Lake City, which was about a two-and-a-half-hour drive from Vernal. It was necessary for the two to go together for a drug buy. More than likely, the driver and his accomplice would be snorting or main lining cocaine on the trip. Even I got so good with a needle I could shoot up while driving.

I had not yet had the pleasure of meeting the Butcher. I only heard of him through Slate, and Slate drew a pretty descriptive picture.

It was a mere fluke that eventually brought the Butcher and me face to face. Slate had been talking to Easterman about me and vice versa. Easterman had scheduled a buying trip to Salt Lake City on a day when Slate was unable to go with him. Slate suggested to Easterman that he take me and assured him I was a safe choice; I was not an informer, and I could be trusted to be in his inner circle. Easterman agreed.

Slate told me, "Don't expect to be along for the buy. More than likely, Todd will drop you off somewhere; he'll go make the buy and then come pick you up."

"Okay. That's cool." I was as excited as a little kid going to the circus.

When we got to Salt Lake City, the Butcher dropped me off at a convenience store, and he disappeared around the corner. I hung around the convenience store, inside for a while and then outside. My nerves were on edge when I saw him pull into the parking lot. If the truth were known, he may have been watching me from a distance just to see if I was on the level with him. He pulled up to the door, got out, locked his car, and went into the restroom. When he returned, we both got in and drove back to Vernal. He told me he had purchased a kilo of cocaine for two thousand dollars. I spoke when I was spoken to, but I asked him nothing directly about the deal. What he wanted me to know, I knew he would tell me.

We got back into Vernal about dark, and he dropped me off about a block from home. *I wanted so badly to impress this vile man.* Before I got out, I stuck out my hand and said, "Hey, man, thanks for taking me along. You got it made, ya know. Call me again. I'm available. Ya know, for whatever." He never acknowledged my desire to shake his hand. He didn't speak. He just nodded one time.

I was so impressed and totally in awe of this diabolical man. Little did I know how in awe I was to become.

Easterman called me the next time he needed to make a trip to Salt Lake City and the next and the next. The more time we spent together, the more his confidence grew in me and the more adamant I was to be part of this man's inner circle of dealers. After three months of being in his company, Slate was completely out of the picture and was no longer my source for buying cocaine. I got it directly from the Butcher and moved in to become his right hand.

He called me early one morning before I was even up.

"Hey, Foster. I've got a little collecting to do tonight. Wanna go along?"

"Todd, I will if you need me. You know that."

"All right. I'll pick you up at eight o'clock tonight at Miner's Keg. Be by yourself."

"I'll be there."

I could hardly contain myself at work that day.

I rushed home, cleaned up, and was at the bar by seven o'clock. I paced myself on beers because I wanted to be alert and attentive when we made the collection stop.

I had a stool on the end of the bar where I could watch outside. I checked my watch every couple of minutes. About 8:07, I saw his Lincoln pull into the lot. I made my way to the door, and he drove on by me and backed into a parking space at the far end of the parking lot. I wasn't sure what to do, so I lit a cigarette and watched in his direction. After a few moments, he turned off the headlights, so I wasn't sure if he was getting out or what. His car door never opened, and then I heard him start the engine. He turned the headlights on and blinked them one time. I took that as my cue to walk in that direction. When I got directly in front of the car, I saw him reach over and open the door on the passenger's side, so I got in.

"Well, Foster, you ready?"

"I'm ready. Just tell me what I need to know."

"Nothin.'"

"Nothin'?"

"Nothin.' You're going to learn a lot tonight. Just watch and learn."

We headed southwest, out of town on Highway 40, when I got up the nerve to ask, "Can I ask where we're going?"

"Roosevelt. I got a customer just outside o' town there that don't like paying for his drugs."

About half an hour later, we could see the small town lights of Roosevelt. The Butcher turned onto an off road and about a quarter of a mile later slowed down to a crawl.

"Right there's his house," said Easterman. We drove very slow past a nice-looking two-story older structure with a detached garage and a couple of old sheds out back. I could see a swing and playground equipment in the back. Easterman drove on by and then turned around. He turned off his headlights, and we drove back. He stopped just short of coming completely in front of the man's house. There were lights on in all the windows, upstairs and down. The inside door was open, and we could see a television playing across the front room.

Easterman got out, never completely closing the latch on his door. He walked around to the back of his Lincoln and opened the trunk. He took out a tire iron, a .380 caliber handgun he stuck in his belt, and a long-bladed knife he stuck in his boot. He handed me a pipe.

"Let's go collect."

We walked across the yard and stepped up on the front porch. The Butcher never bothered to knock. He opened the screen door and stepped in. The man, who was shirtless, jumped to his feet, and his wife stood up beside him.

Easterman never said a word. He walked over to the woman and shoved her back down on the couch and grabbed the man and shoved him out on the porch.

"I'm here to collect."

Easterman growled as he swung the tire iron into the back of the man's head. Blood squirted on the screen door and on me. The man fell off the porch onto the lawn, and the Butcher never lost his gait. He continued to beat the man anywhere he could strike him with the tire iron until the man lay motionless in the yard. Blood covered the man's face and upper torso. I could hear ribs cracking, and the smell of death rose up from the ground. I looked back to see the woman in the house, and she was nowhere to be seen.

When the Butcher was satisfied that he had beaten the man to within a final breath of life, he said, "Come on, Foster. Now we're going to collect the interest."

We went back into the house and took anything and everything of remote value. Easterman shattered the TV screen with the tire iron, and then we went to the bedroom where the woman was hiding. I wasn't sure what was going to happen there. She screamed and ran to another room. Easterman started ravaging through bureau drawers looking for anything of value to take. Any and all jewelry he could find, he shoved into his pockets. By this time, two children had come down from their beds upstairs and cowered in the dining room with their mother. The man's wallet was lying on the bureau. Easterman took the cash and threw the wallet aside. He then ransacked the closet, looking for the woman's purse. He found it on a hook and took the wallet. Satisfied that he had everything of value, we left.

The man still lay motionless on the ground, and the Butcher took one last kick at him in the head as we passed. I could not believe what I had just witnessed. I had collectors coming after me in the past, but nothing like this. *I was in awe!* And the sad part of this was I wanted to be just like Easterman the Butcher.

At that particular time, I would have licked the blood from this man's shoes to be part of his operation. He had everything I wanted. People feared him and, in a sick, twisted, evil way, respected him. I thought that was the image of a successful man. After all, I never had any other kind of influence in my life. All the men I had ever known were angry, hateful, abusive, pitiful creatures of evil. All I knew was survival, take from them before they take from you, hurt them before they hurt you, and in my sick and crippled mind, I thought Easterman had it all.

I got what I wanted. Easterman continued to call on me to accompany him to Salt Lake City on drug buys. I went with him on collection runs. I became his protégé. I was his in-house pit bull. Guys who feared the Butcher feared me.

The team of Easterman and Foster had a user by the name of Wrangler. I had no idea what his real name was; we just called him Wrangler. He'd been a good customer, so we took a chance and fronted him about five thousand dollars worth of cocaine. The deal was Wrangler had buyers and would be able to pay for the drug in two weeks. In two weeks, Easterman sent me to collect. I was ruthless. I didn't go anywhere without carrying firearms, knives, and I always had tire irons and clubs under the front seat of my vehicle. I found Wrangler in a bar. I knew the bar well. I'd spent plenty of time there myself, contributing to the cash flow. When he saw me come through the door, he gathered four or five guys around him. Somebody on the sidelines said, "Ain't that Easterman's pit bull?"

"Yeah."

I pushed my way through Wrangler's cover of cowardly bodies. "Come on, Wrangler, we need to step out back." They knew my reputation, and no one offered to interfere. Wrangler picked up a bottle of whiskey as we passed the bar. We stepped through the back hall and passed the restrooms, made a left through a back storeroom, and I opened the door for Wrangler to step outside.

He smashed the bottle of whiskey against the doorframe as he stepped out and turned to take a swing at me with the splintered bottle. I kicked him before he could swing, and he buckled under the blow. I beat him bare fisted until he was covered in blood. When he couldn't get to his feet, I pulled my knife and put it against his jugular.

"I did this tonight just because you're ugly. But in forty-eight hours, the down payment is due. Forty-eight hours, Wrangler. You got forty-eight hours to come up with five grand. Next time, you won't walk away from our little meeting."

I walked over and picked up his splintered bottle and threw it down beside him.

"Here. Use this on your cowardly bodyguards. They're more your speed."

I reported back to the Butcher about our little meeting. I knew he would hear about it the next day. News traveled fast through the drug rings. In forty-eight hours, Easterman went with me to make our collection. We knew Wrangler would keep a low profile, so we went to his apartment. His vehicle was gone, and the place looked deserted. No sign of him anywhere. We went from bar to bar for the better part of the night, but he was not to be found. More than likely, he skipped the country, as most indebted users did. I had done it myself. But it seemed, sooner or later, they came back. Running is the bewitching call that gets a user or a dealer killed.

Several months passed, and Easterman had pretty much given up on ever getting his money.

There were places in the mountains that had become popular gathering spots for druggies and drinkers. Usually it was close to a river where the land was flat and sparse of trees and foliage. It was the ideal place for a bonfire.

Most weekends were spent hanging out with other cocaine freaks and keggers. There was always a plentiful supply of beer and hard liquor, and drugs flowed freely. There were snorters and mainliners. The ultimate high was to drink a fifth of Jack Daniels and then shoot or snort cocaine. When on a cocaine high, every muscle, from the wrinkles in your forehead to the curl in your toes, felt rigid, and you had the sensation of running all the time. We would spend entire weekends wasted and high, and rare was the exception when there wouldn't be several cases of overdosing.

One night, I had just shot up with cocaine, and the high was intense. I was just getting my lips wet with a bottle of whiskey when I looked across the yard on the other side of the fire and thought I saw Wrangler. A girl was leaning up against me, and I pushed her away and got up. I started in the direction of my target, and every step I took, my temper rose.

As I got to the bonfire, I picked up a rather large log and walked around the backside of the fire. It was Wrangler all right. He was standing with his back to me smoking and drinking. I stepped up behind him, and without a word, I swung the timber against the side of his head. I saw teeth explode from his mouth. His head burst open at the temple, and he fell. When the blood splattered on the ground, I continued the beating and kicking. Two or three times he fell directly into the fire, and I drug him out by the feet and bashed him with one crushing blow after another. My goal was *not* to knock him unconscious because I wanted him to know what was happening, so I busted the log across every other part of his body. I could hear bones crack in his legs and ribs. When I had expended every ounce of rage on him, I pulled my handgun from my boot and shoved it in his mouth. I cocked the trigger and threatened to blow his head off right there.

"Wrangler, unless the Butcher gets his money in a couple days, you'll be wishing I had blown your brains out tonight."

When I stood up, I realized the horror had been witnessed by scores of people. I also realized my reputation held because no one came to Wrangler's defense. I looked back at the tortured mass on the ground. The fire had singed his hair into knots, and he didn't move. His eyes were wild; his body was convulsing.

I continued to hang around with keggers and frequented their parties where I maintained my reputation as a pit bull. At times, I was out of control. Initially, I was accepted for what I was, but eventually the drugs and alcohol turned me into someone even my druggie and drinking friends didn't like.

I continued to accompany the Butcher on his buying trips to Salt Lake City. Never did I meet or even see the suppliers who he made the buys from. That was just not done. He always dropped me off before he made the final leg of the trip and then picked me up when the buy was made. I knew they had done an investigation of me to make sure I wasn't an informant, but no matter how I tried, I never fully gained a hundred percent of Easterman's trust.

Easterman began stringing out for days, and I suspected he was using methamphetamines along with mainlining cocaine.

The effects of meth are similar to cocaine. The meth user will experience a euphoria followed by excitement and extreme energy. It works by speeding up the brain function and other parts of the central nervous system. Cocaine goes to work on the brain to bring about a surge of body strength and self-confidence. Many think they are capable of taking on any challenge. Cocaine highs come on very quickly but are short lived. The crash comes as fast as the high and leaves the user with raw nerves, short temper, deep depression, and weakness, and often times they become very violent.

The Butcher had the characteristics of a psycho, and as time went on, his behavior became more bizarre than normal. Even I didn't like to be around him because of his uneven temper and nervousness. Word was out that he was faulting on his deals and the suppliers weren't getting their money from him. This made me nervous because anyone who knew the Butcher knew his pit bull.

Easterman came to me one day a nervous wreck. He was waiting for me when I got off work in the oil field. I saw his Lincoln in the parking lot away from the field. As I walked to my car, I tried to avoid looking in his direction, but I saw him coming toward me.

"Get in, Foster."

"Hey, what's up, man?"

"We need to talk."

"Yeah, sure. What's goin' on? You need me to collect for you?"

"No, Foster, ain't nothin' like that."

"What is it, Butcher? You're sweatin' up a storm. Are you all right?"

"I need you to do somethin' for me, Foster. Somethin' you ain't never done before. I need you to knock over a bank."

"What?"

"I'm serious, Foster. I need ten thousand dollars by the end of the week."

"Butcher, I ain't robbin' no bank! I'd never get away with it; you know that! I can sell for you and collect what I can, but come on, Butcher. *Rob a bank?*"

"Think about it, Foster. Right now, that's all I'm asking. Just think about it till tomorrow. I'll pick you up tomorrow night, and we'll talk. Now I gotta get outta here."

He took off, throwing dirt and gravel in my face. I couldn't believe what he was asking of me. I drove home and checked my stash. I could sell a couple thousand for him, but there was no way I could sell ten-thousand-dollars worth.

Instead of picking me up at work the following night, he went to the bar and called me to the back room.

"Well?"

"Butcher, I can't. If you need me, I'll stand with you against the guys who fronted you the goods or I'll take care of them for you, you know that, but I ain't robbin' no bank!"

"All right, Foster. All right." And he slipped out the back door. I stood there and watched him through a smoky, dirty window-pane as he drove away. Now what was I to do? I'd let the Butcher down. That didn't set well with me, and I knew it didn't set well with him.

Sunday night came, and I needed to make a buy. I had guys at work I needed to supply with cocaine on Monday, and my stash was getting low. Easterman had a girlfriend, Monica. I called her late Sunday night and told her I needed to make a buy. Did she have the goods there?

"Donnie, I'm terrified. Can you come over?"

"Yeah, sure. Is Easterman there?"

"He's outside. Donnie, I don't know what's happened, but I know it's something bad."

"Can you tell me about it over the phone?"

"Okay, but if he comes in, I'm hanging up."

"All right. Just tell me what happened."

"Two guys came to collect the ten thousand dollars on Friday night. Todd had been here with me, and all night he kept pacing the floor. I don't know how many times he shot up with cocaine, and he was drinking heavy. Two guys came in, and the three of them went back to the bedroom. Donnie, I could hear them talk-ing, and then they were scuffling around. After a minute, the scuf-fling stopped, and I heard two gunshots. I was afraid to go in and see what happened, but then Todd came out and locked the door. The door has been locked since, and Donnie, I'm scared. Todd is like a crazy man. His eyes are wild, and he yells about everything. I'm even too scared to ask him what's behind that door."

"Okay, I'll come over."

I didn't know if I was doing the right thing or not. I was going for Monica. I didn't know what I would find in Easterman. I stuck a gun inside my belt and left. Monica lived just a few blocks from me, so I walked. As I got nearer to her house, I could see Easterman standing on the porch. From across the street, I could tell he had been taken over by a spirit of evil. His arms were tight against his side and every vein in his arms bulged like a road map. I could see the rising and falling of his massive chest as he breathed. There was a grave coldness about his stature. It was like rigor mortis of the living, and his eyes held ashes from a pit. There was nothing, nothing in his eyes that resembled anything human. At that moment, his mind had been transported somewhere other than the here and now. I stood there, unable to make myself cross the street. I had never come face to face with anything as fiendish as this. I don't think he ever saw me. I turned and walked away. I didn't go directly home. I really don't know where I went or when I got home. I do know it stirred something inside of me to take a sobering look at myself. The man I once so admired had become a demon. Would I end up like that? Or perhaps I'd be the dead stiff behind the door. I was surprised at myself for not being able to confront the man I so admired and wanted to be like. Now I feared I might be.

I never saw Monica or Easterman again.

I am afflicted and needy; hurry to me, O God! You are my help and my deliverer; O Lord, do not delay!

Psalm 70:5 (NASB)

Right after I cut my ties with Easterman, Paula and I moved across town. My addiction had total control of my life, and now I had to find a new dealer. The next contact I found was a cocky little Mexican named Enrique.

I continued to work in the oil fields, always high and always an accident waiting to happen. Within a short time, two major accidents cost me my job.

Because I had been off work for so many weeks, I had to do something to supplement the meager income Paula was bringing home, so I contacted Enrique one night to discuss selling drugs for him. When I told him about working for the Butcher, he told me to meet him the next night on the outskirts of town. There was a little dive bar there called Club Lillian. I knew it was pretty much a Mexican hangout. He told me to be there by eleven the next night. He told me, "Don't come up to me. I'll come to you."

I was there most of the evening and shooting a game of pool when this heavyset Mexican walked up to the pool table and said, "You Butcher's pit bull?"

I said I knew Butcher, and he motioned me to follow him outside. Enrique was in the backseat of the longest, shiniest black Cadillac I'd ever seen. The bulky Mexican opened the door and crowded me next to the car with his oversized body and said, "Get in." I got in because I was sandwiched between him and the open door. I bent down and looked in to find Enrique smiling with a big cigar in one hand and a drink in the other.

"*Buenas noches,* my friend."

"Evening, Enrique." I got in, and the bulky one slammed the door. The driver took off, throwing gravel from the dirt road. Enrique reached in his pocket and pulled out a cigar and offered it to me.

"Thanks," I said. I unwrapped the cigar and stuck it in the corner of my mouth between my back teeth. Enrique already had a lighter flicked, and I drew several times while he held the flame to light my smoke.

He wanted to know about my time with the Butcher and where I thought Easterman was. I told him about the last night I saw him but never mentioned the things Monica told me. We talked about the kind of users I thought I could sell to and how confident I was that I would get paid. I answered by telling him I saw to it the Butcher always got his money, and that seemed to satisfy him.

The whole interview lasted less than an hour. I answered his questions, and he took me back to Club Lillian. The bulky Mexican was there to open the door when the Cadillac came to a stop. I got out and stood by the open door looking back at Enrique. All he said was, "I'll be in touch." The bulky one slammed the door, and the driver sped off in a determined fury.

The next day, I got a call from one of Enrique's men.

"You got money to buy the goods."

"I can buy some but not a lot right now."

"Enrique's willing to front you the goods for a couple weeks if you think you can make good on the deal by then."

"Sure. I'll make good." We set up a meeting for the next night, and I was back in the business of selling cocaine.

I was a good dealer. I knew the game. I'd been trained by the best. I was developing a confident relationship with Enrique, buying on a regular basis. He made a fresh buy one night and offered to front me more than what I was prepared to buy. I knew he trusted me, so I accepted the overage of cocaine. It made me indebted to him for about seven thousand dollars. The guys I sold to at work were running a tight ship on me, and there was speculation among the big bosses that I was dealing drugs. Things at work got tight, and I was coming up short on money, and my two weeks were running out.

At the end of two weeks, I called Enrique before he had a chance to come to me. I told him I was going to need a couple more days. I knew I was taking a dangerous chance, but for the next several days, I neither saw nor heard anything of Enrique or his men. I made another phone call, telling him I could pay part of it but would have it all in another week. My excuses were lame, and I knew it.

I got home late one night after shooting up on cocaine and drinking hard liquor for several hours. I walked in the house and went to the bathroom and stripped down to just my jeans. I ran cold water over my face, trying to clear away some of the gray haze in my head. I thought I heard a knock on the door but let it go and ran my wet cold hands through my hair. The cold water felt so good on my scalp, face, and neck.

There was that rattle again, and this time I was sure it was someone knocking. I turned the lights back on through the house as I made my way back to the front door. I flipped on the porch light and looked through the peephole and saw Enrique standing on the porch.

Before I opened the door, I thought about what I was going to tell him. I was running out of excuses for reasons why I didn't have his money. This time, for a change, I thought I would blame it on family. I unlocked the deadbolt on the door and opened it a crack. Enrique pushed his way in, and what I didn't see from the peephole were the two enforcers he brought with him waiting out of sight alongside the porch. They rushed in, and Enrique pulled a gun on me.

"It's time to pay up, Foster."

I started to reach around to pull what money I had out of my back pocket when the two enforcers took over. One of them threw a jab that broke my cheekbone. As I was falling backward, the other one grabbed me and held me while the first enforcer pounded me like I was side meat. They beat me with tossing blows that threw me back and forth between them until my eyes were so swollen that I couldn't see. My jaw and my cheekbone were busted, my nose was broken, my ribs were cracked, and my face was so swollen you couldn't tell where one feature started and the others stopped. There was blood all over the room, and what furniture wasn't busted over me was busted from the fight. I totally lost that fight.

That ended my relationship with Enrique.

I was too busted up to go back to work for several days. Paula was at the end of her wits with me. She was living in fear for the kids and herself and didn't try to hide it. She had envisioned all kinds of horrible things happening to the kids because of my lifestyle. She became obsessed with their safety. There was no spark left in her eyes, and even in my selfish, despicable way, I knew I was dragging her and the kids deeper and deeper into the pit with me. I cared for Paula. I truly did, and I began to realize what she was living with when I heard Monica's story and then saw what the Butcher had become. How close was I coming to what he was?

I knew she was up to something. I just couldn't put my finger on it until a phone call came one night. It was a call from her aunt Gracie in Alaska. She was reluctant to tell me too much about the call. She just said they've been thinking about her and thought they might make a trip to the lower forty-eight sometime soon.

A few days later, Aunt Gracie and Uncle Archie showed up at our door. She tried to act surprised, but I was sure she had a hand in their being there. Her acting abilities weren't that good.

I had never met any of her relatives other than the ones in Texas. They talked on and on late into the night of how special she was to them as a child, how she spent more time with them then she did her own parents, yadda, yadda, yadda. Finally, long after midnight, Paula asked them to spend the night, to which they readily agreed.

Not once did they comment on my appearance. They had to notice, or else they thought Paula married one ugly bruiser. Nobody looks like I looked and was normal. I was still healing from the beating I took from Enrique's men. My face was still swollen, especially around my nose and eyes. There wasn't a spot anywhere on my face that you could lay two fingers side by side without touching a black and blue mass or open wound. I still wasn't walking totally upright because my ribs were broken. No, I was sure they had an ulterior motive for their visit. If I were to make a guess of their motive, I would have guessed that they had come to take Paula and the kids back to Alaska with them.

I was up before anyone else the next morning. It's hard to sleep when everything hurts. I was at the table drinking coffee and smoking when Paula's uncle came into the room.

He poured himself a cup of coffee and walked to the refrigerator, "Got any milk for the coffee?"

"Paula keeps some in there for the kids. Sleep okay?"

"Slept great, but I'm an early riser. What time does Paula get up?"

"Seven, eight, just depends."

"Good. That'll give us a chance to talk."

I wasn't in the mood to talk, but I motioned toward a chair across the table from me. Uncle Archie was a distinguished-looking old gentleman. He still had a head full of thick, gray hair with just a bit of a wave and a classy gray moustache. He wore a bracelet and carried himself well.

Maybe if he ate he wouldn't talk, so I said, "Want some cereal? We got the kinds the kids like, but you're welcome to what we have."

"No thanks, just some coffee. Tell me. Looks like you ran head first into a grizzly and her cubs. What happened, Donnie?"

How much had Paula told them, I wondered. No reason to lie.

"I owed a guy some money, and he couldn't wait for me to pay him back, so he brought his boys over and paid me back for keepin' his money, I guess."

"It must have been a pretty good chunk to treat you as bad as they did. How much did you owe him, Donnie?"

"Seven grand."

"What did you owe him that much money for?"

"Come on. Arch, don't play dumb with me. I'm sure Paula told you the whole story. It was drug money. I sell drugs, Arch, that's what I do. I was havin' a hard time collectin,' and that's just the way it is in the drug world. Drugs run high, and patience runs low."

"How bad is your drug problem, Donnie?"

Nobody ever asked me that before.

"How bad is my drug problem? Look at me, Arch! Do you think I'd take this kind o' beatin' for a short weekend snort? How bad did Paula tell ya? Whatever she told ya is probably right!"

"How 'bout drinkin,' Donnie? How bad is your drinking problem?"

I really wasn't up to this conversation so early in the morning, and he was getting on my nerves, but I answered, "I drink, Arch."

"Hard liquor? Beer? One drink? Two? Ongoing? All day? Give me an idea."

"Look, Arch! I don't owe you nothin'! I know why you're here, so the quicker you can pack up Paula and the kids and get them outta here, the happier you all will be!"

He was getting under my skin. My coke supply was running low, and I hadn't had a fix yet this morning. My nerves were raw, and my patience was thin. I knew why he was there, now why couldn't he just get what he came after and get out?

After a short period of silence, Uncle Arch spoke.

"Donnie, Grace and I care very much for Paula and those kids. Because we care for them, we care about the people who touch their lives. That includes you, son. You have more influence in their lives than anybody does."

I stood up and kicked my chair back under the table.

"Donnie, please, give me just a minute. That's all I ask. Now, I know this is an uncomfortable conversation for you, but I'm not a fool. In my younger years, I was out there trying all that stuff too. I know what it's like. Grace and I would like—"

I cut him off! I had to take control of the conversation. There was no use making up excuses. He knew all there was to know, so I said, "Arch, I'm high and I'm drunk twenty-four hours a day, seven days a week. Is that what you wanted to hear?"

"All I want to hear is the truth, Donnie. Truth is the only foundation we can build on. We want to help Paula, and I think one of the best ways we can help Paula is to focus on helping you, but you've got to give us that chance."

"If you're worried about my habits causin' Paula and the kids to starve to death, don't be! I ain't afraid to work, Arch. Now I'm only going to say this once. I know Paula called you about me. Give me credit for being smart enough to figure that out! I'm sure she's fed up with me and the things I do. I know she's scared for herself and the kids, so if you came to get them out of here, I'm okay with it! I won't stand in her way or yours. Just don't hassle me, Arch!"

"We didn't come to get Paula and the kids. We came to get you." With that statement, he caught me completely off guard.

"Me? Why in blazes would you come get me?"

"Donnie, you need to get out of this place before you get yourself killed. You need to address your drug and alcohol problem. You need to get away from people who are no good and who keep supplying you with the means that will eventually kill you. Donnie, I want you to go back to Alaska with Grace and me. I can get you on one of the oiling rigs at Kenai. Paula said you worked for one of the biggest oil drillers in the country in Texas. Donnie, it's the same company that's drilling in Kenai, and with your experience, you'll have no trouble getting on as part of the crew. Paula's cousin lives in Anchor Point, and they have a place for you. It's about sixty-five miles to the oil fields, but you can make good money and in a month or two bring Paula and the kids up there with you. Donnie, these drug lords you deal with are interested in one thing: money. They don't care whether you live or die as long as you continue to line their pockets. Look at you. Is it worth getting yourself half killed over? There's a better life out there, Donnie. Paula deserves better than this, and the kids don't deserve any of this. Go back to Alaska with us. Get a clean start. Whaddya say?"

"You just don't get it, do ya,' Arch? I don't want your help. I ain't cut out to live in a well-bred society. I ain't like you! I've got a reputation here, and it just happened I wasn't on my toes when these guys busted in my house. I can take care of myself, and I've got a good job, so drop it, Arch. I don't need your help, and I ain't goin' to Alaska. Take Paula and the kids if you want, but I ain't leavin'!"

"Well, I encourage you to think about the kids, Donnie. Keep in mind they're children; they're impressionable, and they deserve better than this. I can't believe you want them to have a life patterned after your own. Just think about it, Donnie. Give them that much. Just think about it.

For some time, neither of us spoke. If I'd had this conversation in a bar, I'd have wiped up the floor with the guy by now.

I spun my lighter on the faded placemat and thought to myself, *Who am I kidding? They already have a life like I had. I'm no different than Frank.*

The silence between us was heavy. Arch was right in the questions he asked. Did I want that kind of a life for them? No, but it was the only way I knew how to live. I didn't know what it was like to go to my job and work under my own natural strength and agility with a clear head and a steady hand. I didn't know what it was like to lay my head on the pillow and feel good about the day. I didn't know what it was like to not constantly look behind me for fear I might be taken out or arrested for the pages and pages of charges I had pending against me from Texas to Oregon. For that matter, I really didn't even know it was possible.

Finally, Archie stood up and put his hand on my shoulder. "Give it some thought, Donnie. That's all I'm asking. I don't want you to give me an answer now. Grace and I will be here until tomorrow. Think about it. It's time you quit rotting away before their eyes with your corrupted habits and start providing your family with the honor of a true man. Your kids aren't getting any younger, and the longer you wait, the more conditioned they will be to follow the same pattern they see you laying out for them. Talk it over with Paula. We'll talk later."

Uncle Archie got up and took his coffee out on the porch. I just sat there. Nobody ever talked to me like that. I couldn't decide if I was angry or grateful. He never yelled at me. He never belittled me. He didn't tell me what to do. He just laid the facts on the table.

I needed a fix. Wasn't that my answer to everything? If the problem is too overwhelming, get high and it will go away for a while. I got up and went to the bathroom to inject my first cocaine fix of the day. I was getting so good that I could shoot up with my eyes closed.

Within fifteen minutes, I was feeling good. My body felt rigid enough I could have run to Alaska and back and met Uncle Archie getting up from breakfast. I liked the old guy. He was different than anyone else I ever knew, but I liked him.

I was having a good high. Some highs were good and some weren't. This was a good high.

What do I want to go to Alaska for? There's nothing up there but long nights, snow, ice, freezing weather, moose, and wilderness. At least in Colorado you could enjoy the wilderness with bonfires. Who'd want to sit out in the wilderness in subzero weather? I'd be nuts to go to Alaska. *I have everything I need right here. No, there was no way. I wasn't going anywhere!*

I pulled out my favorite double-edged knife to clean and sharpen when Paula came down for her first cup of coffee.

"Well, how do you like Uncle Archie and my Aunt Gracie?"

"They're okay."

"Is Uncle Archie up yet?"

"He's out on the porch."

She wrapped her robe around her and poured a cup of coffee and slipped through the door. I heard Archie get up and walk across the porch. Through the window, I saw him give her a hug. I never hugged her just to hug her.

"Good morning, darlin.'"

I finished up cleaning my knife and slipped it back in the sheath when Grace came down the stairs. She was a beautiful woman, and I noticed how much Paula looked like her. She and Paula's mother were sisters, but Paula looked more like Grace than she did her own mother. They were from American Indian background, and Paula had the same dark features as Grace. Paula's hair was thick, coal black, and straight, but Grace had a touch of gray. I noticed the facial structure. They both wore the beauty of high cheekbones and piercing dark eyes. Grace really was a beautiful woman. I remembered being attracted to those same features when I met Paula, but somehow between the drugs and liquor, I lost sight of her beauty.

"Good morning, Donnie. My! What a beautiful morning. I just stood in the bedroom and enjoyed the view. Have you been up long?"

"I'm an early riser. I've been up awhile."

"How are you feeling this morning?"

"I'm okay."

"Your wounds look terribly sore, Donnie. Have you seen a doctor about your injuries?"

"They'll heal."

I wasn't in the mood for another come-to-Alaska lecture, so I poured a cup of coffee and went upstairs. I needed to make a buy today because my supply was running low, but I couldn't go out on the streets in the condition I was in.

I knew the word would be out about my encounter with Enrique's men, and I wasn't ready to face that either.

I wasn't working and I wasn't selling, so my funds were diminishing, along with my coke. I called a friend I knew I could buy a small supply from. I don't know what his real name was, but we called him Mort.

Mort said he would meet me later in the day in the parking lot behind Doug's Pub and Grub. I scraped together what I could find and took all the cash in Paula's purse. She was still out on the porch with Grace and Archie, so I went into their room and found Grace's wallet in her handbag. She had a thick stack of bills— mostly twenties and a few fifties and some smaller notes. I took a couple fifties and several twenties and put the rest back like I found it and went back to our bedroom. I heard the door open and the three of them laughing and chattering when they came in.

"Donnie, you up there?" It was Paula. I didn't remember the last time I saw her this happy. I forgot what it was like to see her smile, much less laugh out loud.

"Yeah."

"We're going out for breakfast. Wanna come?"

"No." My high was wearing off, and I knew what that meant. Unless I could shoot up again, I was going to crash. Crashing was part of the game, and when the coke supply was scarce, I learned to avoid the effects of the crash by drinking.

I had a supply of liquor everywhere, so I found a partial bottle I had in the bedroom and flopped on the bed and turned on the TV. Paula came up to get dressed for her breakfast date with Archie and Grace. She looked good. She put on a pair of jeans and a red T-shirt and twisted her thick black hair up on top of her head. She left a couple little hair tendrils hang down around her face, and she looked happy. She really was beautiful.

"You sure you don't want to come with us, Donnie? How 'bout we bring something back for you?"

"No, you go on. Have a good time." I don't think I ever told her before to have a good time.

I heard the car pull away, and I went to check out Archie and Grace's room for more cash. Grace had taken her purse, and I found nothing else I wanted.

It was the middle of the afternoon, and Paula, Archie, and Grace still weren't back. I was glad. I was waiting on my buddy to call me and tell me he was headed over to Doug's. I'd been drinking all day and snorting what coke I had left, and through a broken nose, it wasn't easy.

The phone finally rang, and I was out the door. I sat in my truck and waited until I saw Mort ride in on his motorcycle. He had a couple guys ride in with him. He walked over to the door of my truck, and the look on his face was pathetic.

"Well, look at what someone did to the Pit Bull. Someone said they heard you had a little trouble. No one believed the Bull would let it get this bad. How many were there?"

"Five." There were three, but I told him five.

"You got the cash?"

"Is it good stuff?" I asked.

"The best."

I pulled out what I had pilfered and confiscated that morning. It was about four hundred dollars in all. Not quite enough to buy a half a kilo. He handed over the bag, and I handed him my cash. I wasn't in the mood for conversation, so we parted company.

When I got home, Paula and her aunt and uncle were there. I went in the back door and into the bathroom. It seemed like there were kids everywhere. All I wanted was a little quiet. One of them knocked on the bathroom door, and I turned my tongue loose on him. I jerked the door open and started to backhand the child across the face when I remembered we had guests. I slammed the door. My anger was growing intense, and I had to get out. I grabbed my bag of cocaine off the counter, and when I did, I forgot it was open and most of it spilled on the floor. That was like powdered gold dispersing in the breeze. I swore under my breath and cleaned it up the best I could and put it back in the bag. I was experiencing a severe grate of desperation. There was a fine film of powder I couldn't scoop up, and I wasn't going to let it go to waste.

I raked it together with a wet finger, and it turned into pasty goo. I found a spray bottle of saline solution in the medicine cabinet and poured all but a couple of teaspoons down the drain. I scraped the wet powder into the bottle and shook it. It seemed to dissolve, so I sprayed it in my nose. Within a few minutes, I could tell my *save* was successful. My confidence returned, and I went to join my wife and my guests. Nothing more had been said to me about the Alaska proposal since Archie and I talked that morning. Their flight was scheduled to leave at seven the next morning, so Paula fixed a nice dinner. We ate together at eight o'clock, and they said their good-byes and retired early.

After they went upstairs, Paula came and sat next to me on the sofa. "Donnie, what do you think about the offer Aunt Gracie and Uncle Archie are making to us about going to Alaska?"

"Do you have any idea what Alaska is like? I'm not about to go up there and freeze my behind off most of the year. Job or no job, I ain't goin' to Alaska. "

"Donnie, I know what Alaska is like. I lived up there as a kid. It's beautiful. We could get a clean start in life, and it would be so good for the kids to get away from here. Donnie, if we stay here, you're going to get killed sooner or later. You're either going to kill yourself with drugs or someone like Enrique and his men will put a bullet in you. Donnie, we need to make a change. This is the best offer we're ever going to get."

"If you and the kids wanna go, go, but I ain't goin.'"

Tears started streaming down Paula's cheeks. Funny, I never noticed it before. There was something tender about her crying. I knew she cried and cried often, and most of the time it was my fault, but I always turned away and figured she was weak, and there was nothing I could do about that.

"I just may do that, Donnie." She stood to her feet. Her voice was strong, and she did not waver. "I can't live this way anymore. I *won't* live this way anymore. I don't ever want to see anything again like what took place here the night Enrique and his men showed up. Donnie, they could have killed you, and for what? Look at you. You're a drunken dope head, and there are three kids living in this house watching you. The night after we got married, you told me about your stepdad and Frank and how they had terrorized your life. Donnie, look at yourself. You're just like them. The kids are afraid of you. They're already hanging around with the wrong crowds. There are times I'm afraid to step out the front door. If you want to kill yourself in this world, go ahead, but I'm not going to stick around and watch it happen. If you don't take the offer Uncle Archie and Aunt Grace are making, I will. You've got until five o'clock tomorrow morning to decide. One of us is leaving. Uncle Archie said if you went to Alaska and worked three or four months, you could make enough for me and the kids to come and live up there. If you don't take this opportunity, Donnie, then Uncle Archie is willing to pay for me and the kids to go, and we will go."

With that, she turned and went upstairs. Paula was afraid to stand up to me very often, but this time she spoke her mind. I wasn't sure if I really cared. I remembered the conversation Archie and I had at the table that morning. I'd never had a grown man talk to me the way he did. It was like we were both men, on the same level, without threat to my character, like I could make a decision not based on my fists wrapped in brass knuckles or knives or guns or tire irons. There was no risk between us of who was going to take from the other first or who was going to hurt the other first, which was the code I had been living by. Was it possible to live like that for the rest of my life?

I'd been on a high since my purchase from Mort, and late as it was, sleep was not an option. I decided to take a walk.

It was a cool, brisk evening. Normally I would have been at a bar somewhere. It was good, I guess, that I was so busted up that I didn't want anyone to see me. I wondered if Paula was sleeping or packing her bags.

Seeing her countenance change with Arch and Grace around gave me a fresh look at the woman I married. Maybe I did owe her something better. How does she know I won't go to Alaska and pick up right where I left off here? On the other hand none of the dealers or king pins around here would think to look for me in Alaska. Maybe the offer was worthy of thought.

I walked until about 3:00 a.m. When I got home, I sat down on the top step of the porch. There was a light on upstairs. I figured then Paula was up there packing for her and the kids to go to Alaska. Instead she opened the door and came out and sat beside me. She was in her robe, and she looked beautiful.

"I've been sitting in the front room in the dark waiting on you, Donnie. Where ya been?"

"Walkin.'"

"Donnie, I really want us to try to make a new start. If it doesn't work out in Alaska, we can come back here or go wherever you want, and I'll give you no argument. All I want is a chance, one chance, for us and the kids."

I leaned back on my elbows. "Okay."

Disbelief was in her eyes.

"Do you mean it, Donnie? Do you really mean you'll go?"

"I'll go for three months. At the end of three months, we'll decide if we're going to stay, but don't sever all your ties here. You may need them to come back to."

We sat and talked until Archie and Grace came down with their bags. Uncle Archie shook my hand when I told him I'd give Alaska a try. Aunt Grace gave Paula a hug. Paula and I decided I would go first and get on with the oil rigging crew. As soon as I could afford a place for all of us, I would send the money for her and the kids. Uncle Archie wrote a check to Paula to buy my airfare to Anchorage.

"Just let us know when to pick you up, Donnie. We'll be looking forward to seeing you."

When the taxi showed up, Paula walked to the curb with them, and I went in and shot up.

For the next five days, Paula was a different woman. I continued to yell and scream at her for no reason whenever I was coming down from a high or drunk. She would not antagonize me any further but just turned and walked away. She almost had a spring in her step.

Four days later, Paula drove me to Vernal Regional Airport. There, I boarded a small plane to Salt Lake City. From Salt Lake City, I flew to Seattle. I had a two-hour layover in Seattle, and the thought crossed my mind to scrap the whole plan and take a bus from there back to Roseburg, Oregon. I still had friends in the Roseburg and Sutherlin area, but I also had a list of charges filed against me, and I wasn't ready to risk being arrested there. I boarded the plane at Seattle and four hours later arrived in Anchorage, where I took a local shuttle plane to Kenai.

Thirty minutes later, I got off the plane at Kenai, and Archie and Paula's cousin, Red, were there waiting for me. I knew where Red got his name. He had a head of the curliest, most unruly, red hair I'd ever seen. We stopped at a hamburger place and got something to eat. I had to admit it was the best hamburger I'd had in a long, long time. Uncle Archie climbed in the backseat when we left the hamburger place and insisted I sit up front with Red. It took about an hour and a half to drive to Anchor Point, where Red and his wife Elizabeth lived.

Red had arranged for me to start work as a roustabout on the oilfields as soon as I was ready. He and Elizabeth were opening their home to me for as long as necessary. The oil fields were just outside Kenai, so it was at least an hour drive in one direction.

My position there was to drive a bulk truck of dry cement to the jobsite where it was mixed with water and pressure poured into the drilling hole. We hauled to the barges in Cook Inlet. It wasn't exciting, but it was a job.

For three months I had no connection to buy cocaine in Kenai, but I could buy all the marijuana I wanted. Also, beer flowed freely. It was the drink of everyone in Alaska. Even the cops drank beer on and off the job. Being coke free, I was healthy, felt healthy, and looked good.

I became friends with a little Italian named Marco, a co-worker. We smoked weed and drank together. He had done well working on the oil rigs and offered to rent me an apartment in Kenai. I took him up on his offer and wrote a letter to Paula telling her she could start making plans to move to Kenai, Alaska.

I was only twenty-three and felt like I had lived several life-times. Paula still thought I was twenty-eight.

Exactly two weeks after writing to Paula, I moved my meager belongings from Red's and Elizabeth's and set up housekeeping the best I could in our new little apartment at Kenai. Two weeks later, Red, Uncle Archie, and I picked up Paula and the kids at the Anchorage airport. When she got off the plane, she looked at me like it was the first time she'd ever seen me. I looked good. I looked clean. I was clean. I hadn't snorted or mainlined any cocaine for four months.

We all crammed into Uncle Archie's big sedan for the long drive back to Kenai. The kids were in awe of the landscape. We traveled the Sterling Highway through the Chugach Mountains, and they couldn't look in enough directions fast enough to see all there was to see. I was feeling worthy of their presence.

The two weeks prior to Paula and the kids arriving, I purchased a few inexpensive pieces of furniture and accessories for our home, among which were used beds and bedroom furniture, a dinette set, a couch, and a couple chairs. I had a well-stocked cupboard of paper plates and cups and plastic tableware, thinking Paula would want to buy her own things. The main selection of our pantry menu was geared for the kids—boxes of macaroni and cheese and peanut butter and jelly. I had some bologna and a couple boxes of cereal. That got us by for a few days until Paula could settle herself and do her own shopping.

She had a very significant glow about her. She was a beautiful woman by any standards, but her countenance reflected the hopes of a woman with dreams and expectations for a new and better life. And that's what we had ... for a little while.

One night, after our shift was over, Marco asked me to go to Grappler's Bar with him. His wife had taken a short vacation to the lower forty-eight, and he wasn't ready to go home to an empty house. I hesitated. I knew better than to allow myself that freedom after being clean for several months. I was still drinking beer and smoking marijuana, but I felt I had it under control. I had been cocaine free for months. I stayed out of bars and did my drinking at home.

"Whaddya say, Don-oh? Are you up to a little lie telling over a beer or two?"

"Let me give Paula a call and tell her I'll be a little late." I made my way to a phone in the office in the truck yard. Paula picked up on the first ring.

"Hey, baby, I'm going to be a little late tonight. Marco wants me to go with him to run a couple errands. Don't keep supper waiting. Feed the kids, and I'll be home as soon as I can."

She was less than happy with my story. I could hear doubt and distrust in her voice. I hadn't heard it since she came to Kenai until now.

"Donnie, I'd really like for you to come on home. Please, Donnie, don't do anything stupid that you might be sorry for."

There was that word again: *stupid*. The last person who called me stupid was Frank, and for a split second, that same anger surfaced. Who was she to suggest I might do something *stupid?* I'd been clean for months now, and I didn't need anyone to tell me what I should or should not do. I hung up on her and returned to the truck where Marco was waiting for me with the engine running.

"Let's go, buddy! I told her I'd be home when I got there."

I was pretty silent as we rode along to Grappler's Bar. Anger was welling up. I was tired. I worked hard that day. It was cold. I deserved to treat myself to a night out with Marco. As we rode, I smoked a joint to take the edge off. We pulled up to the bar, and

I practically jumped out of the truck. My feet hit the ground running, and I stormed in the front door and demanded a drink as soon as I got within shouting distance of the bar. The bartender gave me a look of suspicion and poured me a beer. I chugged it and asked for another.

Marco stepped up beside me, "Hey, man, slow down! What's going on? I've never seen you like this. Paula give you a hard time about coming here?"

"Naw. I'm just tired. Just need to relax a little."

I relished in the atmosphere of alcohol and stale liquor smells. It felt good to be there. I felt myself relax, and the chip on my shoulder quickly disappeared.

Marco and I spent a couple hours at Grappler's. After I calmed down, I felt myself ready to face reality. Marco drank a couple beers; we shot a couple games of pool and headed for home.

I wasn't sure how Paula would react, so I tried to behave as normal as possible when I got home. I saw her standing in the window when I drove the company truck in and parked outside the apartment. She could smell the alcohol on me, but I was walking good, talking good, and in a good mood, so she lost the chill very quickly. I guess I couldn't blame her for worrying or even being angry. She had no reason to think I wouldn't get wasted like I'd done in the past.

But as time progressed, that night was the resurrection of old habits. Within two weeks, I was back at the bars on a nightly basis, drinking until all hours of the morning. Marco was getting wasted with me, along with several other guys from work. I was the one they regularly carried home, propped me up outside the door, rang the doorbell, and I would literally fall in when Paula opened the door.

One Wednesday morning, when I was in fairly decent shape, my boss called me into his office.

"Donnie, I think you know why I've called you in here. Your work is under par. You show up under the influence, unable to do your job. I can't trust you with the trucks anymore, and I'm going to have to make a decision. I know the monster that has control of your life. Donnie. I'm a recovering alcoholic myself, so I know what you're dealing with. I don't want to fire you, Donnie. More than anything, I want to see you whip this monkey on your back, so I tell you what. You take a couple days off and come back in on Monday clean and dried out. Let's start over and see what happens. Are you willing to give it another try?"

I said I was, and I went home. That night, Marco came by and got me, and we went back to Grappler's. I had plenty of time to think that day. I knew if I could find a cocaine supplier, I could get by on the job. Shooting up kept me high and counteracted the alcohol stupor. In my twisted mind, I believed if I could find a dealer, I could survive.

That night, I started asking around the bar if anyone knew where a fellow might pick up a little cocaine every now and then. One of the regulars told me to come back the next night and I could meet a dealer. The regular's name was Boston.

I couldn't wait to get back. I was like a little kid going to the fair. I scraped together all the loose cash we had in the house. I knew Paula had been hiding money ever since I started going back to the bars. Our apartment wasn't very big, so it wasn't too hard to find her little stashes of cash.

I drove to Grappler's myself on Saturday night. I got there about nine thirty, and Boston hadn't yet arrived, so I sat down at the bar and ordered a beer. About an hour later, I saw Boston come in with several other men. I didn't know if one of them was my connection or not, so I waited for him to come to me. I kept an eye on them, and from time to time, Boston would glance in my direction.

They had been there about an hour when one of the guys at his table got up and headed for the men's room. He was probably the cleanest looking of the group. He was dressed in flannels and had a rugged, outdoors look about him. Boston caught my eye and slightly jerked his head in the direction the man was going, and I took that as my cue to follow.

I stepped into the men's room, and he was not in sight. I assumed he stepped into a stall. I stood at the sink and started to run water in the pretext of washing my hands. As I was drying, he stepped up beside me. He spoke first.

"How's it going?"

"All right. Nice night."

"You Bosty's friend?"

"I know Boston."

"You lookin' for a buy?"

"You know where I can make one?"

"I think so. How much you looking for?"

"Couple hundred dollars worth."

"Meet me at this address tomorrow night at nine fifteen. You bring anybody with you, and you'll not see me then or ever again."

"Not a problem." He shoved a piece of paper in my shirt pocket and walked out. I waited a few moments before my exit.

I left home the next evening as Paula was feeding the kids dinner.

"Donnie, do you have to go out tonight? It's Sunday night, and I was hoping we could have a quiet evening together. Just you and me, and we'll put the kids to bed early."

"Not tonight. Some other time."

"Please, Donnie. It would mean so much to me to see you make an effort to stay out of the bars. You know your work is suffering, and so am I. We came up here to get a new start, and all the progress we've made is just being thrown out with the empty beer cans. Donnie—"

I pushed her aside. I heard all I was going to listen to. I started to walk away but then turned and said, "Don't crowd me, Paula, and don't tell me what to do. I'll handle my job. I'm not fired yet."

I slammed the door and drove to Grappler's.

Boston was there when I arrived, and I acknowledged his presence but tried to stay clear of him for fear of being watched by some other figure in the ring. I felt the wad of cash in my pocket and thought about what I was doing. Every beer I drank made my decision to see it through seem a little more reasonable. At nine o'clock, I left Grappler's and headed for the location to meet my connection. The deal was made without incident, and I couldn't wait for my first hit.

I went back to the bar before returning to Paula and the kids. When I finally went home, Paula was asleep on the couch. I knew she had waited up for me, hoping I would return early. I told myself she had no clue about the little package I was bringing back into our life. My alcohol consumption was modest. I had to keep a clear head until I had the little bag of white powder securely in my hands. In the morning, work would be good.

I returned to work on Monday morning, as Jack suggested. He seemed pleased with my appearance. He stuck out his hand and laid the other on my shoulder. There was caring in his demeanor. I could feel it.

"Well, Donnie, you're looking good this morning. How was your weekend?'

"It was good, Jack. It was good. Had some quality time with Paula and the kids."

"How do you feel about coming back on the job?"

I was feeling the peak of the high I was on at that particular moment, and I would have agreed to a run with a grizzly bear to keep my job.

"Jack, you have no idea how much I appreciate your patience with my behavior these last several weeks. You really were under no obligation to give me this second chance. If you're willing to take a chance with me, I think I can keep things under control." What I meant was, as long as I had a little cocaine in my pocket, I could bluff my way through anything.

He stuck out his hand again. "Glad to have you back, Donnie. You can pick up where you left off and resume with the job you were on. If you ever need to talk or need someone to get you through a rough spot, I'd be glad to have you give me a call. I know firsthand what you're dealing with."

I liked Jack. He was a good man, but he really had no idea what I was dealing with. I wasn't even sure I fully understood the severity of my problem.

My little plan went on for weeks without the slightest flaw. I could drink all night, snort a little coke, and be good to go by the time the early shift whistle blew. My frame of mind returned to the mindset of addiction. It was all I cared about. I took several hits during the day, and for all appearances' sake, I had my act together and was an honorable employee. I'd found an adequate supplier. The goods were excellent, and I was right back where I was before I moved my family to this iceberg toward the upper crust of the world.

Part of my job was to take my turn to be on call during the night shifts. I was only needed in the event there was an equipment breakdown or blowouts on the wells or any other trouble.

One treacherous snowy night, my phone rang about midnight. I hadn't anticipated going out, so I'd been drinking heavy all evening. I hung up the phone and looked out the window to see a blinding snowstorm, not the kind of Alaskan night I wanted to be out, especially to work. My services were needed at Swanson Valley, so I bundled up, grabbed a bag of cocaine, braved the elements, and fired up my pickup. On my way to the truck yard to get my semi, I stopped by a liquor store and bought several cans of Tequila Sunrises. It might be a long night, and I wanted to be prepared. I drove to the truck yard and crawled in my semi. While I waited for the truck to warm up, I drank a couple tequila drinks. Whiteouts and horrendous winds were making the run to Swanson Valley very hazardous for most drivers, but I'd been drinking and shooting up, and I had all the courage I needed.

I approached a long hill with a very steep grade where truckers were pulling off the road to chain up. I had no intention of stopping to put chains on my truck, but as I approached the bottom of the hill, one driver stepped out in front of me and flagged me in. I rolled my window down, "Ev'ning! What's up?" I knew but thought I'd act interested and ask.

"You been on this road before?"

"Coupla times. Why?"

"You were coming down the road there at a pretty good clip, and I just wanted to make sure you were going to pull off and chain up before you try to climb this grade. You're not going to make it if you don't."

"Ah, I'll be okay. It don't look too bad. I think I can make it."

"Listen, buddy, you better take the time to chain up, or you'll end up putting this rig over the cliff. It's nothing but ice and snow."

The booze and cocaine were running my mouth and overriding my head. I was on a high that gave me the guts of a raging bull and about as much sense.

"I'll be all right," I said and shifted that big old truck into low gear and started the climb. About halfway up the grade, the truck spun out, jack knifing, and slid, dropping the right rear tandems off the road. I could feel the tank teetering over the side of a three-hundred-foot cliff. I jumped out of the cab, and a trucker with chains stopped short of where I was. Once he saw I wasn't hurt, he radioed for a rescue team. I left my bag of cocaine on the seat, so I eased back in the cab to get it and shoved it inside my shirt. When help arrived, they smelled alcohol on my breath and called Jack.

I waited at the bottom of the hill with a member of the rescue team until Jack arrived to pick me up.

"What happened, Donnie?"

He knew what happened. I didn't have to tell him. He took me back to town, and we stopped at an all-night coffee shop. We went in, and he ordered black coffee for both of us.

"Donnie, I can't let this behavior go undisciplined. You know that."

"No, sir, I know that. I slipped up tonight, and I'm sorry. I'm sorry about the truck, and I'm sorry you had to come out and get me."

"What about your habits, Donnie? Do you have any remorse about them?"

I didn't know what to say. If I said yes, he was going to send me to a treatment center. If I said no, I might as well kiss my job good-bye, so I said nothing. I just stirred my coffee. I needed another hit. Coke highs were good, but they just didn't last.

Several minutes passed, and neither of us spoke. Finally, Jack leaned across the table, "Donnie, I can't just throw you out and turn my back on you. There's something about you that tells me you can kick this habit. I want to see you win your battle of addiction."

Did he know about the cocaine or was he just referring to my alcohol addiction? I didn't know.

"Let's see if we can't work out some kind of deal for you. Whaddya say?"

There was no reason to try and fool him.

"I dunno. Let's hear the deal."

"Check yourself into a treatment center and get yourself dried out and then come back and see me. If you stay clean, I'll hire you back."

"I dunno, Jack. I've been this way a long time."

"You have everything to gain and nothing to lose if you really want it."

"Yeah, okay. Why not? I guess I can do that."

He gave me the names and numbers of people and facilities I could contact for help. We talked a while longer, and it was about 5:00 a.m. when he took me home.

"Take the day off, Donnie. You've had a long night."

Okay, maybe he didn't know about my coke habit. With enough hits, I could stay up for days, but I took the day off and took a thirty-day leave from work on the presumption I would get professional help for my addiction.

Kenai was a very small community. Everyone knew everyone, and everyone knew everyone's business. I had no intention of going to a treatment center and never tried to hide it.

It was two weeks into my work hiatus, and I was arrested for drunk driving. Now, beer flowed free in Alaska, but drunk driving was not tolerated. The penalty for the first offense was a mandatory three-day jail sentence; second offense, ten days; third offense, thirty days. I spent my three days behind bars.

I didn't count it a total loss. During my three-day imprisonment, I met a king pin who had been busted, not for drugs, but for some minor offense. As we conversed, it got my foot in the door to again sell drugs. He told me where I could reach him, and when we were released, I bought cocaine from him and sold it in the bars in and around the Kenai Peninsula. Paula was devastated. She lost that special glow she carried when she first came to Kenai. She was looking tired and weary, like she had when I left her to come to Alaska. I also returned to my abusive treatment of her and the kids. But in my deceived mind, I was trying to keep the bills paid. Wasn't that all that mattered? Whenever I left the house, I would travel with six to eight loaded syringes neatly filed in a dart pouch I carried in my boot.

When my thirty-day leave expired, I returned to the main office looking for Jack. He escorted me to a make-do conference room with two other foremen or supervisors. The conversation didn't take long. They knew I reneged on my promise to seek treatment, and they knew my license had been suspended from the DUI, so they denied me work with the company. However, they did say I could reapply for a position after a one-year suspension.

I had several cokeheads as *friends*. There was one we called Digger. His brother was head foreman for one of the biggest roustabout companies on the Kenai Peninsula. They were lenient in the hiring process. There was no pre-employment drug testing, but once they hired you, they had no tolerance for shoddy performance or character.

Digger pulled some strings and got me hired on, but I had to work at Prudhoe Bay, right on the northern coastline. It was approximately 1,040 miles from Kenai to the bay. The job plan was this: the company would fly us in, we worked two weeks, and they flew us back to Kenai. We were off two weeks, and then they flew us back for another two weeks on the job, and that was the schedule. Take it or leave it. I took it.

Several of us were taking a break in a work shelter one day, smoking marijuana. We thought we had the shelter well secured where the smoke smell would stay confined, but we were wrong. It wasn't long before there was a knock on the door and security came in, and we were busted for smoking weed. They confiscated the weed I had on me, *plus* they found my stash of cocaine. Not only did I lose my job, I was officially kicked out of Prudhoe Bay with the understanding I was *never* to come back.

I went home, found another roustabout company, doctored up a couple numbers on my social security card, changed my date of birth back to 1958, and finagled my way into their employ. Where did this company send me? Right back up to Prudhoe Bay. That hitch lasted a short time, and I was back in Kenai and out of Prudhoe Bay for good.

Back in Kenai, trying to make a life for myself, I started looking for employment. Paula had taken the kids and left. I knew it was a matter of time, and I really didn't care. Neither did I try to find her.

Being a respectable husband was not something I ever worked at, and I wasn't about to grovel over a woman. It was easier for me to let her and the kids go than to deal with what I saw when I faced the truth about myself. I was never going to change.

By this time I had a new girlfriend. They weren't hard to come by. Her name was Sarah. Sarah and I had been together for a while, and I thought things were over between Paula and me. I couldn't blame Paula for taking all she was going to take from me and my addictions and my devilish lifestyle.

I thought I had her out of my head until one day I passed a vehicle on the road on the Kenai Peninsula. I was sure it was her sitting next to the driver. I spun my truck around, and I chased them and taunted them until I finally ran them off the road. I bailed out of my truck and busted out his driver's window. My intention was to kill the guy if I could. Paula was screaming while I was relentlessly punching him through the busted window. He managed to pull a knife from his boot. I didn't see the knife until he took a downward jab, just missing my gut. He took a couple more swings at me from inside the truck but never offered to get out. I didn't consider that too great a threat, but I backed off. I went back to my truck with a vengeance to find him again. The next time, I'd be armed, and there would be no barrier between us.

I continued to keep an eye out for his vehicle, and it was only a couple days later I saw him again. I spun around and was in pursuit. This time it looked like he was alone. We ran through the countryside until we were well out of sight or earshot of anyone. He pulled off the main road onto a little dirt road leading to forested area along a river. He stopped his truck. Then, throwing dust and rocks, he spun around backward so his truck was facing me. I made sure the chamber of my handgun was fully loaded and tucked it behind me in my jeans belt. I opened the door and started to get out when he opened his door. He never shut off the engine, but he dropped one foot on the ground, assessing the situation. Then suddenly, he stood up behind the opened door and opened fire. He fired two stray shots before I could shoot once. I stayed behind the door of my truck and fired one shot, more or less just to let him know I too was armed. He jumped back in the driver's seat, jerked his vehicle into gear, and was coming at me with an open door and a pointed weapon. I had only seconds to make my decision, and I lined him up and I shot. His head flew back. I saw the handgun fly from his hand onto the ground. I had to dodge his runaway truck as it flew by me and crashed through the tree line and into the woodland. The only thing I remember seeing as the truck sped by me was the way he slumped across the seat of the truck.

I got back in my truck and sat there. Once or twice, I looked toward his wrecked vehicle in the trees and saw no sign of him moving. My body started shaking and convulsing until I thought I would literally lose all control of all my senses.

Yes, I was enraged to see him with Paula.

Yes, in my twisted, deranged mind, I wanted to kill him for being with her even though I treated her like dirt.

Yes, anger, hatred, and rage were magnified under the distorted influence of cocaine. Had I really done what my enraged heart desired to do? I didn't know. I thought back to the beatings I inflicted as an enforcer for the Butcher. Beating a guy to within an inch of his life didn't bother me, but this was tearing me apart. Why? I think it was because I was on my own. I had no kingpin or drug lord to back me up. I shot a man over a woman. In my demented state, I wondered if it was even worth it.

What was happening to me? At one point, I remember screaming, just opening my voice with a gut-wrenching bellow helped to clear my head. There was no one to hear me but the muskrats, caribou, and brown bear. Would they find him first?

I have no idea how long I sat there. When I finally quit shaking enough, I reached in the glove compartment for a syringe.

Everything would be all right now.

O Lord, oppose those who oppose me;
Declare war on those who are attacking me;
Lift up your spear and javelin
And block the way of my enemies;
Let me hear you say, "I am your salvation!"
How long, O Lord, will you look on and do nothing?
Rescue me from their fierce attacks ...

Psalm 35: 1, 3, 17 (NLT)

I kept a very low profile after this. My idea of going into hiding was to stay out of the public's eye, which meant out of the bars. I was sure I was being trailed. I could feel it. My guilt was so horrendous that at times I felt like a madman. It was making me believe the authorities were trailing me twenty-four hours a day.

I hid for the next couple of days. Finally, late one night, I drank myself into enough courage to drive back to the wilderness, where I'd left the unconscious man in his truck. I wasn't sure I could find the area again, but as I drove out of the town, some strange phenomena created flashbacks of countryside and memory of what I'd seen through angry eyes of hate as I pursued the chase of a man I didn't even know but wanted to kill. Strangely enough, I had no trouble retracing the route. As I rounded the final bend in the path, déjà vu slapped me right between the eyes. An eerie ambiance hung over the woodland where I'd been forced to protect myself and now reentered like a bad dream.

The night was black as pitch with only a sliver of moon visible. It moved in and out of gentle clouds as I approached the winding dirt path where our encounter faced off. Like the memory of a bad dream, my head reeled with the sound of his revving engine as he came directly at me, pointing a loaded handgun at my face. In the stillness of the forest, I again heard the shot as it rang through my head as clear as the day I fired my weapon. Was it my shot I heard or his? I couldn't tell. I played it over and over in my head. It was as clear as the day it happened.

I opened the door of my truck. Did I really want to get out now that I was here? I grabbed my flashlight and turned to put my feet on the ground. I could see the damaged tree where his truck came to a stop. As I stood upright, my heart began to repeat its erratic rhythm, pounding so loud in my chest it vibrated in my ears. I couldn't make my feet walk on. His truck was gone, and the grounds were quiet. I couldn't tell that any other vehicles had been here. Hopefully the guy regained consciousness enough he was able to drive himself out. I had no way of knowing. There had been no local news reports of the likeness of any incident where I might have been accused. That thought and the cool Alaska night breeze cleared my head. Somehow it was soothing. My worst fear was that I would find the scene just as I had left it, but the only telltale sign was the damaged tree. I got back in my truck and started to leave.

I didn't even know the guy's name.

> Know also that wisdom is sweet to your soul; if you find it, there is a future hope for you, and your hope will not be cut off.
>
> Proverbs 24:14 (NIV)

I asked Sarah how she felt about leaving Kenai. Although she really knew very little about me, she knew I was dealing with very deep-rooted thorns. She had nothing to hold her in Kenai, so we packed a few things in our Lincoln Continental and left Kenai, Alaska, late one night. She had a sister, Madeline, in California. She called Maddie and told her we were coming.

As far as I knew, Paula and the kids were still somewhere in the Kenai area. As of yet, I had not been alerted to any steps being taken to legally divorce me or even legal separation. I wasn't one for living by the law, so to me it didn't matter one way or the other.

We headed out of town on Spur Highway and drove up through Anchorage, down through the Yukon Territory, through British Columbia, Washington, Oregon, and into northern California. It was a 3,200-mile trip, and we made it in a little over two days. I had plenty of cocaine and kept it ready for immediate injection, and I could drive for hours.

We arrived at her sister's late in the afternoon. Sarah's brother-in-law, Vic, was a man of like-mindedness with me. He was, of all things, a *marijuana farmer*, so he and I hit it off. He knew what it was like to live in the shadows.

We had no sooner been seated and offered a beer upon our arrival when Maddie's phone rang, and it was Sarah's mother. Although the mother wasn't aware that we had actually arrived, she was calling Maddie to tell her she was concerned about our arrival. Somehow she received word that the authorities were looking for us. That was all I needed to hear. I knew I had better lay low.

Maddie and Vic had a few acres in the northern mountains where forest and foliage grew thick. I stayed up in the mountains and away from civilization. Within a couple months, I turned into the image of a grizzly mountain man. Day in and day out, all I did was shoot up with cocaine, smoke marijuana, and drink. Life was a living hell.

I needed a new identity. I lied my way around, presenting any tangible paperwork upfront. I decided to use the last name of my stepdad, Carpenter. From that day on, I was Foster when I could be, but I became Donnie Carpenter when it was necessary.

Hellish as life was, I never tried to change anything. I kept up my drug and alcohol addictions by selling Vic's crop. He had weed growing in several stages, so there was always a portion to harvest. I would come out of hiding long enough to help him harvest and process the ready growth. He had processed weed ready for immediate sale all the time. That was my expertise. By now, I had a thick beard and long hair, and at times I barely recognized myself in the mirror. I was making my new identity work for me.

From time to time, I would pack up to twenty pounds of marijuana in a large trunk. To create deception of the trunk's true contents, I would add bricks or rocks for weight. I would transport the goods to the airport and catch a red-eye flight to Anchorage. The next morning, I would sell the weed to my connection there I simply knew as Kattman. Then I loaded my bricks and rocks back into the trunk and flew back to California with anywhere from sixty-thousand dollars to one hundred thousand dollars stashed in my bags, pockets, boots, coat, anywhere I could conceal cash. I was a walking ATM. Although I was making a good living, I was digging myself deeper and deeper into the miry pit of destruction. I was a man so smart in the world of deceit that I lost all sense of reason because the biggest man I was deceiving was me.

As the weeks rolled by, I was getting a little braver about letting myself be seen in public. Like I said, I barely recognized myself, and the cocaine kept me believing I had courage, and the booze kept my highs mellowed out.

The phone rang late one night after Sarah had gone to bed. I'd been shooting up all day, and sleep was not an option. I grabbed the phone before it woke Sarah.

"H'lo."

"Is Sarah there, please?"

"She's in bed. Who's this?"

"I'm Sarah's aunt Barbara from Alaska. I know it's very late, but it's quite important I speak with Sarah. This concerns her father."

"Yeah, okay. I'll get her."

Sarah heard the phone and was already coming to see who was calling so late. I could tell by her end of the conversation things were not good.

"This is Sarah... Aunt Barbie! What's wrong? Oh no! When? Was Mom with him? Which hospital is he in? Okay. Is anyone staying with him now? Sure. Of course I'll come. Can you arrange for someone to pick me up at the airport? I'll call you as soon as I know my flight schedule. Of course, Aunt Barbie, you know I will. I don't know if Maddie can come right away or not, but I'll go tell her right now. Please tell Mom I'll be there as soon as I can, and tell Daddy I love him. Thank you for calling, Aunt Barbie. You too. Bye."

"What's going on?"

"It's Daddy. He's had a severe heart attack. Donnie, I have to go be with him and Mom. Aunt Barbie said Mom is a basket case. I have to go tell Maddie. You're going to have to take me to the airport, Donnie. Hopefully I can catch a flight early in the morning if not tonight."

Maddie and Vic were still up when Sarah called on them. As she suspected, she was going to have to go to Alaska by herself, and Maddie would follow as soon as she could. She packed a bag, and I drove her to the airport.

Several days later, she called me to tell me her dad would recover. It was going to be a slow process, but the prognosis looked positive.

It was close to a month into her stay that during one of our phone conversations I asked, "How long do you think you'll have to stay with your mom, Sarah?"

A long silence followed my question.

"Sarah? Are you there? I asked how long you plan to stay."

"Donnie, I'm not coming home."

"What?"

"I got a job, Donnie, and I've been working for about a week. I'm not coming back to California."

"What do you mean you're not coming back? Why not?"

"I can't, Donnie. I have my reasons, but all I'm going to say is if you want to see me, you're going to have to come to Alaska. I have to go now—"

"Sarah! Don't hang up! Sarah!"

I slammed the phone down and kicked the table, swearing under my breath.

There was really no reason for me to stay on in California. I had no job. I was making periodic trips to Anchorage anyway to sell Vic's weed. After a couple weeks, I decided to return to Anchorage. I went straight to Sarah's mom's house, and, to my surprise, Sarah was there. She didn't seem upset that I followed her back to Alaska, so I stayed on with the intention of finding a job.

I had only been there two days when I stopped by her place of employment to take her to lunch. While I was waiting in her office, a man walked in and asked, "Are you Sarah Jewel?"

She stood to her feet and said, "Yes, I'm Sarah."

"Miss Jewel, you are under arrest. You have the right to remain silent. Anything you say can and will be used against you in a court of law."

Her eyes were as big as saucers. He cuffed her and started to lead her out of her office.

"Donnie, call my mom. Tell her I need her to bail me out. Please, Donnie. Go tell Mom."

The officer looked me over and asked Sarah, "You know him?"

"He's a friend of mine." I stood there speechless. As soon as Sarah and the officer were out of the building, I ran. Without Sarah, I really had nowhere to go. I couldn't go back to her mom's. I had no friends or even acquaintances in the area. The only person I knew in Anchorage was Kattman, my drug connection I'd been selling all the bags of weed to from Vic's little farm.

I knew where he lived, so I paid him a visit. I knocked and waited. I knocked again. He had to be home. He was my only hope. After the third knock, I heard footsteps coming to the door. He opened it only a crack. I tried to push my way in, but he stood firm, so I tried to talk to him where I was.

"Whaddya want?"

"Just need to talk to you, Kattman. I need a little help. I was hoping you could loan me about eight thousand dollars to help out a friend that got herself arrested."

Before I could say another word, Kattman told me to get out and never come back and slammed the door in my face. Did he know about Sarah? Did he know something I didn't?

Did Kattman think I was working undercover? Sarah … Vic … Kattman … was this the reason Sarah decided to stay in Alaska?

Talk about not seeing the forest for the trees. For the first time in my life, I realized how screwed up my life had become. I felt like a beaten man. I had no one to trust. I had no one to turn to. I had no friends, and I had no job. I had no place to live. I had no place to go. I was alone. I didn't even have a circle of drinking buddies where I could go and be lost in a sea of faces. Perhaps it was desperation that made me stop and look inward. When there was no one to care whether I lived or died, I began to realize what a lonely man I was in a world that didn't care. I literally ran scared from Sarah's office to see Kattman, and when he turned me away, I found myself in the land of the midnight sun with not so much as a warm place to lay my head. I didn't have enough money to get home, and I was a destitute addict whose next move would have been to become a street beggar.

I just started to walk. I felt the eyes of guilt always on my back, feeling the threat of somebody following me or spying on me. I would turn aside from time to time just to make sure it was my imagination. I was hungry and fished in my pockets for some cash. I had enough to buy a decent meal at a diner, so I went in and ordered the special, hot beef sandwich with mashed potatoes and gravy, carrots, and a scoop of ice cream for dessert.

It was the best food I had for several weeks. Even the carrots tasted good. Most of the time, the cocaine left me with no desire for food, so I ate very little, but tonight the mashed potatoes and hot beef sandwich smothered in thick gravy gave me comfort. I finished my meal and had enough change for a beer. My mind actually functioned on a level of reality. I even began to wonder if fate itself had abandoned me. With no one to encourage or discourage me, I toyed with the idea of turning myself into the authorities just to get it over with. I could see myself as a fugitive running from one thing or another for the rest of my life. Is that really what I wanted?

I paid my tab and walked to an all-night gas station/body shop. There was a television in one corner with some magazines and free coffee. I had nowhere else to go, so I planned on staying there as long as I could. I tried to get interested in what was playing on TV. My head kept going back to, *Get it over with, Donnie. It's now or never. You're finished! You're washed up! Your luck will not last forever! Face the music, and get it over with! Do it! Only a fool would keep running! Sarah's in jail, turn yourself in, serve your time, and then get out and make something of yourself.*

I stayed at the station until the *Tonight Show* went off the air. There was a midnight movie coming on when I left and started toward the police headquarters in Anchorage, Alaska.

Once I arrived at the police station, I walked back and forth in front of the entrance, trusting and then doubting I was doing the right thing. The worst place on all this earth was jail. I *did not* want to go back to jail. I swore repeatedly in the past I would do all in my power to never go back behind bars. My jail experiences in the past were absolute hell, and the little devil perched on my shoulder kept reminding me of my prior experience.

The headlights of a cruiser startled me back to reality. It pulled into one of several empty parking places, and two uniformed officers got out. My first instinct was to run, but my feet didn't budge. The officers started to walk past me, and then one of them stopped and turned around.

"Hey, you! Do you need something?"

"Uh...what?"

"Can we help you?"

My head was working in slow motion, but, as was natural, my tongue was firing like a speeding bullet. "I wanna turn myself in."

"How's that?"

I faltered. The voice in my head was saying, *Just walk away, Donnie. Just walk away.*

"Did you say something?" he asked again, this time taking a couple steps in my direction.

My throat felt shaky, and my tongue felt thick, but I said, "Yes, sir. I'm Donald Foster, and I want to turn myself in."

"Mack, get over here!" he called to his partner, and the two of them escorted me into the building and set me down in a secured area.

I really don't remember much about the inquisition, but I do remember telling them I knew there were warrants for my arrest, and I was tired of running.

They ran a check on all my priors and officially booked me on various drug charges, DUIs, and domestic abuse, but there were no charges or warrants for attempted murder for the man I shot. They extradited me back to Kenai, where I went to trial and received a two-year sentence in Kenai Wilderness Correctional Facility (KWCF).

Working out in the gym one afternoon, I struck up a conversation with an inmate we called Watts. We had talked on numerous occasions, and I knew he was soon to be released. Like me, he was in for drugs. He was excited about gaining his freedom but had no intentions of going straight.

"So, Watts, where are you going once you get out?"

"I got a connection at Anchor Point. He'll have some plans for me. How 'bout you? How much longer you got?"

"Couple months."

"Got any plans?"

"Nope. Most of my bridges have been burned. I've got no plans and no one to go home to."

"Tell ya what, Foster. I can help you get on your feet if you want to come to Anchor Point. Ever been there?"

"Used to live there."

"We've got a tight ring in Anchor Point if you wanna give it a shot."

"Oh yeah? I got a little time. I'll give it some thought."

Wow! An open door, and I was not even out yet. I kept that possibility in the back of my mind.

At the end of the two years and one day, I was called in to the warden's office, "You're going to be a free man in a few days, Foster."

Those *few days* seemed like a life sentence, but when the day finally came, I received what financial means I was granted and my personal belongings. Paula had divorced me, and prior to my release, I learned she took the kids and went back to Cave Junction, Oregon, to her mother. Sarah remained in Alaska. As soon as I hit the streets, I went directly to a motel room and called Watts.

"Watts? Donnie."

"Are you out?"

"Got out yesterday. That offer still good?"

"Yeah, we'll work something out. When can you be here?"

"Coupla days."

"Okay."

He gave me an address in Anchor Point where to meet him.

"I'll meet you there, and we'll talk."

"I'll be there."

I jotted down the address but knew exactly where I was to meet him.

I used part of the money to buy a ticket to Anchor Point and then met him at the designated location. He looked better than he did while in prison. His clothes were expensive, and he was driving a nice pickup.

We talked about me being a drug runner. He knew I had no money to pay upfront, so he fronted me ten pounds of marijuana and enough money to travel back to Kenai to sell it for him.

I caught a small plane back to Kenai and then checked in to a cheap motel and started my runs the next day. Before my first twenty-four hours were up in Kenai, I sold all but a couple pounds of weed for anywhere from four hundred fifty dollars to six hundred dollars a pound. I had the money in my pocket and enough weed for myself for a while. I went back to the motel room. I threw the cash on the bed and counted it. I had a bundle of cash well over four thousand dollars and nothing but an open road ahead of me. Watts would never think to come to Oregon looking for me. He should have known better than to front an ex-con that much product.

I also knew my parole officer wouldn't be looking for me yet because I'd been out of jail one day shy of a week. I called one of the contacts I sold to that day, gave him a sob story, and asked if he would mind driving me to the airport. He obliged, and I bought a ticket to Medford, Oregon. I burned Watts for the weed, violated my parole, and I was going back to Cave Junction, Oregon. Who knows, maybe I could find Paula.

Early the next morning, I hitchhiked the fifty-eight-mile trek from Medford to Cave Junction. It was a nice town, so I set about trying to find work before looking for Paula. I landed a job with a small sawmill. We made the ends for watermelon crates and other boxes for shipping and storing fruit.

On the job, I met Jeff, a real cowboy—boots, buckles, and hat. Jeff liked weed and booze. He had a cute little wife named Cherry. I spent time with Jeff and Cherry on weekends, and Jeff and I hung out in the bars almost every night after work.

Cherry met Jeff at the door one night after work and said Abby, a friend of hers from California, called earlier in the day and wanted to know if she could come and stay with them for a while. Abby found herself in a relationship with a very abusive guy, and the two of them abused themselves with addictions to metham-phetamines. She asked if she could please come to get away from her abuser and hopefully the addiction.

Cherry was a sweet and caring girl, and Jeff was okay with the girl coming. Abby showed up a few days later. She was the ugliest female body I ever saw. She was skin and bones, knock kneed, and gangly, but something about her face was very attractive.

She wanted nothing to do with me or Jeff. She had been

burned by the male species one too many times. She hid out with Cherry for the first few weeks, and I saw her only occasionally. She and Cherry would bring lunch to Jeff and me at the sawmill every day.

I tried to be a gentleman whenever I was around her. I liked her, and the selfish side of me wanted more than just a casual relationship with her, but she wanted nothing to do with me. I was a druggie and a drinker, and she wanted no part of that lifestyle anymore.

As time passed, she dropped her guard and began to trust me. I hid my addictions well when around her. Would I be willing to change for her? Sort of. What happened was this: I became an alcoholic addicted to cocaine who learned to hide my addictions very well. I admired her diligence to abstain from drugs, but I became an artist at hiding mine. I didn't have as much trouble cutting back on the booze, but I never changed my drug habits. I expanded my drug consumption to include methamphetamines, which was the very thing Abby was running from. I fell in love with their effects, and they totally changed who I was. Cocaine highs would last only a short time, but a good meth fix would last eight to twelve hours. It was a new kind of high, and I loved it. I also found it to be very lucrative. I became a meth dealer, as well as cocaine.

I had my own apartment, and Abby was living with Jeff and Cherry. When she thought I was trying to cut back on my addictions, she began to spend more one-on-one time with me. Our relationship was strictly platonic because she wanted it that way. As our relationship moved along, it drifted away from platonic, and eventually Abby moved in with me.

Jeff and I arrived at work one day to find the little sawmill in flames. It was suggested a lit cigarette carelessly tossed ignited the blaze. Nevertheless, I was out of job and looking again.

I contacted a local businessman in Cave Junction, and he hired me to operate a backhoe. The backhoe work kept Abby and me in groceries and rent. The meth highs were ego boosters, and I grew into confidence that I could run and operate my own business. It had to be something with low, low overhead. I finally decided I would be a window washer, and I started my own business. I put out flyers around the local businesses and did quite well. Most of my accounts were commercial, and we floated along successfully.

The town of Cave Junction didn't have its own law enforcement but had police substations. The county sheriff's department would stop by the substations at least once daily to read reports and handle any issues on the register. If law enforcement was ever needed, someone would call the authorities in neighboring communities. Of course, it would take anywhere from twenty to ninety minutes for an officer to respond, but all in all, it was pretty much a quiet little town.

As the months passed, I learned that one of my customers, Phillip Ghetty, was a law enforcement officer. Until then, I had no idea. Once I found out that little piece of information, I befriended Phil, and we became very good friends. As always, my motives were self-centered. I figured the day would come when I might need a friend like Phil, especially someone in his line of work. It never hurt to score some points however I could.

THE AGE OF FALTERING AND RETURN

THE CATALYST: **REBELLIOUS THINKING**

… the seed is the word of God;
The ones along the path
are those who have heard.
Then the devil comes and takes away the word
from their hearts so that they may not believe and be saved.
And the ones on the rock
are those who when they hear the word
receive it with joy. But these have no root;
They believe for a while and in time of testing
fall away.
And as for what fell among the thorns,
they are those who hear,
but as they go on their way they are choked
by the cares and riches and pleasures of life
and their fruit does not mature.

As for that in the good soil,
they are those who, hearing the word,
hold it fast in an honest and good heart,
and bear fruit with patience.

Luke 8: 11–15 (ESV)

Things were going well between Abby and me. She came to trust me not to abuse her even though she still had no idea how much doping I was doing. I knew she had three children she wanted to bring to Oregon from California.

I surprised her one weekend. We went down to O'Brien for a day in the mountains. I asked Abby to marry me. She accepted, and we set a date and bought our license. A few weeks later, we drove back to the mountains. Abby wanted to be married by a man of the clergy. I didn't care. But I cared for Abby and wanted to get off on the right foot, so we scouted around for a pastor to do the job. We searched the Yellow Pages and finally found one who answered his phone. He was Pastor Jacob DeBaine. He pastured the flock of an Assembly of God Church. He readily admitted he didn't feel comfortable just marrying us on the spur of the moment but said he would be glad to perform the honors if we would be willing to come back to him a couple of times for some premarital counseling.

"Donnie, what can it hurt?" Abby pleaded.

"All right, but I'm not listening to a bunch of preaching and Bible rambling. I just want the dude to marry us, that's all." We obliged, and I apparently gave the man all the right answers.

We went back up to the mountains on a Saturday afternoon. Jeff and Cherry were the only other people with us. It was a beautiful outdoor ceremony, and we became Mr. and Mrs. Donnie Foster.

A few days after the marriage, I decided I needed to pull out all the stops concerning who I really was. We finished dinner, and I asked Abby to go for a walk with me. There were some things I needed to tell her.

I found it difficult to make small talk, so I just blurted right out, "Abby, I'm an alcoholic, a doper, and a drug dealer. I've been covering up my true self ever since I've known you, and I don't want to do that anymore. I want you to know what you've married."

Looking back, what happened next was probably one of the most pitiful things of my past. She just looked at me, and within a couple weeks, she became what I was. She couldn't beat me, so she joined me. She started using methamphetamines again.

Abby and I were so deep in debt because of our drug addictions that we lost the apartment we were in. We were forced to move into a rat-infested house owned by Abby's brother, Walt.

Through all the drugs and lack of money, I never had to part with my motorcycle. I borrowed or stole to have some cash but never once considered giving up my bike.

I had a Harley, and I started riding with a guy in Cave Junction we called Flaming Joe. He told me he was a member of the King's Rollers Motorcycle Club. He invited me to sit in on the club's meetings. I was mean, and I was ruthless. They allowed me to go on drug runs with them by way of sizing me up to be a prospective member. I fit right into their circle because I could do anything just as good or better than anyone of them could do. I knew I was definitely King's Rollers material.

Abby was so hurt when I started riding with the club. She was disappointed and devastated that I would let myself be included in their circle. Nevertheless, she stayed with me.

It's a funny thing when both parties of a couple are addicts. The woman will stay with the guy no matter how rotten life gets. The reason she stays hinges between security and safety or out of fear of leaving.

I was selling drugs to Walt, which was part of the deal to let us live in that rat hole.

Along the front of the property was a row of trees that hid the house from the public eye. There were two smaller buildings on the property that Walt offered to let me fix up and use as a meetinghouse for the bike club. It turned into a rather quaint and secure hideaway where we hung out and made meth. We used the other building to hide the goods we stole. Every weekend, we held our drinking and doping parties there. From the road, our little hideaway was out of sight, and the booze and drugs flowed freely.

My little window washing business was failing because I was slothful in order to do my drug thing, and I was not dedicating the time I needed to satisfy my clients. I was in debt up to my neck, and Abby was at the end of her rope.

I became so desperate to maintain the methamphetamine habit that I was stealing anything I could in order to meet my addiction. Through my little window washing service, I learned of a local businessman who had a nice array of weapons he collected. He had shotguns, rifles, and handguns. On a weekend of cashless panic, I burglarized his home, taking all the guns I could find. Some I sold to pawn shops, some to individuals, a couple guys in the bike club bought one, and a couple I kept. What I didn't know was the wife of the man's home I burglarized was a sister to one of Flaming Joe's drug connections who lived in the wilderness country of southwest Oregon.

Two or three weeks passed. Late one Saturday night, Flaming Joe and three of the guys from King's Rollers came by the house in an old beat-up car. They were going to re-up and asked me to go with them. I crawled in the car, and we sped out on what they called a miracle mile ride. We drove for what seemed like endless miles out into backcountry in no-man's land. I was beginning to get an uneasy feeling.

We finally stopped at a dark and secluded cabin out in the middle of nowhere. One by one, we got out of the car and went in. Three other guys and I milled around while Flaming Joe disappeared behind closed doors to talk to the man that lived there.

When Joe reappeared, we left. This was all very strange procedure. It wasn't long until we pulled up in front of another off-road cabin. We all got out and went in. Joe introduced the man living there as Mac. Beers were passed around, and again Joe and Mac disappeared.

I noticed the three men left to wait with me had an edge on their behavior. Something was in the air, and I didn't know what.

After several minutes, we heard footsteps coming back into the room, and the three moved in around me. I got vibes like I was being entangled in a thorny hedge. Two of them shoved me down onto an overstuffed chair. The third man put his forearm across my throat, and Flaming Joe stepped up. He raised a revolver to my temple. The man who lived there stepped up and pointed his weapon directly at my forehead.

"Hey, man. What's goin' on?" I stammered.

"We want the guns back, Foster!"

"Guns? What guns? What are you talkin' about?"

"Your prized goods you've been sellin' around. We want 'em back! All those guns you stole belonged to Mac's brother-in-law."

"Hey, dude, I didn't know! You gotta believe me! I had no idea who I was taking 'em from. Do you think I'd be so stupid as to take guns from someone you know? Man, I ain't that crazy!"

There was more conversation, and I was sweating. Mac finally spoke up and said, "There's no use killing 'im until we get the guns back. Take him out now, and we'll never get 'em back."

The arm across my throat lifted, and the guns dropped.

Joe stared hard into my eyes and said, "I'll see to it he gets your stuff, Mac. Come around in a couple weeks and pick up what we have."

We drove back to Cave Junction with little conversation. The two in the front seat mumbled from time to time, but the two in the back with me were quiet.

One person I did not want to involve in this was Abby. But addicts go to whatever means are necessary to satisfy their ruthless drive for satisfaction.

When we got back to my house, the entire pack followed me to the door. They were there to take Abby's car as collateral. Her little

Mazda RX7 was parked in front of our house, and they ordered me to get the keys and the title. Flaming Joe walked right in beside me with a gun in my ribs. With every step, he told me if they didn't get what they were there for, it wasn't too late to kill me.

I woke Abby and told her I needed the title to her car and the keys. In a haze of sleep, she questioned my request. Joe stepped into view and took over the conversation. Abby's pleading broke through his anger, but when he left, he made sure, under no uncertain terms, if the guns weren't retrieved in a timely fashion, he would be back to get the Mazda.

I had no money to buy the guns back from the pawnshop. I remembered an old farmer on the edge of town who purchased two of the shotguns. I decided the next morning to go back to him first. I told him I needed to have them back. I gave him some song and dance about how they had been my dad's and I didn't know my brother wanted them and yadda, yadda, yadda. In the course of the conversation, I mentioned I had to buy some back from the pawnshop but didn't know how I could do it. I was broke. At some point, the old gentleman took my desperation to his heart. Before I left him, I had the guns he bought, and he gave me enough money to buy the ones back from the pawnshop. There had to be a spirit more divine than human nature at the heart of the old gentlemen. Thanks to him, my chances of survival were improving.

I managed to satisfy Flaming Joe and paid off the guys in the biker club with meth and cocaine if they would return the guns they purchased from me. I was losing confidence with the King's Rollers, and I was feeling the pressure of the law moving in on me.

I was creating a living hell for myself and Abby and the kids.

"Donnie, let's get out of Oregon. My kids are suffering here because of the way we live, and I want something better for us. Please, Donnie."

"Where do you want to go?"

"Anywhere. I don't care. Just away from here."

What she suggested was sounding like a good idea. I truly felt it was just a matter of time before the law caught up with me.

"Donnie, my brother Jack lives in Bakersfield, California. I know he would let us stay with him until we can get ourselves established there. Have you ever been to Bakersfield?"

I didn't tell her, but I heard Bakersfield was known as the meth capital of the world. She came to Oregon from Bakersfield to escape her abusive relationship, but if she wanted to go, I was game.

"Call your brother and see what he says."

My first job in Bakersfield was laying pipelines underground. I was in the trench digging and laying the pipe to be connected and fused. The weather was mild and in the midforties. Due to the drugs in my body, I was sweating like a marathon runner—a dead giveaway to anyone who's trained to recognize the evidence of drugs. My foreman approached me and said, "Foster, are you all right? You're wringing wet with sweat. You aren't sick, are you?"

"No, just hot, boss. It's hot in that trench. I'll be okay."

"Look at me, Foster." I knew he was checking my eyes.

"Go get a test, Foster. Right now."

"Excuse me? What kind of test, sir?" I tried playing dumb. Sometimes it would work.

"You know what kind of test. Go clock out and don't come back until we know your tests are clean."

Abby's brother provided the urine for the first test when I hired for the job. This time, I had no one to take the test for me, and it came back dirty, and I was fired.

Not ever holding down a job but always looking for one seemed to be my way of life. It was always a good front for selling drugs. With all of my oil field experience, I could land a job with no problem. It was keeping them I had trouble with.

Abby was unhappy with the whole mess and pleaded with me to go back to Oregon where she could be close to Cherry and Jeff. I knew Abby was serious about moving when she agreed to move back into that rat-infested house if we had to. That's just what we did.

The house had a toilet but only a dirt floor in the bathroom. The rats were as comfortable there as we tried to be. The whole scenario was horrible. Abby and I fought night and day. I was always on a drug high and looking for the next fix. We had Abby's three kids with us, and we were not offering them a good life. The King's Rollers club was still meeting in the building out back. I stayed away from them for the time being.

Abby immediately found a job at the Cave Junction grocery store. Mostly, she stocked shelves and worked as a checkout cashier. She worked as much as she could just so she wouldn't have to be home in that rat hole or around me. I can't say I did anything to make life good for her.

One night, she packed up the kids and met me in the kitchen.

"Donnie, I'm taking the kids, and I'm leaving. I can't stay here any longer."

"Where are you going?"

"I'm going to go stay with Phyllis until I can find a place of my own."

"Who's Phyllis?"

"A lady I work with. Donnie, she's the nicest person I've ever met. She offered to let the kids and I stay with her for a while. I've never ever been around anyone who makes me feel like Phyllis makes me feel. There is something so special about her; it makes me just want to cling to her."

Phyllis Rowe was a middle-aged woman in her early fifties who befriended Abby. I could see a change coming over Abby, but I didn't fully understand until now that it was the influence of this woman named Phyllis.

"And just what makes old Phyllis so special?" I asked sarcastically. My pride was hurt, and I didn't want anyone else giving Abby something I couldn't give her and didn't even know existed: peace.

"Donnie, she talks about how much God loves me. She talks about living a life of peace and joy. She really lives it, Donnie. I can see it in her. She talks about God's mercy, and now she's showing me that kind of mercy by letting me and the kids stay with her. Donnie, nobody's ever treated me like she does. There is something so different about Phyllis."

"Oh, a Bible-toting, gospel-preaching woman, huh? Well, I never figured you for one to listen to that kind of nonsense!"

"Maybe it is nonsense, Donnie, but she's different. She has something no one else I've ever known to have. If it's nonsense, then it's nonsense, but right now that nonsense is comforting to me, and I'm going to take her up on her offer. Good-bye, Donnie."

And just like that, she was out the door. I didn't sleep that night. I shot up and was on a screaming high all night. I went back out to the clubhouse and hung out there a while to drink. Only a couple guys came around that night. Back at the house, it was just the rats and me. I watched a couple scamper between the boards in the wall, and as they tried to run and hide, I thought how similar we were.

The same week that Abby left me, I heard there was a series of old-fashioned revival meetings in town. I had a feeling Phyllis was dragging Abby to the meetings and knew if that were true, it would be only a matter of days before she came back to me.

I tried to fill my off time doing productive things. Early one evening, during the week of the revival meetings, I decided I'd clean up my Harley and then ride it around the block where the meetings were being held and see if Abby was attending them. When she didn't come back after the first couple of days, I thought, *Geez! Maybe Phyllis did talk her into going with her,* although I couldn't imagine Abby sitting through any church service.

I soaped my bike down and was squatted on my haunches,

rinsing it with the hose when something in the breather caught my eye. I turned the stream of water away from the bike and took a better look. There in the reflection on the breather I saw a very distinct set of horns. They were sitting atop a head that didn't look like me, but something in the eyes looked like my eyes. I was stunned at what I was seeing. I dropped the hose, and my hands started to shake. I knew the vision was representing me as Satan.

I turned off the water and sat down on the stoop of the house. I didn't feel scared, but I felt extremely vulnerable to something I couldn't identify. I felt my strength completely wiped out. I felt used.

I got on my Harley and headed down the street. If Abby was at that church, I would find her and, if necessary, drag her out in front of everyone. Nothing like this ever came over me before. I didn't like it. It felt as though it was something beyond my control, and I liked to be in control.

I could see the little church in the distance. The closer I got, the angrier I got. I pulled into the parking lot and, as a sign of protest, revved up my bike for the benefit of anyone who could hear.

I parked at the front entrance and dismounted my bike. I glanced at my reflection in the breather one more time, and the image was gone. It did, however, give me a chance to size up my appearance. I realized I was dirty, sweaty, covered in grease and oil, and smelly but proceeded to enter in at the church foyer. In front of me were two massive, artistically sculptured doors. I assumed they led into the sanctuary. I wasn't feeling quite as confident at this particular moment, so I stood there trying to decide exactly what I was going to do.

"Excuse me, sir. May I help you?" spoke the voice from the man whose left hand was gently resting on my shoulder. I saw no one anywhere when I walked through the front door. He startled me, and I spun around and stopped myself before I swung at him. But then I couldn't take my eyes from his face because I knew I'd seen that face before, but where? Was it the face of someone in a picture? I had a flashback of the ornaments on the walls at Jerome's sister's house of the man on the cross. It really was not the same face, but something in those eyes held me to that remembrance.

He stuck out his right hand and introduced himself as Andrew. "Welcome to our service. I'm Andrew."

I shook his hand and said nothing. Then Andrew spoke again.

"God wants me to pray with you, if I may."

"Man, you ain't doin' nothin'! Just back off and leave me alone!"

"Well, you must have come in for a reason. Can I help you in any way at all?

"I'm just looking for my wife."

"Is she here for the service?"

"I dunno. I think she might be."

"Okay. Please take a look around and see if you see her." He opened one of the huge doors. The sanctuary was packed, wall-to-wall people. I stepped inside and walked to the nearest aisle. I took about five steps down the aisle and saw her halfway up in the middle of the pew. I could tell it was her by the leather clip she wore in her hair. It was a leather wrap with a stick through it. I loved it when she wore her hair up like that.

I stopped at the end of the aisle row she was in, and she had her head down. My discourteous behavior was causing enough unrest among the congregation, and she sensed something out of the norm and lifted her head. When she saw it was me creating the rustle, she burst into tears.

Although my presence was distracting from the evangelist's message, he never missed a beat until Abby started to cry. He stopped in midsentence and asked, "Young lady, is this your husband?"

She nodded her head, and I could hear mutterings of disapproval from every pew.

"My beloved, God's Word will not return unto him void. Did we not pray that God would speak to the heart of this dear girl's husband within these last twenty-four hours and draw him into the fold?"

Amens came from everywhere.

What was going on? Nobody here saw me in the last twenty-four hours, not even my own wife. What in blazes was he talking about?

"Young man, your dear wife knelt at this very altar less than twenty-four hours ago and called upon the Son of God to forgive her sins and cleanse her from all unrighteousness. She turned her heart over to do the will of God and asked the dear folks here to pray for her husband. We prayed that twenty-four hours would not depart before that very thing would come to pass. My dear friends, see here before you the sovereign hand of the Almighty, faithful to answer the prayers of the righteous."

To tell you the truth, I don't remember too much of what took place at that moment, but I do remember someone talking with me and explaining the love of Jesus and his gift of love and mercy to forgive me for all the sinful things I'd ever done. It was more than my doped-up mind could conceive, but I took a leap of faith into something that made no sense. I believed what they told me, and I stepped out in trust and let the congregation pray over me, and I dedicated my life to do the will of God.

Whoa!

That was my first taste of love—real love, not the kind the world speaks of but a deep compassionate love for me, a wretched, lousy, worthless man.

The world wants a love where it's a two-way offer, but I had nothing to offer back to the one who died for me but to stand there in my greasy, oily, stinky, sweaty sinful self and say, "Here I am, Lord. Save me."

Before the meeting was over, the congregation prayed over me and anointed me. I didn't know what it all meant; I just knew I felt different than I did when I walked into the foyer and stared at those huge intimidating doors that were separating me from life and love. I just didn't know it was life and love I didn't have. The more I realized I didn't know, the more I realized I didn't know! It was awesome.

Well, Abby and I were among the last to leave the service that night. I couldn't get enough of being with those people, and I didn't want the night's activities to end. I realized I had never experienced a drug-induced high that exhilarated my joy like that. I kept waiting for the crash when the high would wear off. It didn't.

Brother Bob, the evangelist, offered himself available to my questions or needs at any hour of any day.

"Here's my number, Donnie. You call me anytime you need someone to talk to." I promised him I would. I turned to hug this man once more before I climbed on my Harley to head home.

"You know," Brother Bob said with tears welled up in his eyes, "you came in here a stinky, smelly, filthy sinner inside *and out,* but you're leaving with a brand-new heart as white as snow. Now, all this didn't clean up the outside yet, but the new man is born in your heart and God will clean it all up from the inside out one day at a time. He'll rid you of all the smelly, stinky sin that you have been a slave to. Don't *just* trust him, Donnie, *depend on him;* seek him in all ways. He'll never let you down, Donnie, never."

We started to leave the church when someone called my name. It was the church's full-time pastor. He approached Abby and me, and when I saw him, you could have knocked me over with a feather. He was none other than Pastor Jacob DeBaine, the one who insisted we attend some premarital counseling sessions before he married us. He didn't seem at all surprised to see me. "Donnie and Abby, I knew you would be back."

"Hey, man, how'd you know that?" I wanted to know everything, and I wanted to know it all *now.*

"I've been serving God long enough to know when he sends someone in that is hurting and searching; he may let them stay away for a while, but sooner or later, he will bring them back. Here is my phone number and my address. I want you to call me anytime of day or night whenever you feel like you need someone to talk to."

Abby and I walked outside and down the steps together. Neither of us spoke. My motorcycle was right in front of the church, so she stopped there with me. I didn't know what to say, so I put my arms around Abby and held her. We stood in an embrace, and we both cried. It was an embrace like I never felt before. She was warm and gentle. She felt sweet and needful.

In those few moments, I realized any other time I embraced a woman it was for my own selfish pleasure. Holding Abby in those few moments, I felt, for the first time, that the puzzle of our life was now intact. The missing pieces had been found, and the picture was complete and, with a little work, the lines between the pieces would disappear and we would have the makings of a masterpiece. It felt so right, yet I didn't know if she was ready to come back to me or not. I knew I wanted her to come home in the worst way, but something inside warned me not to push.

"Things are going to be okay now, Donnie," she finally said.

"I want them to be okay, Abby. I have a lot of changes to make, and I don't know if I can make them all at once, but like Brother Bob said, it will come from the inside out one day at a time, and right now, I feel inside like I want everything about me to change. Will you help me?"

"I'll help you if you'll help me. I know Phyllis will be there to help us if we need someone. You'd like her, Donnie. She's like a second mother to me."

"Abby, in the worst way, I want to ask you to come back home tonight, but I don't know if you're ready. I'm going to ride my bike on back to the house. I'll leave the light on in case you'd like to bring the kids and come on home. If not, I understand. There's not much there to offer you but a lot of bad memories and bad living conditions. If you don't come back tonight, please call me tomorrow. Okay?"

She nodded her head, and I walked her to her car. I embraced her again before she left. "Donnie, we have nothing ahead of us now but the opportunity for a new life, and now we have a new power to achieve it. Let's not mess it up."

"Good night, Abby."

She got in her car, and I watched her drive away. As I stood there by myself, I thought, *What just happened here tonight? Was all of this real, or am I going to wake up and find it was just a dream or worse yet a hallucination from a bad dope trip?*

Then I remembered seeing the reflection of the head with the horns in my bike, and I tried to recall the vision just as I saw it. Try as I would, I could not pull that vision into any mental focus.

I got on my bike and started back to the house. For the first time I could ever remember, I rode at a modest speed and in no hurry. What was this gentleness in my spirit? Something new, that's for sure, and I was wallowing in it.

I parked around back and went in the side door. *Now what?* I thought. Normally, I would have gone straight to my stash of coke or meth and shot up for a good high. Could I still do that now that I took this big leap to become a new man? Would it really matter if I shot up every now and then? Cocaine didn't last very long, and truthfully, I didn't see the danger, nor did I see the error in my thinking.

I started toward the bedroom where I kept my stash, and I remembered the power I felt in the parking lot while I was holding Abby. Had I only imagined the inner strength that upheld me then to want to be the kind of man she could be proud of?

I opened the bureau drawer and pulled out my bag of cocaine. I rested my palms on the bureau and wrestled with myself over this decision. Maybe just one more hit for old time's sake. I heard a vehicle and looked up to see headlights reflecting in the mirror. I stepped to the window, and it was Abby. She had come back with the kids.

I shoved the bag of cocaine back in the drawer and met her as she came in.

"I decided we needed each other tonight, just to make sure we get off on the right foot."

All I could do was nod my head. Brother Bob's words reverberated in my ears. "Don't *just* trust God, Donnie, *depend* on him, and he will never leave you or forsake you."

Abby put the kids to bed, and then we retired. Abby was exhausted and fell asleep immediately. I lay there with a million things going through my head. I even saw the kids in a different light when they came charging in the house. Finally, I got up and looked at the clock. It was a little after three. I quietly walked over to the bureau and opened the drawer that held my drugs. I lifted the bag out, and I heard Abby stir. She sat up when she realized I wasn't in the bed beside her. Then she saw me at the bureau.

"Donnie, what are you doing?"

"I was getting ready to take care of this. Wanna help me?"

"I don't know. What are you going to do with it?"

"Come on. Let's go flush it down the toilet." I really hadn't consciously made that decision, but at the moment, it seemed like the perfect response.

She got out of bed, and we took all the meth and all the cocaine we had in the house. We carried it to our dirt floor bathroom and flushed several hundred dollars worth of drugs out into the sewer where it rightfully belonged. I ran my fingers through my hair, and my head felt smooth—no horns—and my heart felt clean. I would win the war, one battle at a time.

I still had a plentiful supply of marijuana in the house. I didn't have the strength at that point to give up the weed, but I had begun cleaning up my act by destroying one type of seed from which horns will grow.

That's when life took a brand-new turn and things started to get crazy.

Behold, God works all these things, twice, in fact, three times with a man, to bring back his soul from the pit, that he may be enlightened with the light of life.

Job 33:29–30 (NKJV)

I still hadn't told Abby about the charges pending against me in Alaska. I knew she needed to know. I also knew it was something I was going to have to take action on. I could not, nor did I want to, run the rest of my life.

It was a Saturday afternoon, a few days later, when my buddy Phil, the law enforcement officer, pulled up in the yard. He got out of his car and stuck out his hand. We shook hands. It was good to see Phil again, but I doubted he was here on a social call. We exchanged the usual greetings, and then Phil said, "Donnie, it looks like we might have a problem. I have a warrant for the arrest of Donnie Carpenter out of Alaska. Seems he's a felony fugitive. There are some investigations in progress, and I received word they think you might be Carpenter. If I could just see your driver's license, we can clear this up."

My heart was in my throat, and my mind was telling me to run and not fight.

"Sure, Phil. My wallet's in the house. I'll be right back."

I went around to the back door, and Abby was at the stove stirring something that smelled good. It was now or never.

"Abby, I have to tell you something real quick. Do you see that man out there? He has a warrant for my arrest. Abby, I'm a fugitive from Alaska. I don't know if his warrant is drug deals, parole violation, or attempted murder, but you have to help me so if he comes in here to talk to you, you tell him …" I started to tell her what to say when she stopped me.

"You know what, Donnie? I'm not going to lie for you. If we really believe in this God we turned our lives over to, we're going to have to trust him."

I grabbed her by the shoulders. "Abby, you don't understand. Now you listen to me—"

"No, Donnie, you listen to me. I'm not lying for you."

I felt the old anger rising up. I turned and walked away from her. I went back out to face Phil.

"Phil, Abby's put my wallet away, and she can't find it right now. Can you wait here until we find it?" I needed some time.

"Sure, Donnie. I'll be at the substation most of the day tomorrow. Just bring it by." He got in his car and drove away.

What? He just drove away? He stood face to face with me a wanted fugitive, and he just got in his car and drove away? Was he crazy? I freaked out! I thought, *I can't do this. I am not going back to prison.*

I went back to the house. Abby met me at the door, but I refused to look at her. I went right to the bedroom and threw a few things in a bag. All I wanted was a good stiff drink and a cocaine fix.

"Donnie, where are you going?" Abby grabbed my arm as I pushed past her.

"I don't know, but I'm not going back to jail." I got on my bike, and I left.

I really don't remember where all I rode, but I ended up along a river. I parked my bike and sat on the shore for hours. I weighed my options, of which there were few, and I prayed. In my heart of hearts, I knew Abby was right. Never before had I ever entrusted my demise to anyone else to handle. I've always managed my own problems my way, and now she was telling me I had to trust someone I didn't even understand. I knew God loved me, I felt that. But there was no way I could sit back and wait when I couldn't see any evidence that he was going to do anything.

At one point, the thought passed through my head, *Well, Donnie, if you could understand God, then you really don't need him. Why would you even need a God you can understand? If you can understand him, then you can figure all this out yourself.* It was obvious I couldn't figure it all out myself, and besides, the tactics I tried in the past weren't working very well, so obviously I needed to trust a higher power than me.

After sitting there for what felt like hours, I finally said, "Okay,

God. It's going to be your way. You're going to have to deal with this. You chose to love me, and you accepted me with all my ugly past. If you can remove my sinful past, then I have to trust you to take care of whatever my sinful past carries with it." I got on my bike and started to go home.

In the distance, I could see the steeple of the little church where I asked God to save me. I remembered the pastor telling me that night, "Anytime you need someone, Donnie, day or night, you call me."

I turned onto his street and stopped my bike in front of his house. I walked up to the porch and rang the bell. I heard his foot-steps come across the floor, and when he opened the front door, there sat Abby and the pastor's wife.

"Come in, Donnie. We've been praying for you."

"Abby, what are you doing here?"

"The same thing you are. We need help, Donnie. Not just you, but *we* need the help of someone who can show us what to do."

The pastor spoke up, "Donnie, we've been praying that you would turn all of your past over to God to deal with. You trusted him to forgive that past, so that means you're no longer carrying it, but he is. However he sees best to deal with it, it will be to bring glory to him. You have to let it go, Donnie, and let God have it *all*."

"I just don't know if I can go back to jail."

"Donnie, if God allows you to go to jail, he will go with you, and he will remain with you. He will use you there in some way. You have to trust him. There is no other way."

My head was swimming. Nothing was making any sense. I had to test the water and see if this guy knew what he was talking about. If not, I better get out now. It was sink or swim. I didn't know about walking *on* water yet.

"Okay. Where do I start? Should I call Phil?"

"Your warrants are from Alaska, so I would say let's try and get in touch with the Alaska parole department. Let's go right to the target."

It took several phone calls, but we finally reached the parole office.

"Hello. Alaska parole department; how may I help you? This is who? Where are you, Mr. Carpenter? You did what? Really? Can you tell me about it?"

"I know there are warrants out for my arrest, and I want to turn my life around and do what's right. I've given my life over to God, and I want to let God have control of my life."

"Okay, Mr. Carpenter. This is what you need to do. Go down to the police department there in Cave Junction and turn yourself in. Tell them who you are and give them my number. I'll get the ball rolling here, and we'll be back in touch with the authorities in Oregon. Something you might want to do to help your case go in the right direction is get as many letters of recommendations as you can and send them here. Testimonies from people who know you can help your case immensely. In the meantime, we'll get you faced against these new charges and help you get your life going again."

Turn myself in? I couldn't do it. I could not do it. The very suggestion that I might go back to jail was a dread I could not willingly step into.

"Well, how about starting with soliciting friends for letters, Donnie? That will at least keep you busy until you hear from Alaska."

I spent the next three days calling everyone on the church roll and anyone else in Cave Junction that knew me and knew I wanted to be a new man. By the end of the fourth day, I had a book. Abby got it ready to mail.

On day number five, as I pulled into my driveway, Phil pulled in behind me. He got out of his car, pulled his revolver, and said, "Don't move, Donnie. It's over." He arrested me. He cuffed me and put me in the back seat, and he drove out of town.

"Where're we going, Phil?"

"Grants Pass. Why'd you lie to me Donnie?"

"I didn't want to go to prison. How long was it before you knew who I was?"

"I've always known. I had your photo in my car."

"Why didn't you arrest me, Phil?"

"God told me to give you time."

What? Was this guy a Christian? He was a Christian!

"God said to give you time, Donnie, and I did. But now God says it's time to act, so I had to do what I had to do. It doesn't mean God's turned his back on you; it just means it's time now to take some steps in the right direction and see what God has planned."

He booked me and put me in a cell. Two detectives came in and started questioning me about some unresolved Oregon murders in and around Grants Pass and Cave Junction. There was no mention of the man I shot in Alaska. They moved me to an interrogation room where videotapes were played of me at various Cave Junction hangouts; there were guns being fired, to which I had no information to give them.

"Come on now, Carpenter. Make it easy on yourself. We're willing to strike some sort of deal with you if you'll turn state's evidence and help us out here."

"I'd be signing my own death wish to do that. Look, I just want to take care of my own wrongs. I've turned my life over to God, and I want to make changes in the man I am, but I'm not signing my own death wish."

"If that's true, Carpenter, and you want people to believe you're a changed man, then this is your first opportunity to show that you are willing to change. The old Donnie would hide the truth and protect evil. Is that what you mean to do?"

So I turned informant. I told them what they wanted to know. By being honest, a burden was lifted from my shoulders that I cannot explain. At the time, I didn't know the verse, "Ye shall know the truth, and the truth shall set you free," but I had the most awesome sense of freedom lifted from my conscience. It was as though all that information was no longer mine to carry and hide. I was free from it!

The next day, I appeared before the judge for my extradition hearing. He talked with the district attorney. He talked with the attending officers. He talked with the detectives, and then he turned to talk to me.

"Mr. Carpenter, this is the first time in I don't know how many years of my sitting on the bench that we've caught a fugitive and have to let him go. There are no charges against you here. You'll have to turn yourself in to the authorities at Kenai, Alaska, but, Mr. Carpenter, you are free to go."

One of the officers was first to speak, "What?"

"That's what I thought, *what,* but the warrant has been canceled, and you're to contact your parole department and set up arrangements to fly yourself back to Kenai, Alaska."

I sat down right where I was. I just heard a judge speak who was blown away by what happened. We had an officer who was blown away and screaming *what.* And we had my God, who was starting to unroll the path for my life.

"Case dismissed."

I called Abby, and she came to Grants Pass to pick me up. We were loving life.

"Abby, God is giving me another chance! He's giving me another chance, Abby!"

We drove directly to Pastor DeBaine's house, and within minutes, we had people there cheering and rejoicing in what God had done. I was experiencing something I never even knew could exist: peace. It was an overwhelming peace, because I learned in this one incident that as long as I told the truth, God would look out for me. Truth is the gear that turns the wheel of freedom.

I didn't have to be in Kenai for two weeks. After the first week passed, I called the parole office just to check in and talk with my caseworker.

"I'm going to put you on hold for a few minutes, Mr. Carpenter. I'll be right back."

I didn't know if that was a good sign or not. After a few minutes, she came back on the phone.

"Mr. Carpenter, I apologize for taking so long, but I just wanted to make sure the transcription notes in your file are correct. It seems that we've taken all this back before the court, and after hearing you've turned state's evidence and considering all the letters of recommendations you sent us, you know what? All prior charges have been dropped, and you are no longer wanted in the state of Alaska."

"What?"

"That's right, Mr. Carpenter. You're no longer a wanted man in Alaska, so I say to you, have a good life and continue to serve the Lord!"

I dropped the phone. I was ecstatic! I'd have done back flips if I'd known how. I could not believe the hand I was dealt in this life because of a power in heaven called God!

I dropped the alias of Carpenter and started using Foster, my birth name again.

For the next year, life was great. I was clean from coke and meth, but I still smoked marijuana. My biker friends would come around, and I would tell them about God, so they quit coming. I was in church every time the doors were open.

Brother Bob returned within that year for another two weeks of revival services. This time, he traveled with a tent crew who set up the massive tent in a vacant lot in a little town near Cave Junction. He asked me if I would be security guard around the tent, and I agreed, but not before I posed the ultimate question, "Pastor Bob, why would you call on an ex-thief to do security?"

"Because only an ex-thief would know how the real thief works."

Abby and I left our old rat-infested house behind and started following Brother Bob and his evangelistic crew. Traveling with the revival crew was a tremendous growing experience for Abby and me. One trip took us to Hemet, California, which was about forty-five miles from Palm Springs. I remembered I had a grandfather in Palm Springs, although, as a kid, I seldom saw him. I contacted him from Hemet, and one afternoon, Abby and I drove to his home.

I was excited to share my newfound faith with someone in the family. Granddad listened intently and encouraged me to remain faithful to the path I was on and not look back.

He told me I had an uncle, Bernard, living in Grants Pass I knew nothing about. He thought years ago that Uncle Bernie "joined up and became one o' them Mormons." Having lived in Utah, I was familiar with the Mormons but knew nothing of their religion. He also told me Uncle Bernie had a carpet cleaning business, and Granddad encouraged me to contact him when I got back to Oregon. Granddad just couldn't remember the name of the business.

Driving back to Hemet, Abby and I talked about the possibility of returning to Oregon, looking up Uncle Bernie to see if he might be interested in hiring me. It was the prospect of a good job in a good circle of family and acquaintances.

Granddad said, "Boy, you need to stay clean away from them boys out there in gangs that's thieving and carryin' on. They'll drag you right back down in their pit, Donnie. Stay away from 'em, ye hear?"

A week after we returned, I started looking for Uncle Bernie in Grants Pass, and within days, I located him. He had an unlisted personal number, so I went through the Yellow Pages of carpet cleaning businesses and called them one by one. I had called all the As through the Ls and was going through the Ms when I called Mountain Fresh Steamers and got this:

"Good morning, Mountain Steamers. How may I help you?"

I gave this number the same old line I'd given every carpet cleaner that answered for two days.

"Hello. Uh...I'm trying to find a relative of mine that runs a carpet cleaning business, and I'm just going through the Yellow Pages, hoping I'll find the right one. His name is—"

"Donnie, is that you?"

"Well, yeah, my name is Donnie. I was looking for my Uncle Ber—"

"Donnie, this is your Uncle Bernie. I've been waiting for your call. I got a letter from your granddad saying you might be calling me. Boy! It's good to hear your voice!"

"Well, good morning, Uncle Bernie. I'm sorry to say I don't remember you, so I'm kind of embarrassed to be calling. I was hoping we could meet whenever it's convenient for you."

"I would love that, Donnie. Your granddad said you're married, so I would like to invite you and your wife to come to dinner on Saturday. How 'bout it? Can we count on you?"

"We'd be honored, Uncle Bernie."

He gave me directions to his home, and we drove to the neighborhood. I was so excited that we were about thirty minutes early, so we drove around until it was time for us to arrive.

Uncle Bernie had a nice home, nothing extravagant but very nice and in a nice neighborhood. My hands were sweaty, and I felt as giddy as a kid when I rang the doorbell. I'd been living around people who never questioned my appearance. When Uncle Bernie opened the door, my appearance set him back a syllable or two.

I stuck out my hand and said, "You must be Uncle Bernie. Hi, I'm Donnie, and this is my wife, Abby."

"It's so good to meet you both." He shook our hands and welcomed us to his home. We met Ella, his wife, and saw pictures of all his kids. We sat down to the most fabulous home-cooked meal I will never forget: homemade rolls, roast beef, mashed potatoes and gravy, asparagus, and a seven-layer cake of fudge and cream. I shared with him my new life experience, and we talked about many things but very little about my past. Finally, Uncle Bernie said, "Donnie, have you got a good job?"

"No, sir. Not right now. We've been traveling with the tent revival ministries, but their tent revival season is over for a while, so we're going to have to settle down."

"Would you like to work for me? You'd be working with the rest of the guys cleaning carpets in people's homes and some businesses. It's hard and heavy work and sometimes some long hours, but I'll pay you good, and I think you could do it."

"Uncle Bernie, if you're willing to give me a chance, I'd be honored to accept the offer."

"Well, Donnie, I do have a couple requirements before we seal the deal. You're going to have to shave and get your hair cut. And you're going to have to keep yourself clean shaven and neat."

"Not a problem, sir. Not a problem."

For the next year, I showered daily and kept my hair neat and my face clean. Uncle Bernie treated me better than any man in my life ever had. He was like a father to me and even signed for Abby and me to purchase a mobile home. We set our home in a small mobile home park in Rogue River, Oregon, and life was sweet.

We found a quaint little Bible church in Rogue River, and we loved it. We treasured the friendship of the people there. I gave my testimony at every opportunity I had. Anyone I came in contact with heard my testimony within the first two minutes of our meeting. People were astounded at the power God revealed in and through me and with the changes taking place in my life. I was so excited about the potential ministry I could have with addicts and people who were in the gutters of sin just like I came from. They were my people. I knew where they were emotionally. I knew where they hurt. I knew their weaknesses. I knew their hopelessness. I also knew where to find them. God was upholding me in his strength on a day-to-day basis, but I was still smoking marijuana.

As time went on, Uncle Bernie trusted me with anything he had. He gave me a cleaning van with all the equipment in it. I was feeling God's love by the people he was surrounding me with and the people I was worshipping with.

Uncle Bernard never preached Mormonism to me, and I never questioned his religion. I didn't agree with his religion, but he held to his faith as though he was the archbishop.

Abby and I were in church every time the doors were open. I was bringing in business for Mountain Fresh Steamers by cleaning the homes of people in our congregation. Uncle Bernie even offered a discount price to first-time customers in our little congregation.

We had the most awesome group of friends at the little Bible church. Every Sunday night after the service, several of us couples would meet at a local restaurant for pie and coffee, and the fellowship would last long into the night, sometimes until they started turning the chairs over on the tables getting ready to close.

> You, therefore, beloved,
> Since you know these things beforehand,
> beware
> lest you also fall
> from your own steadfastness
> being led away
> with the error
> of the wicked;
> but (rather) grow
> in the grace and knowledge
> of our Lord and Savior
> Jesus Christ.
>
> 2 Peter 3:17–18 (NKJV)

Among the couples in our group were some great friends, Josh and Martie. They were regulars and always loads of fun. I noticed over the course of a few weeks their attendance began to slack off. They would miss a Sunday morning here and there and then began missing every Sunday night. They loved our after service get-togethers as much as anyone, so I was very puzzled why they were pulling away and nobody seemed to know the reason. I asked around, but no one knew anything nor had anyone talked with them or been able to reach them. Something was definitely and seriously wrong. After several weeks of this, I took it upon myself to check it out.

It was another Sunday night absence, so on Monday, I called Dale, Josh's brother, who was a long-distance truck driver. I asked him to go with me after work, and we would drive up to their place and see what the problem was.

"Yeah, Donnie. I'll go with you. Someone needs to look in on them."

We made our plans, and then, in the middle of the afternoon, Dale called back and said the dispatcher was sending him out on a long haul, and he would not be able to go until the following week.

"Man, I can't wait a week. I'm going up there tonight."

"Well, take someone with you, Donnie. Don't go alone."

"Oh, I'll be all right. I'll find them."

When I got home, I told Abby I was going up to their place in the mountains and see why they'd distanced themselves from us all.

"Donnie, don't you think you should take someone with you?"

"What is it with you and Dale? Don't you think I can handle this myself? That's the same fool thing Dale told me to do, 'take somebody with you.' I'm just driving to their home. I just want to know why they've not been in church, and then I'm coming home. It's not a big job. I can handle it."

She wouldn't let it go. "Donnie, call the pastor before you go."

Angry, I picked up the phone and dialed his number. Before I could even ask him if he was interested in riding with me, the first words out of his mouth were, "Donnie, take somebody with you. Don't go by yourself."

That did it! I slammed the phone down and cranked up my

truck and started up the mountain. They lived in a quaint little hideaway high up in the Siskiyou Mountains.

As I approached his property, I saw Josh coming out of a shed. When he saw me, he went back in, shut the door, and then came back out. He met me at the driver's door of my truck. I pushed my way out of my truck and slapped him on the back and shook his hand.

"Hey, man. What're ya doin? Where ya been? I've been worried about you."

"Oh, I started a new job. I'm rolling rocks for a jewelry company for fairs, you know, agates and stuff like that."

"Well, hey! Let me see what you're doing."

"No, they're in the process now—"

"Oh, come on, man. Let me see what you've got going in there."

Reluctantly, he opened the door to his little shed. I stepped in first and as soon as my feet cleared the threshold, I knew I was under direct attack by the enemy of my soul. The air was filled with the aroma of methamphetamine smoke.

Up until my conversion, I had ingested meth, injected meth, stuck it in every open place of my body, and drank it, but never smoked it, and Satan knew it! And God knew it. That's why he sent so many messengers that said, "Don't go up there alone."

"Josh, are you smoking meth?"

"Yeah, Donnie, I'm smoking meth."

"I didn't know meth could be smoked. How do you do it?"

"Wanna try it?"

"Yeah, I'll try it. I've done it every other way. So meth can be smoked, huh?"

That night was the beginning of another round of hell. Satan knew I never smoked methamphetamines, and he hit me right where my strength was thinnest. He knew I wouldn't be able to deny myself that one hellish temptation when the aroma hit my senses. I stayed with Josh for a couple hours smoking and reestablishing my love for getting high. It was a different kind of high, but my flesh reunited itself with what my heart had victory over.

I woke up the next morning and never called Uncle Bernie to tell him I wasn't going to work. I drove right back up to Josh's and bought my own supply. I showed up at work late that afternoon after I got back. I don't know if anyone on the crew suspected what I had been doing. No one mentioned my unexplained or unannounced absence that morning.

Smoking meth finally was not good enough, so I went back on the needle. I was going to church on Sunday morning and evening, praising the Lord. I never missed a Wednesday night prayer meeting, even though I would be stoned out of my head. I was living a sick and twisted life again, and for what? They were the dead things of the world, and dead things reap death.

> I will say to God, "Do not condemn me,
> But tell me what charges you have against me.
> I am guilty...I am full of shame.
>
> Job 10: 2, 15 (NIV)

Prior to returning to my addiction, I had developed a nice little bank account, and within a short time, I depleted that. Bills weren't being paid, and Abby was concerned about the utilities being shut off, and I simply shrugged it off. I was lying at home to her and lying at church. I was back in the pit, spinning in the vicious circle of addiction.

I hid it pretty well at work for a while, but then my work became inferior, and customers were complaining to Uncle Bernie. To meet the demands of my addiction and to keep Abby off my back about the bills, I started stealing from the homes of people who trusted us to come in and clean their carpets. I stole money, jewelry, and credit cards, whatever I could find.

Customers were calling the authorities, who then questioned Uncle Bernie, but because he had done an honest business in that area for so many years, customers were reluctant to suspect him and doubted it was anyone from his crew.

Uncle Bernie called us together and told us all about the missing things from the homes and cautioned us not to do anything to lay suspicion on ourselves. He also informed us he had been called by the Mormon Church to go on a mission's trip and would be out of town for a couple weeks. He told the other employees he was leaving the keys with me and if the guys needed anything out of the usual supplies, they were to call me. *He was leaving the keys with me!*

I had keys to all the vehicles, warehouse, and to Uncle Bernie's own house. One day on the job, I let myself into his house and ransacked his office. I found his checkbook and tore out several blank checks. I forged his name, filled in the amount, and gave them to my crack buddies. I cleaned the little Bible church at Rogue River and stole the sound equipment, video cameras, and money I found in the main office. I took all of the stolen merchandise to Josh, and he would make runs to California and sell it. We'd then split the money.

I got home one evening, and Abby met me at the door. "Donnie, I'm not stupid. I've seen you going downhill for the past month. I know why, and I want you out." Just like that, I was out.

I had a camper top for my old truck, so I put it on and headed out. I lived in my truck until Jody, a girl who tended bar, took me in and let me live with her. I was going down, and I was going down fast.

I got a phone call at the bar one night from Josh. He said he was in the Rogue River jail and asked if I could come down. So I went. I walked in and saw Josh in cuffs and being interrogated. He looked at me and then turned his head and said, "That's him."

They immediately escorted me into a private room and started asking me questions about the stolen merchandise. My addiction had me believing I could lie my way out of anything, so I denied knowing anything about it. When they realized I was useless to their questions, they brought Josh in and asked him in front of me if I was the one who stole all the stuff. I looked him square in the eyes, and I don't know if it was out of loyalty or fear, but he could not say to me, "You know you did it," so they had no choice but to let me go.

I knew it was just a matter of time before I went down.

I went back to the bar and waited for Jody to get off work. When we left, I purposely left my wallet on a chair at a table on the backside of the room. We got to the car, and I fumbled around acting like I just realized I didn't have my wallet.

"Jody, did I give you my wallet?"

"No, Donnie. You never gave me your wallet."

"Look in the seat. I can't find it."

She dug around and disgustedly said she found no wallet.

"I'll bet I left it at the table. I hope the cleanup crew didn't find it. Give me the door code, and I'll go check."

"Oh, for cryin' out loud, Donnie. I'll go check. You know I can't give you the code."

"For Pete's sake, Jody. Just give me the code. If the cleanup crew found it, you're not going to be any threat to them. Let me go in. I have a better chance of getting it back than you do."

She had worked hard and was tired and ready to get out of there. She gave me the code. I let myself in, found my wallet on the chair, and left.

I knew it took the cleanup crew a couple hours to finish their chores, so I waited until I knew the place was empty and I drove back to the bar. I let myself in via the code and stole everything of value. I knew guns and knives were kept in the offices, so I broke in and took those. I stayed in my truck that night and didn't go back to Jody's.

I called her the next day, and she never pulled any punches with me. The cops had questioned her as an employee and one who had the door code. She admitted to me that she told them she gave me the code and now they were looking for me.

"Donnie, if you want to leave Oregon, I'll go with you. Tonight, after work, I'll walk to the little coffee shop around the corner. Pick me up there."

That was good enough for me. I picked her up, and we headed back to Grants Pass. I had been stealing things from church members' homes that I knew had gone south for the winter. One gentleman had a nice pickup parked in his garage for the winter that I planned to steal, and tonight seemed like a good time. Before we left town, I went after the pickup. I broke into the garage and found the keys. I drove his truck, and Jody drove mine, and we headed for California. When I got there, I painted the truck.

We didn't stay in California but a few weeks. I was so high on my addiction that I really didn't care about anything anymore. I was no longer a thieving junkie without hope, as I was in the past. I was now a thieving junky *with a conviction so heavy on my shoulders I didn't want to live before the God I trusted and now had failed.* I had come to the point where I wanted to die. I didn't deserve to live. God had to be angry with me. He wouldn't let me die! Or maybe living was my punishment.

I was losing the war on depression. The highs weren't high enough; I wasn't *coming down* from highs; I was crashing! My nerves were raw, and the booze was never enough. I was losing control, and my lifestyle was an ever-tightening noose around my neck. In desperation one night, I decided to try something I was told *never* to do. It was a sure death sentence, and I was ready to end this nightmare.

Jody was in the room with me when I pulled out a syringe and shot straight air into my veins. When she started yelling and screaming at me I told her to get out. I got up and nearly threw her out the door. I waited for whatever was going to happen, to happen. But it didn't.

When Jody thought the worst was over, she came back into the room with her hands over her mouth expecting to find me laid out and gone. I saluted her when she stepped through the door.

"Donnie, are you okay? What is wrong with you? Why did you do that?"

Why try and explain? I just got up; we packed our belongings and left California.

We were on our way back to Oregon, and I was following Jody in my newly painted, stolen pickup. She took the lead driving my Subaru truck. We were headed north on a very curvy, hilly road traveling about eighty miles per hour when we could.

I was driving on a meth high and in a state of mind that was dangerous to me and anyone on the highway with me. I really don't remember if I was doing it on purpose or because of my state of mind, but I had my own little game going back and forth over the middle yellow lines. The road straightened out somewhat, but the incline was increasing.

It was second nature to me to always be on the lookout for cops, and as we moved along up the mountain pass, I thought I spied a patrol car coming in my direction some distance away. He obviously spied my erratic driving because he turned his vehicle around, and as I passed him, he began his pursuit. He was playing my game. I increased my speed and, on a double yellow line, passed the little truck Jody was driving. Once in front of her, I could keep him at a decent length behind me once we got back into the curves, as I blazed my own trail up the mountain road.

I made up my mind that I was not going to jail. This was going to be the final run I would ever have to make. I would either kill myself or that cop was going to kill me. Either way, it was going to be over.

Checking in my rearview mirror, I could see him gaining on me and hoped my little truck wasn't getting hot. I kept watching the sides of the road. I saw an opening where I could put the truck over the cliff, and I was ready to make my move. In a matter of moments, it would all be over, and I would never have to run again. The opening was just ahead. I looked back to see Jody one more time before I would end it all.

The truck died. The truck just died! The incline stopped it quickly on the side of the road.

I bailed out just as the cop pulled to a screeching stop several yards behind me. He exited his car, and I started toward him yelling at the top of my voice, "You're going to have to kill me, pig. Go ahead! Pull the trigger! There's only one way you'll take me outta here! Shoot me, you slimy swine! Shoot me!"

I was walking straight at him, expecting him to pull his revolver and stop me. Instead, he simply side stepped me and took me to my knees with his billy club. He cuffed me and all but dragged me to his car and threw me in the passenger side. So far, he hadn't said anything, at least nothing I heard.

He left me sitting there still dazed and walked back to meet Jody. By now, she stopped, and once she saw there would be no gunfire, she got out of the Subaru and started toward the action. I saw the officer talking to her. She kept her head down and kept shaking her head. I knew she was crying but had no idea what she was telling him.

I still had it in my head I was not walking away from this. I managed to squirm my skinny self around to where I could get my arms at my side just enough to flip the door handle, and I bailed. By running just a few yards down the side of the road, I was going to jump off the cliff and hope I crashed, killing myself on the rocks below or drowning in the river. I knew I didn't have time to be particular.

Run and jump, Donnie. Just run and jump was what was going through my mind as my feet pounded the shoulder of the road. I saw an opening, and I jumped, bailing off the side of the cliff.

Some days, nothing goes right.

As I bailed out into the air, the most excruciating pain blew into my head. It dazed me as it flung me back onto the shoulder, my blood splattering everywhere. At my point of execution, I jumped head on, right into a protruding limb about the size of a ball bat that caught me right across the front of the head and knocked me back on the ground. With my hands cuffed behind my back, I was at the mercy of floundering velocity. I finally heard the cop speak, "Son, you're going to have to do better than that if you're going to kill yourself."

He cleaned me up and drove me back down to northern California and threw me back in jail.

When the cops searched the pickup, they found meth in the truck and meth on me. I had been committing credit card and ID fraud for the last three months. Jody took them to where I had all the stolen goods stashed and told them anything they wanted to know.

I knew this was it. I knew it was the end. I had no one to make my bail. I had no one to care whether I lived or rotted in there. Finally, one day I told myself, "Foster, you've always been a loser. It's the only thing you're good at."

Even dying in prison didn't scare me, so I became every inmate's worst enemy: a rat, an informer. I found I could get things in my favor by being a rat, so while my investigation was taking place, I told on everyone or anyone I had to. I told the authorities anything they wanted to know. I decided I wasn't there to make friends. I was where I was because I didn't have any choice except to be where I was, so I might as well hold nothing back. What did I have to lose? Most rats die in prison, and I was okay with that too.

I was laying on my bunk one night just wondering who it might be that would knife me in the men's room or slit my throat in the prison yard or even hang me in the boiler room. All kinds of things could happen. There were inmates in my cellblock alone that would have knifed me and not thought twice about it. Seldom were attacks of that nature reported. That's just the way it was.

Just as I was dozing off, I heard a voice run through my head. "Donnie, here's my number. You call me anytime you need someone to talk to."

I sat straight up. It was the voice of Brother Bob. It was as real as if he had stepped into my cell. I lay awake the rest of the night, anxious for the dawn. I heard his voice and saw his face hour after hour.

The next morning, I asked for privileges to call Brother Bob. Within a few short hours, he was in the visitor's lounge praying over me. I told him what happened—how Satan slipped in when I wasn't paying attention and how I let everything go bad after that. Brother Bob's advice was as simple then as it was the last time I needed help. "Tell the truth, Donnie, just tell the truth. If God wants you in prison, then prison is where he is going to use you to further his kingdom."

I went to trial and did as Brother Bob said; I told the truth, the whole truth, and nothing but the truth. The truth shall set you free, if not physically, at least spiritually and emotionally. I held nothing back, and my spirit felt free. God honored my step of courage, and I only received a four-year sentence. I was sent to San Quentin.

San Quentin will make or break an inmate. You either get tough or you lose. My nerves were shot, my hope was gone, my life was worthless, and I knew it. I didn't know if I'd even make it out of San Quentin alive or if some barbaric inmate would slit my throat at some point.

In the solitude of my cell, one night, I just started to weep. Nothing in particular triggered it. I just started to weep. There in the power of the weak, I started to pray. I don't remember what I prayed for; I just prayed. In the midst of my torment, I lifted my head and there on my cell wall was the shadow of three crosses. I couldn't take my eyes from them. An unfamiliar light was shining through the bars, and God broke through the stench of where I was and he showed to me the promise of himself: "I will never leave you nor forsake you."

My gaze was glued to the scene on my wall and drew me into the entrance of God's peace that passes understanding. My attention never wavered until a man stepped up to my cell door with a prison guard at his side.

"Donnie, I'm the prison chaplain. May I come in?"

I couldn't answer. I just stood there. The guard turned the key, and the chaplain stepped into my cell.

"Donnie, I was ready to leave tonight when God told me to come to this cell and pray for the man in here. May I pray with you?"

I dropped to my knees, and he sat on the edge of my cot with his hands on my head and he prayed.

I slept well that night.

Within a short time, I was transferred from San Quentin to Corcoran State Penitentiary, Corcoran, California.

From there you will seek the Lord your God and you will find
Him if you seek Him with all your heart and with all your soul.

Deuteronomy 4:29 (NKJV)

Corcoran was a prison of riots and outbreaks over many issues. It was a life of survival of the fittest. I had all the access I wanted to meth, cocaine, and marijuana among the inmates.

Once again, I fell flat on my face. I fell back into solving my problems the way I always had—with drugs. My addiction soared, and I began owing drug debts in prison. I still had not learned to find my strength in the only one who could set me free from old habits.

In an effort to get a handle on this vicious cycle, I learned there was a small Bible study group of men in the prison. I started hanging around their Christian circle, hoping to get a foothold that could pull me out of my pit. Once you became affiliated with that group, the rest of the inmates considered you weak and a coward. I tried to sit in on their study groups but always kept one eye behind me.

I was leaving that circle one evening when another inmate shot off his mouth starting with, "Hey, Bible man!" I mouthed back, and he took a swing at me. Before I could react, it was broken up, which wasn't good. It labeled me as a sissy, weak and afraid, and put a hit on my head to be dealt with as such. Inmates don't like weak, sissy, scaredy cats. My pride wanted to prove them wrong, so now I had another issue to deal with.

Corcoran Penitentiary is operated by levels. Some of the yards were governed by the inmates' own code of social status according to any number of things: the crime you committed, your order of seniority, where you are from, or even the section of the state you were from. When I got to level one yard, they sent their main shot caller to me. I was lifting weights and working out and trying to mind my own business. I'd heard about the guy, and as I got up from the weight bench, he approached me.

"I hear you're from Oregon, Foster."

"Oregon? I ain't from Oregon."

"No? That's what I heard."

"Well, ya heard wrong."

"Where ya from?"

"Coalinga, Bakersfield, and parts unknown."

"Well, Mr. Coalinga, Bakersfield, and parts unknown, I don't much care for sty gravy from your area."

He moved in closer with a twenty-five pound barbell in each hand. He put his ugly face next to mine, trying to intimidate me. "You know, Foster, I can kill you right here in this yard, and ain't nobody going to stop me. Ain't even nobody gonna watch. They'll all look the other way."

"Maybe."

He just shook his head.

"This is the way it's going to be, Mr. Coalinga Bakersfield. Anything you got from here on out is mine. You understand? You got food, you bring it to me. You got cigarettes, you bring 'em to me. You got clothes, you bring 'em to me. That's the way it works in here. This is my yard, and you're my property."

I stood up and walked away. I decided then and there that I had two choices: I could survive to have as decent a life as possible or I could die fighting in prison. I opted to live.

I made that decision work for me in Corcoran. The truth had been my sword in the past. I would not fear the truth anymore.

The communication between the two state boards hadn't caught up with all the facts yet, so I thought I would speed the process along. The next morning, I went to the captain and told him, "Hey, look. I'm still a wanted man in Oregon."

Before the day was over, I went from level one yard into level three yard. Level three is maximum security. Well-known inmates like Charles Manson were held at level three. It was a yard of riots and uprisings. Was I digging the hole deeper for myself? It seemed like it. Stabbings took place on a regular basis.

Soon after I was transferred there, the whole yard went down over an uprising, and we were all locked down in solitary confinement for ninety days.

Another time, they were searching the grounds for someone or something. We never always knew the reason. When this happened, we were ordered to hit the ground, facedown, and not move. We were in this prone out position one afternoon when the inmate next to me turned his head to see what was happening. There was an armed guard standing next to him on his blind side, and I witnessed the guard put his boot right through the back of the guy's head. What you witnessed stayed in your head and was never talked about.

I had all the drugs I could want. It was in prison my addiction to cocaine and methamphetamines now included heroin. I got heavily indebted for heroin to a Hispanic inmate known as Pagano. I lived in the shadow of death every day. Once I started shooting heroin, I started losing a grip on everything. I didn't know if I should live the way I'd lived the first thirty years of my life, the new way, or give up entirely, throw in the towel, and put an end to my life any way I could. Oh, I considered my options, but in prison, that sort of thing is heavily guarded against. About the only way I could have been successful would have been with an overdose of drugs.

The only thing that kept me from doing it was the mail. Day in and day out, I continued to receive letters from Brother Bob's church and Christians I knew on the outside. I knew they were praying and trying to encourage me.

Late one afternoon, while we were outside, I had come to the point where I was tired of always watching behind me. I was tired of this hellish hole and had pretty much talked myself into over-dosing that night after lights out. The prison debt I had hanging over my head for drugs was going to be dealt with one way or another, and I knew I'd lose. At least if I took my own life, I had the satisfaction of knowing, in my own sick, twisted way, that I'd won for the trophy of my life. Nobody in this hell pit would have the pleasure of taking it.

Walking around the yard, I'd thought this through so thoroughly that I almost felt a huge burden lifted, knowing the decision had been made and the act would soon be done. It was the only way I could comprehend ever being free.

I took a deep cleansing breath to assure myself I made the right decision when the ear-piercing alarm sounded for us all to hit the ground, facedown, and spread eagle. I assumed the position.

It was hot. The heat radiating from the tarmac was sickening, so I turned my face into the simple breeze that dusted along the ground. I had an uncanny sense of what was taking place around me. Once in position, I held fast. I'd seen too many inmates twitch in the slightest and heard the steel-tipped batons of the guard crack a skull. The back of my throat tasted of toxic waste. I opened my eyes to see where the guards were standing. Instead of heavy boots, intimidating of ruthless authority, I saw the tiny feet of a fallen sparrow less then a yard from my face. I could almost smell its sickening carcass, yet I couldn't take my eyes from the stiff and lifeless form. I wanted to kick it free for having died in this hellish place. I was in no way free to respect its lifeless form. It was a bird, for heaven's sake, a dead bird! Why was I so drawn to stare at something so worthless?

I was aware of loud and boisterous voices around me. Guards were yelling, and boots were pounding with heavy running steps on the tarmac. Inmates were screaming obscenities and batons were chiming through the air, hitting their targets, and the dead bird never moved.

That's you, Donnie.

I knew better than to speak, but those words were echoing in my head. My thought responded, *What's me?*

That sparrow, Donnie. That's you. My eye was on that sparrow, and I watched it fall to its death. Donnie, do you want to die like this simple bird here in this place?

I knew it was true. God's eye was on that sparrow, and I knew his eye was always on me.

I focused my attention back on the lifeless bird. My soul erupted in a deep exhaustion, tired of the struggle going on in my body and mind.

No, God, I don't want to die like this bird, but I don't want to live like this anymore either. I don't want to carry the guilt of you calling my name, oh, God, and I'm not here because I've died under the yoke of a slave to Satan, chained to my sin. I don't want to die because my spirit was crushed under the weight of disobedience. I don't want to slip into a godless eternity, nothing more than a simple speck on the tarmac like this bird. I've tasted of your holiness, oh God, and I know you are good. Help me, oh my God, and I will surrender these addictions that keep me enslaved to their deceiving satisfaction. God, I want to live! Oh, God, help me to live! Tears were burning my cheeks as they fell against the asphalt. God had stamped the seal that was to bolt the door against the enemy who no longer was to have control of my every thought. The pains of labor of my rebirth had begun. Death was beginning to overtake the life I knew as a slave to Satan. God had breathed his spirit across the hot asphalt, where I identified with the bird.

I don't know how long we were prone out under the security check, but when it was over, I stood to my feet with a new spirit of hope. I went back to my cell and flushed my drugs down the toilet. The next morning, I went to the captain of yard C and told him I had some inside people after me, so they started proceedings to have me moved two hundred plus miles north to Folsom State Prison, level two yard.

It was a new start. Not like I would have planned, but nevertheless a new start. I arrived in Folsom and began to pour myself into the Word of God. I was in chapel every day, and God planted a hunger in my heart for his Word.

Chapel services and small group Bible studies helped me to recognize my need for a one-on-one relationship with God's Son, Jesus. Jesus, not just a name out of history, God's Son, God's gift to me and to people *like* me, the one God sent *with no strings attached.* It was Jesus who died the death I should have died like the sparrow. God gave his one and only Son because he desired to have a relationship with me. Why?

My first steps of faith following my experience at Cave Junction were proof to me I could trust God. I had trusted in God, and he showed himself to me. Unworthy as I was, *God loved me enough to meet me on my level.* Now he was ready to show me what made me worthy of his love, and *it sure wasn't me.* I've never been worthy of anybody's love, and especially not the love of a holy God. *Only God's own love is worthy to come back to himself.* God's love makes me worthy to love him back. How is that possible? I was beginning to understand when I learned I had to come to the end of myself, of *who* and *what* I thought I was. I had to recognize and admit my unworthiness and my insufficiencies. I had to confess I was nothing, I had nothing, and I would continue to be nothing outside of the love of God. I had to come to the bloodstained sod at the foot of the cross bearing the slain Son of God with nothing but a broken and contrite heart, and I had to trust the love that hung there. I had to trust the love of the one God provided to be there. When I made the choice to do that, *God's own love came back to himself through my faith and obedience* in his precious Son.

The deeper I got into his Word, the more I realized my earlier relationship with God was a what-can-you-give-me mentality. Why would God want to give me anything? Why would God even be bothered with the likes of me? But God did want me, all of me, just as I was, with nothing but my wretched, sinful, needy, empty self—a dead and worthless piece of clay. That is exactly what he wanted. Now he had something to recreate from the inside out. Now he could begin the healing, but first I had to understand that I continued to be my own biggest enemy. God was helping me to see life was not about me. His offer is so simple: "Give me you, all of you, and I'll do the rest." Once I offered him my nothingness, now *he had something to work with. Wow!*

As God's mercy lifted me again from the pit at Folsom, his grace allowed me to learn the skill and become a certified welder. I renewed my vow to God time and again that I would give up all forms of addictions, and *in my heart, I meant it,* but Satan refused to release my thought process from his despicable vice of lies, and I couldn't get my head to work with what my heart knew was right. The battle raged on.

After all these years, I began to hear from Mom. She had moved back to Indiana and encouraged me to come back there when I was released. Somehow she knew about the biker clubs and knew my life had been on a steady downhill spiral.

I finished out my term in Folsom. Abby divorced me, and I knew there still had been no paperwork forwarded from Oregon, so charges were still pending there. I had no one but Brother Bob and the people who never ceased praying for me. In the weakness of my flesh, I still needed someone to lean on.

My social skills were based on my need for survival, and although I knew my duty to God was to serve him with my life, I *still* hadn't learned the do-unto-others thing yet. I guess the best way to describe the struggle going on between my heart and my head is this: I wanted a change *in* my life, but I really didn't want to change my life.

One week before my release from Folsom, I went before a hearing committee to see if there were any outstanding warrants for my arrest hanging out there as far as the California jurisdiction. I was told there were none. I found it hard to believe but finally decided it was because of the aliases I used for all those years. I was Donnie Foster when convenient and Donnie Carpenter when Foster was questionable.

It was a Saturday morning. They put me on a train. I was a free man.

WHEN VICTORY SLIPS AWAY

THE CATALYST: **RETURN TO DEPENDENCE OF SURVIVAL THINKING**

But the Lord said to him,
Go, for he is a chosen instrument of mine
To carry my name...
For I will show him how much he must suffer
For the sake of my name.

Acts 9:15, 16 (RSV)

I was a free man. Funny, but you don't just automatically become a free man. Your depressed mentality, which has been under the oppression of jail cells, prison bars, locked and bolted doors, armed guards, fear, self-survival, not to mention the influence of drugs, all of this hinders the word *freedom* from taking hold of your thinking. Being free with no one to watch over you doesn't make you free in heart or spirit. That whole being free concept takes time to adjust to and to accept. You can't just shake the whole self-preservation and survival lifestyle with an I'm-gonna-do-what's-right counter-attack. It just doesn't work that way.

I sat down in the coach car of the train, and my head was going in circles. I knew I was a survivor. Like the cat, I had used up most of my proverbial nine lives. I was going to survive this, but right now I could really use a drink.

I got up to go to the dining car but stopped at the restroom. As soon as I closed the door behind me, my eyes fell on a man's wallet dropped next to the toilet. I picked it up, and without giving it a second thought, opened it and took out the cash. There was a little over a hundred dollars, and I pocketed the money and put the wallet deep under the debris already in the trash receptacle.

The train trip from California to northeast Indiana took several days. Each day, I was able to relax a little more and became less tense in my new world of freedom.

It was night when we arrived in Waterloo, Indiana. When I stepped off the train, the first face I saw was that of my mom. Next to her stood a man I assumed to be her escort or husband. There were a few other relatives there to greet me. As my feet touched down on Indiana soil, I felt my first sense of freedom. It was so surreal, but somehow I knew life was going to be good from this point on.

My orders at Folsom were to go directly from the train station to the parole office in New Haven, Indiana. It was late, so I checked in first thing the next morning. I met my parole officer and filled out the paperwork and listened to my orders, which I'd heard it all before.

While I was writing, signing papers, and listening, I was checking out a business behind the parole office. It was a truck and trailer business, and I was already making plans.

We finished up at the parole office, and I shook my officer's hand. I was going after my first job as a free man.

I walked over to the business feeling very confident. I carried myself with confidence through the front door, where a middle-aged gentleman met me.

"Hi, there! Can I help you?"

"Well, sir, I hope so."

"Sure, buddy. Whaddya need today?"

I looked at the name above his left shirt pocket. It said Wilford Gilbert. "Mr. Gilbert, I'm an ex-con. I just got out of California prison where I earned my certification as a welder, and I need a job. Would you be willing to give me a chance?"

There were several seconds of silence. I thought, *Donnie, you better get used to this.*

"An ex-con, huh?"

"Yes, sir, Mr. Gilbert, I am. I served time all up and down the west coast but was just released from Folsom State Prison in Folsom, California, where I completed my sentence and learned the art of welding. It would mean an awful lot to me if you could give me a chance to prove myself."

There were several more long seconds of silence. Finally, Mr. Gilbert stuck out his hand to shake mine and asked, "Can you be here at seven tomorrow morning?"

"Yes, sir, I can!"

That night, I couldn't go to sleep. As I lay in bed, anxious to be on the job, in the morning, God showed me something very interesting. In my mind I relived, in fast forward, my life as an adult.

God kept me alive and healthy and allowed me to escape so many accidents that should have claimed my life. He delivered me from an obvious life imprisonment to serve minimal sentences—the knowledge of drug related murders and attempted murder charges, prison yard fights, drug charges, drug addiction, and drug-related death. And why? Because God had a plan, I, as of yet, knew nothing about. It wasn't God who was taking this long, deep look into my life. He was allowing *me* to take this long, deep look into my own life. I realized I had been spared for a reason. What? I didn't know, but I knew God was just beginning to teach me his way.

I gave up all hard drugs but could not surrender my love for alcohol or marijuana. I went to work at North East Indiana T&T Repair faithfully but frequented the bars every night where I stepped out back to smoke my weed. That taste for alcohol and marijuana addiction was still with me. I kept replaying the promise I made to God in prison but could not get a handle on keeping my word to him.

I had to check in with my parole officer every week. It took no longer than the first week for me to decide I didn't like her. I went in with an attitude and started to question her intelligence about how things were going to change, but she was a lot smarter than I gave her credit for. We got off on the wrong foot, and at the time, I really hated her because she wouldn't listen to a thing I had to say.

I reluctantly went back the second week and waited in the waiting area much longer than I should have. I was getting irritated and thinking I would soon make a scene if I didn't get called back. I threw down the magazine I'd been reading when two uniformed police officers walked through the door.

"Are you Donald Carpenter?"

I couldn't say I was, and I couldn't say I was at one time, and I couldn't say no, so I said, "I am."

"Stand up, Mr. Carpenter. We have a warrant for your arrest."

"*What?*"

"We have warrants from the state of Oregon to place you under arrest. Anything you say can and will be used against you in a court of law."

My first response was to lie, but then my memory kicked in. I remembered going through an Oregon court several years back to learn there was another D. Carpenter on the court records who was born the same month and year as I was. I remembered his physical statistics as a little guy, about 140 pounds, with tattoos all over. I was over six feet and 220 pounds. His description did not fit that of mine.

"Look, you have the wrong guy. Yes, I am Donald Lee Carpenter, but I think you're looking for a short, little guy covered in tattoos, also by the name of Carpenter." They chitchatted back and forth, made a few phone calls, and said I might be right. Unless they were absolutely certain I was the one they wanted, they had to let me go until they could redo their homework, so again I slipped through.

I knew better than to stay where the law could find me, so I ran from my mom's house. I called an acquaintance of the family and asked if I could stay with him for a few days. He obliged but let me know he had a young lady and a couple kids living in the house with him. They were both more than gracious in opening their home to me.

I was only there a few short hours before I realized I had moved into an arrangement of nonstop verbal pounding toward the young lady. Her name was Kelly, and she had beautiful hazel eyes and two very young and adorable children: a two-and-a-half-year-old daughter and a one-year-old son. I was used to verbal abuse to women, having been abusive myself, so at first it didn't bother me that he would lash out at her with very degrading and belittling comments. But as the days wore on, I began to observe the hurt his words carried. It began to get under my skin.

I had made my home with them for several days, coming and going, mostly just to sleep, clean up, and go out almost every night. At times, I went alone, but frequently the three of us would go together, bar hopping and drinking.

One Saturday night, my generous house parent (as I jokingly referred to him) became very foul-mouthed to Kelly. In the short time I had been in their home, I found her to be too sweet a girl for the likes of his kind. I never witnessed any physical abuse against her, and I was not immune to the sound and the fury of an overly obnoxious drinker, but tonight, the tongue lashing toward her was getting to be a gigantic burr under my saddle. I could see his tone and verbiage were beating her spirits down and destroying her on an emotional level. A couple hours passed when I finally decided I'd heard enough, and at some point tonight, I would tell the young man so.

As we left the bar and walked to the car, the foul and disgusting tongue let loose on her again for no reason. I looked at those hurt and broken eyes, and I could tell her pride was deeply wounded. She never said a word in retaliation. She walked around to the driver's door and got in behind the wheel. The raging bull got in on the passenger's side. I crawled in the back. He wouldn't let it go, and I could see the tears rolling down her cheeks, but she never took her eyes from the road or her hands from the wheel.

From the dark of the backseat, I finally blurted out, "Shut up, man. Just shut up!" I tried taking a couple swings at the back of his head out of my own anger. The abuse continued as though I wasn't even there. In the midst of all the havoc, Kelly kept her head. Instead of going to our home, I looked up to realize we were sitting in front of my mom's house. Her abuser stumbled out of the car and went inside.

I was seething mad. I got out and went around to the driver's door and opened it. Still shaking and in tears, her knuckles were wrapped around the steering wheel, her head resting on her forearms.

"Hey, come on. Are you okay?"

"I'm okay. Donnie, what's wrong with him?" She dropped her head in her hands, and all she could say was, "What's wrong with him? He's crazy, Donnie. What's wrong with him?"

I didn't think letting my own anger show at this point was a wise thing to do, so I made light of the conversation.

"He's an idiot. Come on," and I took her hand as she stepped out of the car. She smoothed back that beautiful dark hair and grabbed her handbag from the front seat. She had stopped crying and turned toward the house. "Aren't you coming in?"

"If I go in there, I'll kill the little twerp! I'm going for a walk."

I turned and took a few steps to realize she was right behind me. I slowed my pace until our steps fell in sync.

We walked several steps in silence when Kelly finally spoke. "Why did you do that, Donnie?"

"Do what?"

"In the car. Why did you stand up for me? Nobody's ever done that before. Why did you?"

I was so angry that I couldn't even answer her question. I could feel my teeth grinding, and my head was pounding from the tightness in my jaw, and I just kept walking.

Several paces farther, she spoke again. "Donnie, I am so sorry about all this. I know he doesn't mean all those things he was saying. He's drunk, and you know how he is when he's been drinking. Try not to be so angry. One angry person in my life is enough."

We continued our pace. Again, she spoke, "Donnie, I'm not sure if you're just angry at him for being who he is or if you're angry at him because of me. My family has witnessed this behavior from the beginning. At first, they tried to help me, but recently, it's been like, 'If you aren't going to do something to help yourself, we don't want to hear it anymore.' And they just backed away. I guess I can't blame them. Then tonight, not until tonight, has anyone ever tried to step up and protect me. That's a pretty awesome feeling. I don't know if you meant it that way or not, but it meant a great deal to me to see you defend me. I guess I need to know, Donnie. Even under the rage tonight, you're the only person who ever listened to what goes on between the two of us. You're the only person to ever stand up to him. I just can't believe you did that. I know this sounds crazy, but under all of your rough and rugged appearance, I saw the heart of a man who knows how to care. You're different, Donnie. Other guys I've known don't have that quality. I can't put my finger on it, but it's like … oh, I don't know how to say it … it's sort of like—"

"Come on, girl. Tell me what you're thinking."

"You're going to think this is stupid."

"Maybe. I've heard stupid things before."

"All right, but don't laugh at me."

"I promise. Not so much as a grin."

"It's like a spirit of hope about you just wanting to be acknowledged. Does that make sense?"

I stopped walking and turned to face that gentle voice. I was dumbfounded. Did she say she sees me as a person of *hope?* That's the last thing I ever expected anyone to find in me. I've never been hope to myself, much less to anyone else. I didn't know what to say.

She didn't realize the impact that comment made on me, and she continued, "No one has ever looked at us and recognized the anger he carries in his heart. No one has ever bothered to see the disaster in my life because of his anger. You see that, Donnie, and because somebody finally sees it, that gives me hope."

Finally, I could speak. "Look, Kelly, I think I got angry tonight because that abusive man in the car *is me.* That's why I got so mad. That was me tonight at the bar! *That was me!* That's the way I've been, and for the first time, I saw myself in somebody else. I couldn't take it, Kelly. It ripped my gut out to know that was me! Look, he made a point with me tonight, and I don't want to be like that anymore. I want to change, but I don't know how. I can't change what I am. I have been what I am for so long that only God can change me, only God."

"Do you believe in God, Donnie?"

"Yes, I do believe in God, and I believe God can change me. I know I have so many hang-ups that need to be changed, but when I see the ugliness of life outside of God and I see the way evil corrupts the mind, cripples the heart, and destroys the spirit like that idiot in the car tonight, I want to run from it. I want to change it. But I also want to change *me.* I don't know how it's going to happen. I know it's not going to happen over night. I guess God's going to have to set up that timetable too. I don't want anger to be the ruling force in my life. I don't want to live without the hope that I can never be anything but what I am.

"Donnie, I don't know anything about God, but I think if you truly want to change, you *can* make it happen. And if God is the answer, then you have him in your corner to coach you."

"God is the answer, Kelly. That's the only answer! I know that. I know it in my heart. I just have to figure out how to get it to my head and work with him. Anger comes too natural and too easy. It's the way I've always tried to solve everything, and guess what, I'm finally finding out it doesn't get me anywhere. Tonight I got a real picture of how ugly it is when I see it and I hear it in someone else."

"Well, I just want you to know how grateful I am. It made me feel I am worthy of being cared about. Thank you. And thanks for letting me tag along with you. I needed this. I should probably head back to the house and see what kind of horrible tales are being told. Are you coming?"

"Yeah, come on. I'll walk back with you. Hey! That was some cool-headed driving! You're okay, girl!"

We arrived back at the house. When we stepped through the door, several pairs of eyes glared at us.

I looked at Kelly's big, gorgeous, hazel eyes, and I knew they were ready to spill over with tears, and I knew she needed a good cry. She'd had enough tonight, and I knew it. She walked on past everyone and disappeared behind the bathroom door. I wasn't in the mood to talk to anyone, and I sure wasn't in the mood to listen. I turned and left. I recognized the wounds of an emotionally wounded woman, but I didn't know what to do for her.

Before that night was over, her boyfriend kicked me out of their house.

I had no other place to go except back to stay with Mom. The following morning, I went to work with a multitude of feelings. I watched the clock and stayed busy to make the day go faster.

What was going on? I felt like my heart and my head were tugging in opposite directions, and my body was trying to adjust to the discontent in my soul. This was supposed to be a new start, but it didn't seem like life was changing too much.

For the next several days, I carried through with my routine. Get up, go to work, clean up, and go bar hopping.

One night, I retired early. I dozed in and out, hearing the television in the adjoining room where Mom's husband was watching some annoying sitcom. Awakened by loud voices and footsteps in the house, I pulled my pillow over my head and turned over. The voices were speaking as voices of authority, and I got out of bed. I was pulling on my pants when the door opened, and from the light in the hallway, I saw the silhouettes of two officers standing in the doorframe with pistols drawn. I put my hands in the air and waited for someone to speak.

"Are you Donald Carpenter?"

"I am."

"We have a warrant from the state of Oregon for your arrest. Turn around and put your hands behind your back."

I felt the familiar cold steel rings wrap around my wrists while they read me my rights.

Once incarcerated in the Allen County Jail, the court set about to extradite me back to Oregon to face charges. I really had lost track of what was still pending there. I knew there was burglary, grand theft auto, drug charges, and didn't really know what else. What I *was* sure of was this: I knew this was the end of the road. I would not get another chance.

Between the Oregon and Indiana paperwork, it took about a month to get everything in place, which gave me time to think. Also, beneficial to me within the short time I was in the Allen County Jail was an introduction to the prison ministry available to inmates by the jail chaplain. This man played a very meaningful role in helping me come to terms with my destination in Christ.

His visits created positive thinking about my destiny if I remained on the road I was on.

During the duration of making preparation for extradition, I had time to do some serious thinking about where I'd been, where I was, and where I had the choice to go. Where I'd been was not a working plan, so it seemed to be time to adopt another plan. I spent days reflecting on what I knew to be the truth according to the Word of God versus what I knew to be of my own making. Living according to my own standards was the plan in operation. It wasn't working, and it never did. Brother Bob's words replayed in my head over and over, "Just tell the truth, Donnie. Just tell the truth."

> Turn away my eyes from looking at worthless things;
> Revive me in Your way.
> Turn away my reproach which I dread
> For your judgments are good;
> Behold, I long for your precepts;
> Revive me in your righteousness.
> I will speak of your testimonies …
> And will not be ashamed …
>
> Psalm 119:37, 39, 40, 46 (NKJV)

I was thirty-nine when I arrived in handcuffs at Grants Pass, Oregon. The system already had a court date set for me when I arrived. I remembered the letters I petitioned friends and acquaintances to write back in Cave Junction when I thought I would be facing charges in Alaska, so while I awaited my hearing in Oregon, I contacted Brother Bob and several people in Grants Pass that knew me from the church. I also contacted a few that I had stolen from.

The main context of each letter simply stated that I was back in Oregon to appear in court to face charges against me, some of which had been violations against them. I told them I had found peace with God and that I was trying to turn my life around. I expressed a personal apology to each one for my behavior and asked them to please pray for me. I also wrote a short note to Kelly. Although I didn't expect a reply, I told her I would appreciate hearing from her if she cared to write. She wrote faithfully for a while.

> Give great joy to those who have stood with me in my defense...
> Then I will tell everyone of your justice and goodness
> And I will praise you all day long.
>
> Psalm 35:27, 28 (NLT)

My day in court arrived. "Will the court please rise?" I stood and turned around to see a handful of old acquaintances seated in the courtroom alongside Brother Bob. They offered signs of encouragement to me. Among them were people I robbed.

As I turned back, I saw a judge taking his seat I had never seen in the courtroom before. I asked the officer seated next to me if he knew anything about the judge.

"All I know is he's been filling in for Judge Whitesell while he's out of town."

I didn't know if that was good or bad.

"Will the defendant please rise?"

I again stood before the Oregon bench and listened as the judge read aloud the charges against me. I listened and knew my sentence would be long. When the judge quit reading and looked up at me over the narrow glasses perched on the end of his nose, the calculations I had run up in my head told me I was looking at a sentence of one hundred and four years in the Oregon penitentiary. My first thought was of the guys already incarcerated there, against whom I had turned state's evidence. I would definitely be on their hit list. More than likely I would die at their hands. My heart fell and shattered on the chains around my feet. Even if I only did half the time, fifty years was a lifetime for me.

My heart immediately asked, *God, what are you doing? I'm just beginning to figure this thing about trusting you, and now, what are you doing?*

Then there was one other thing I thought I had going for me. I had developed a good friendship with the young lady who told me she saw hope beneath my brash exterior. Even though I was kicked out of their home, the young lady and I had begun a friendship back in Fort Wayne. I discovered what a special lady she was. I worried about nobody being around to protect her from an abusive companion. I realized she was one lady in my life I would look after and protect when she needed protecting. I asked her to write to me during my absence. I worried about the way she would be treated. I wondered how long she could endure under the verbal abuse. I hoped she would let me know how her life was going.

I also realized how my own attitude had changed. Several years ago, I would not have cared. Today, I cared. Today, I still had the taste of hope in God, and I knew life could have meaning and be lived as a gift.

As I stood before the court, I knew the judge was speaking, and yet I didn't hear him speak. I couldn't focus on what was going on around me. I remembered Brother Bob telling me, "Donnie, if God allows you to go to prison, he will use you there as a witness for himself."

I was firing up urgent one-word prayers before the throne of mercy as dozens of thoughts were scrambling for priority in my head. Brother Bob's words resounded in my head. *Just tell the truth, Donnie; just tell the truth.*

Somewhere, in a faraway voice, I heard the judge say, "Does the defendant wish to make a statement?" Then he repeated his question, "I said does the defendant wish to make a statement? *Mr. Carpenter!* Do you wish to make a statement before sentence is passed?"

"Yes, Your Honor, I do."

Now what was I going to say? I had the court's attention, and there I stood, feeling as naked and vulnerable as a baby.

"What do you wish to tell the court, Mr. Carpenter?"

"Your Honor, I'm here today because this is where I belong. I'm here because I've come to a dead end. I know I can't move ahead with my life until I've dealt with it.

"I can't go back and undo any of it, but I can beg the court's forgiveness and the forgiveness of the people I have wronged and abused. Seated behind me, Your Honor, are people whose homes I burglarized. I want to say how sorry I am for what I did. I'm not sure why they're here, if it's to offer me support or to see for themselves that I get what I've got coming, but for whatever reason, I want them to go from here knowing I am not the man I was.

"Your Honor, sitting back there is a man who played a very important part in helping me to see there is hope of recovery. Brother Bob Kurko there taught me of the forgiving love of God through his Son. He led me to seek repentance for my past and showed me how to have a new life through God.

"Your Honor, I'm guilty. I'm guilty of every one of those charges you read. I know the debt I owe to society is fair. But you see, Judge, the judge of this universe has forgiven me. Brother Kurko back there can tell you all about that. The human side of me begs the court's mercy for leniency.

"I know God is the only one who can look into my heart and truly know that I am a changed man. That's all, Your Honor."

It seemed like forever before anyone in the courtroom spoke. The judge removed his glasses and cupped his hands over his brow. Then he leaned back in his big black chair and thought for a few moments, rocking back and forth. The bailiff stared at me with scrunched up eyebrows and a look of question and disbelief.

Finally, the judge sat upright in his chair. He took a long, cleansing breath before he said, "Does anyone of the court wish to make a comment?" His eyes and the bailiff's eyes scanned the courtroom. I heard the shuffle of a hand being lifted up in the back and then someone standing to her feet.

The judge acknowledged the patron behind the bar, "Yes, ma'am. What is it you wish to say?"

"Thank you, Your Honor. My name is Millie, and I'm here today for Donnie."

I wanted more than anything to turn around and see who it was. I didn't recognize the voice or the name. I tried a side glance and saw one of the ladies I guessed to be of Brother Bob's group clutching a white hanky in her hand, and she started to speak.

"Donnie's path has crossed my own in the past. Some of his struggles had an adverse affect on my husband and me. When we heard he had been returned to Oregon to stand trial, we determined in our hearts to stand beside him as an advocate and pray the people he has treated unjustly can forgive him. We pray with God's help that will happen. Once we made the decision to stand with him, God encouraged us both that Donnie would have a special place in his service. We believe that our decision to forgive a man of God's choosing will encourage him to be an instrument in God's hands. I believe, if given another chance, God could have great plans for Donnie.

"You see, Your Honor, I am aware of the countless times God spared his life, and I believe there must be a reason. We believe that somewhere down the road God is going to use Donnie to bring lost souls into the kingdom of God. He has a past that will give him an understanding and a familiarity with lives much like his own, and he will be able to touch their spirits far better than anyone else.

"That's all, Your Honor. Should any of the charges read here today bear our name, it is our desire that the court would exercise extreme leniency in pronouncing Donnie's sentence as far as we are concerned."

When this dear lady sat down, I stood there with tears coursing down my cheeks in a flood of emotion. Who was this woman? Why was she doing this? Had I violated their home and their privacy? Did I take things from them to sell to support my ugly lifestyle? Why are they asking for leniency on my behalf? No one ever did anything like that for me. My whole future was at stake in this room, and so was theirs. How did she know I wouldn't make them an easy target and come back to them to do more harm if I were allowed to go free? I felt I had stepped into another dimension where only the redeemed are free to stand. I was afraid to hear what the judge had to say. I knew if Judge Whitesell were sitting on the bench today, he'd throw all this out the window. He knew the old Donnie too well.

"Mr. Carpenter, this is an unusual hearing today. My record shows that the state and your attorney have reached a plea bargaining agreement, but in light of the comments made in these last few minutes, I would like to reevaluate this case. We'll take a brief recess and meet back here in thirty minutes."

> I will rescue you from your own people …
> I am sending you to them to open their eyes
> and turn them from darkness to light
> and from the power of Satan to God …
>
> Acts 26:17, 18 (NIV)

When the judge stepped back into his chambers, I sat down at the table. The tears wouldn't stop, and I couldn't wait to throw my arms around Millie and thank her for her comments. When I finally gained a little composure, I raised my head and looked back where she and Brother Bob were sitting. She was bent over in her seat, as were several others, and Brother Bob was on his knees beside her. They were praying. I wanted to be there with them, but I was restricted and had to remain at the table for the defendant.

My attorney put his hand on my shoulder. "Are you okay, Donnie?"

"Yeah, I'm okay. Do you have any vibes from the judge?"

"Well, you know, Donnie, the state of Oregon has presumptive sentencing. Under this code, there will be a mandatory minimum for your charges. All we can do is wait and hope someone is hearing the prayers of your friends back there."

Just a few minutes short of a half-hour recess, the chamber doors opened and the bailiff called us to stand. The judge took his seat, and we took ours. I was sweating like a marathon runner, and I knew everyone could hear me shaking like a paint mixer.

My mouth was dry, and my head was swimming.

"Will the defendant please rise?"

I stood to my feet and faced the judge.

"Mr. Carpenter, this has turned out to be an unusual case in this courtroom. I'm not sure even I understand what all has taken place here today, but I feel that I have been in the presence of something totally unfamiliar.

"Over and over, I read the list of charges against you. I thought and rethought the evidence. I played and replayed the things I heard here today. I was taken aback by your demeanor. I've never heard testimony from a victim like this lady in the back gave for you, a wholesome forgiving testimony from a lady who definitely has every right to want the book thrown at you yet asks for leniency for you.

"Mr. Carpenter, if I sentence you according to each charge brought against you in this courtroom today, do you realize you are looking at one hundred four years in prison time?"

"Yes, sir, I do. I did the calculations as you read my charges."

"Against my better judgment, I am going to grant this fine lady's sincere request and trust what you've told the court, Mr. Carpenter, to be true. The court will grant leniency on your sentence. For the charges read at the beginning of this hearing, I am sentencing you to four years in the Oregon State Prison. Sentencing for the combined charges will run concurrent. Mr. Carpenter, you owe this lady your life. Court dismissed."

I went numb. Did he say four years?

"Hey! Four years, Donnie! You got four years!" It was my attorney talking and patting my back and trying to shake my hand. I did hear him right. He did say four years. I immediately looked back to find Millie's face. She was smiling and lifting her hands toward the ceiling, and Brother Bob's head was bowed, and I knew he was giving thanks. I pleaded with the bailiff to give me a moment to thank Millie before he led me out.

I caught her eye and motioned for her to come forward. She came to the bar that separated court personnel and participants from the spectators, and I threw my arms around her neck and wept like a baby. My breaths were shallow and taken in quick gasps. Brother Bob was trying to embrace us both. All I could say was, "Thank you! Thank you! Thank you! Ma'am, I can't thank you enough. Thank you!" I couldn't regain enough composure to ask her who she was. I could only thank her.

I felt the bailiff tugging at my arm, and I didn't want to let go of my dear Millie. I owed her a debt I could never repay. Finally, my attorney said, "Come on, Donnie. It's time to go."

I started to pull away when Millie cupped my face between her palms. "Donnie, look at me. Promise me you will go with God and let his will unfold over you and find the vision he has for your life. Become the warrior for him he is calling you to be."

All I could do was nod my head.

> You have delivered my soul from death; Have you not kept my feet from falling that I may walk before God in the light of the living?
>
> Psalms 56:13 (NKJV)

The bailiff led me in the direction of the cellblocks. Before exiting the courtroom, I glanced back again and Millie was gone. I was too numb to really understand what just happened, but I know the power of God was in that courtroom and his amazing spirit spoke through the heart of someone on my behalf. It was enough to know his eye was on me as it was on the fallen sparrow.

It wasn't long until they transported me to a correctional facility farther north in western Oregon. When I arrived there, I was pretty much on my own as a follower of God. There was no support of fellow Christians. There was no ministry like I had in Grants Pass, and I soon fell right back into some very bad habits. I was smuggling in cigarettes, dabbling in illegal drugs, smoking on work crew jobs, and letting my joy for the Lord wear off. I realized I was calling or relying on God as it was convenient for me but not taking his instruction serious when my head wasn't on the chopping block. My heart knew better. My heart knew I was allowing my head too much responsibility. Even in my disobedient behavior, God was keeping his eye on me.

The warden called me in one day. "Carpenter, we're moving you out of here. I have orders here to transfer you to a correctional facility on the coast. You'll be transferred there within the week."

I'd heard about this place I was to soon call home. The facility was unique in the fact that it had been quite successful by the operation of a military-style boot camp within the program. I was given the option of participating in the boot camp. I jumped at the chance.

I was the oldest guy in the program. I remembered my experience at boot camp in Texas but decided to try it anyway. I loved the physical side of it. I was getting myself together. We ran every morning, jogged up the mountains, and physically, it was a godsend. But I still couldn't take authoritative personnel *in my face.*

We had a female instructor who took great pride in her position. She loved getting in our faces and yelling at us. I couldn't take it. It was Smokey Bear hats and Lackland Air Force Base all over again. It was one thing to have a man yell at me, but I had an altogether more serious hang up about a woman in my face and yelling. Maybe it was male ego; I don't know. I just knew I couldn't take it.

She lit into me one day, and I fired back. While my mouth was running down, and I was running out of foul and abusive air, someone was flipping handcuffs on me. Outside of my own voice running amuck, the last thing I heard was the click of the lock on my solitary confinement cell.

As the guards walked away, one was yelling, "Scream all ya want, Carpenter! Ain't nobody gonna hear ya in there!"

He was wrong. Somebody did hear me in there. God heard me. When I had time to cool off and stop my ranting and raving, God moved in beside me in his very gentle way. *Donnie, it's your anger. Don't you get it? It's your anger that causes you so much pain and adversity. Donnie, you must learn to deal with your anger, and I am here to help you. Trust me, Donnie. You have to trust me.*

During the last leg of my sentence, Kelly's letters stopped coming. I was very hurt and had no clue why she quit writing. I treasured her friendship, and many were the times I replayed our walk and conversation over and over in my head. I continued to write to her, asking for an explanation but never received an answer back. I was pretty sure someone back in Indiana was behind her silence. I was hurt because Kelly dropped me with no explanation, which didn't seem like her. I began to worry that her boyfriend may have gone too far and physically hurt her.

When it came time to make a decision about staying in Oregon or returning to Fort Wayne, I knew I could not concentrate on my plans at hand until I had some definite answers concerning Kelly. I knew her silence would continue to plague my mind. I had to find out for myself.

It was August 1999 when I completed my sentence for the crimes I committed in Oregon. I decided to follow my heart rather than stay in Oregon and follow my original plan.

Oregon had set up a parole contract agreement with the state of Indiana to handle my parole, and I was under the same agreement in Indiana as I would have been had I remained in Oregon.

When I arrived in Fort Wayne, I learned that Kelly and her two children were still in the same relationship as when I left. I learned my mother befriended her.

We were all at Mom's house one Saturday when Kelly and I found ourselves alone. It was the first opportunity we had to talk with no one else around. I started the conversation with a little singsong to set the mood. "It's good to be back home again in Indiana."

"It's good to have you home, Donnie. How are you?"

"Well, Kelly, I'm a little hurt and a little confused."

She cocked that cute little head and raised an eyebrow. "Hurt? Why are you hurt?"

"How would you feel if you were in prison and your best friend just quit writing to you and never told you why?"

She dropped her head and remorsefully said, "I'm sorry, Donnie."

"Why, Kelly? Why did you quit writing? Just an explanation would have helped me understand, but nothing. Faithful writing and then nothing! Did your boyfriend make you quit?"

"He didn't make me quit."

"What did he do? What did he say, Kelly?"

"Oh, I don't know, Donnie. It was just easier to quit writing than to listen to him and everybody else around here all the time."

"Listen to what?"

"Promise me you won't get angry with them. I've struggled with this since I wrote the last letter."

"You know I won't be mad at you. What did they do, Kelly? Tell me!"

"Donnie, they said I had no business being friends with you because you were no good, a loser, and nothing but trouble. They said awful things about you, and I didn't know if they were true or not. It was just easier to back away than to listen to them."

So that was it? I should have expected as much. At least it was a decision fueled by someone else and not Kelly's own lack of interest that stopped her letters from coming.

I had my answer, but I also had purpose to stay in Indiana. Kelly still needed someone to evaluate her relationship and call it what it was: abuse. I couldn't change that, but I could let her know I saw it for what it was and at least be her sounding board if she needed one. It was the first time I ever felt respect from the opposite sex, and I had so much respect for her.

> Seek the Lord your God and you will find Him if you seek Him with all your heart and with all your soul.
>
> Deuteronomy 4:29 (NKJV)

Several weeks later, a situation arose that drove Kelly to her knees before God. She came face to face with the saving knowledge and *power* of Jesus and gave him her heart. Her spiritual growth was like a delicate bloom, flourishing in the peace she found in Jesus. She shared her experience with me and, through her new life in Christ, we learned to pray together, and we began attending Follower's Freewill Baptist Church together.

When God enters into the heart of a new child, Satan takes it real personal. He definitely does not like the idea of losing one of his slaves to the kingdom of God. With her newfound faith, Kelly found the courage to carry on, having left her abusive relationship, to establish a life on her own. Kelly was growing spiritually, and I still had a lot to learn.

One night, some friends and I went out to treat ourselves to something a little special. We ended up in a little nightspot on Fort Wayne's north side. When I had a few beers under my belt, I could be quite the loud mouth in the bar. I was being quite vocal when some guy mouthed off to me, and I hit him. *Would I ever learn?*

He and I wiped each other up pretty good by the time the police showed up. I got in one last lick by smashing a beer bottle in his face.

When I saw the police, I started to leave out a side door just as the guy I'd beat up started yelling, "That's him! That's him!"

Somebody grabbed me, and the police started asking me questions.

"Okay, buddy, calm down now. What's your name?"

At this point in my life, I was under the name of Foster, and my parole was under Carpenter. So I told them I was Donald Foster. They phoned headquarters and learned there were no warrants or parole violations out under the name of Foster, so they called it a mutual combat and let us go.

I was still under parole policy and obligated to report to my parole officer on a regular basis, so several days later, I checked in. I showed up on time and sat down in front of her desk. I noticed she was a little on edge but didn't know if it was me or maybe she'd had a bad encounter before me. I hoped the latter was the case. I sat there quite a while as she looked over paperwork and then she finally spoke.

"Donnie, I have something here that's pretty disturbing. I know you weren't arrested, but I have a report that you had contact with a police officer. I know you violated your parole by public drinking, and you were involved in a barroom fight. Wanna tell me about it?"

My heart fell through the floor. How did she know when I used the name Foster?

I just dropped my head and said nothing.

"I have to tell you I've contacted the Oregon parole office, and we're sending you back, Donnie. I have no choice but to send you back to Oregon." I knew she meant it.

Oh, dear God! Would this ever end?

You did not choose me but, I chose you and appointed you.

John 15:16 (NKJV)

It took about three weeks for Oregon to issue and send out the warrant to have me sent back. Paperwork complete, I arrived back in Oregon and was taken directly to the parole office. The first thing they told me was I was there to stay. They were not going to let me leave the state, so I was not going back to Fort Wayne.

"May I please say something?"

"What is it, Carpenter?"

"Look, dude, I screwed up. I know that. I decided to go out for an evening with some friends, and I know I should have laid off the beer, but I didn't. Some guy mouthed off to me, and I took a swing at him before I thought. That's an old reflex I know I need to work on, but I have responsibilities back in Fort Wayne, and I have a good job with a great employer who stuck his neck out to give this ex-con a chance. Please reconsider. Please."

They took me from the parole office back to the jail, and I spent the next two weeks in the holding tank, which was my penance for parole violation. Somewhere someone had to be praying. I was angry and wasn't on praying ground for myself, but even through it all, God did not forsake me, nor did he turn his back on me. With my time served, I was released and taken to the parole office.

"Mr. Carpenter, we've checked your story about your responsibilities in Indiana. We contacted your boss in Fort Wayne, and he is willing to give you your job back. But we're sticking our necks out sending you back there."

He handed me an envelope. "Here's a plane ticket. Your flight is scheduled to arrive in Fort Wayne at three tomorrow afternoon. Your parole officer there is expecting you as soon as you get to town. Whoever picks you up is to take you directly to see your parole officer. Is that clear?"

"Yes, sir. That is clear. Thank you."

I boarded my flight, and although I had a window seat, I saw nothing of the view. I can't tell you if anyone even sat in the seat beside me, because God began to occupy my mind with thoughts about the place I was in. From God, my heart was hearing, *Donnie,*

I've told you before; you have to address your anger. Anger is a sin of very great weight that so easily besets you and keeps you from running the race of faith. It must be dealt with before you do anything else. Trust me, and I will direct you if you are willing to let me lead you. That was all I could think about.

My plane touched down on the Fort Wayne runway, and my family was there to meet me. I did as I was told and reported to my parole officer. I don't remember much about that visit because I was so focused on what I needed to do concerning my anger. It was like a wasp in my overalls, I had to take care of it ASAP.

As soon as I got home, I went immediately to the Yellow Pages in the Fort Wayne phonebook. The first consultant ad I saw advertised for anger management as well as consulting service for substance abuse. I scanned the page for other options, but my eyes kept coming back to anger management and substance abuse. Was this the group God had in mind? I was sure they were all going to be the same—little rooms with couches and chairs, full of psychiatrists and therapists—but it was a start, and I had to start somewhere. The only thing to do was to find out. I called the number, and I made an appointment. I was expected the following Wednesday at 1:30 p.m.

Once the appointment was made, I wasn't sure if I was ready or not. I really didn't need some psychiatrist messing with my head. Maybe I should just cancel and work it out on my own. Well, I'd wait until the day of the appointment. Maybe I'd just work right on past the 1:30 hour and say I couldn't leave work. Anger? White lies? At this point, I couldn't see that it mattered much.

Wednesday arrived much too quickly. I worked through my lunch break. In the days prior, I found when I had time to think, I could think of nothing else but this appointment. All morning, I wrestled with the whole idea.

Donnie, you can't continue this path you're on. What you've been try-ing for these last forty years is obviously not working. What ground you are gaining, you are losing by the lack of control of your own temper. It's time to try something else. How bad do you want to change? How bad, Donnie? I was sure this was the voice of God speaking to my heart.

One o'clock came, and I punched out. I drove myself to the appointment. I didn't want to be dependent on anyone else driving me in case I found myself in a predicament and I wanted to get out of there in a rush. I was almost as nervous as I was standing in the courtroom in Oregon awaiting my sentence. The enemy was pounding my emotions, wanting me *not* to keep this date.

I stepped up to the reception desk.

"Hi! How may I help you?"

"I'm Donald Foster. I have an appointment."

"Just have a seat, Mr. Foster, and someone will be with you shortly. Would you like a cup of coffee or cool drink?"

"Yeah, sure. I'll have a cup of coffee."

I took a seat across the room, and the receptionist returned with my coffee. My hands were shaking so bad I was afraid I'd spill it, so I set it down on the end table next to my chair. Within minutes, I was called to a consultation room. I forgot my coffee.

I took a seat and waited. The door opened, and this burly guy stepped in. Was he my anger management therapist? He stuck out his hand and gripped mine like we were going to Indian wrestle. "Hi. My name's Mullinax. Wyatt Mullinax. It's nice to meet you, Mr. Foster."

Just the handshake on this guy was intimidating. I knew immediately it would not be in my best interest to lose my temper with him. Even his voice was intimidating.

Instead of losing my temper, I found my defenses surfacing. I wasn't about to let any anger show on this first visit, but I could be defiant. I decided real quick I wasn't about to give this guy the time of day. He might be big and he might sound tough, but what did he know about the world I came from?

Mr. Mullinax seated himself across from me. "Can I get you something to drink? Coffee? Coke? Water?

"I'll have a coffee." I figured I might as well ask for another one.

When he left the room to get my coffee, it was all I could do to stay in my seat. My head kept telling me, *Get out, Foster. This guy's going to mess with your head, so get out before he comes back.*

The door opened, and Mr. Mullinax set my coffee in front of me.

"So, tell me about Donald Foster."

"Whaddya wanna know?"

"Whatever you want to tell me. I'd like to know a little about what's going on in your life right now. I'd like to know what your life has been like up until now. Just wherever you care to start."

The vibes I was getting in this room were grating. I wasn't sure I made the best choice. I decided up front I might have made a big mistake.

"It's a long story, and besides ..." For a few brief moments, my head went blank and then my agitation exploded. "What in thunder would you know about the kind of life I came from anyway? You have no idea how I feel or what makes me tick. I could talk all day about the life I came from and you wouldn't have a clue! You sit here in your fancy office with your books and your fancy padded chair, and you don't know the first thing about life on the outside! This whole place is a joke, man, a screamin' joke!"

Mr. Mullinax stood his six-foot frame to his feet and slapped his Paul Bunyan-sized hand on the desk and leaned over breathing directly into my face.

"Now, you let me tell you this, young man. I came from *exactly* where you are! I've been there, Foster. I've been there, so don't pull this crap of an attitude on me!" And with that, Mr. Mullinax proceeded to tell me his story. He never sat back down but paced as he spoke, relating recollections from somewhere deep inside. For the next several minutes, I sat there with my chin on my chest and my mouth open. I listened to the testimony from a man whose lifestyle was so like my own. Piece by piece, his story unfolded until he said,

"Now, Foster, just how much do you think I *don't* know about where you've been or where you are? You're talking to the chief, man! I'm here to help you, Foster, and I know *how* to help you because I know *how* the gut cries when a man feel hopeless—when he's tried all the wrong things that seem like the right things, when nothing works and life goes from bad to worse. But you get this, Foster. I can be of no help to you unless you're willing to commit yourself to listen, to learn, and to apply the truths I'm going to teach you. I'm not teaching you the wisdom of Wyatt Mullinax. I'm going to teach you the truth according to the Word of God. Now, I've got room in my classes for anger management and addiction recovery, but you make up your mind whether or not you're willing to commit to it. If you're not willing, don't waste my time."

I knew this man at one time sat exactly where I was sitting today, in the seat of defeat. I also knew this man had hold of the truth that would not fail if I put my trust in God and his Word. I wanted what Wyatt Mullinax had.

"Where do I go to sign up?"

I gathered up the information, along with my schedule of classes, and walked out to my car and got in. I don't know how long I sat there. I opened the windows, and for the first time, felt like I could breathe in true breaths of promise. Maybe I was just caught up in the hype from Wyatt's testimony. I didn't know for sure, but I did know I didn't want to be suckered into anything that was just going to take my time. I didn't want my temptation for hope just scratched or my desperation tickled to again fall away from the grace of God.

As I thought back at the countless times I would regress and turn back to my old life, I realized God never shut me out. He was steadfast. He was sure. He was always there.

It was I who walked away.

It was I still hanging on to the things I thought I needed in my life to survive.

It was I who kept picking up the old habits and strapping on my back that heavy weight of disobedience that kept pushing my heart away from following after the truth.

Instead of turning to the God of my salvation and trusting the promises of God to deliver me, I'd take the bait, which pulled me into battle, and I'd wage it again by myself against myself. I should have learned a long time ago my methods were for losers.

It was my own choices that kept me playing with the deadly destructive things of the world.

I had tasted of God's love and mercy since that day my anger took me into that little church looking for Abby and I ended up finding mercy.

I knew something had taken place that day.

I knew for certain hope was attainable, not by anything I could do, but I learned the priceless commodity of truth.

I knew there was healing in repentance.

I knew I would never be alone as long as I walked with God.

I also knew there was a force out there ready to perch on my shoulder and take me down. It happened every time I wasn't moving forward, learning from and depending on and trusting in the God who showed me mercy.

God had performed some kind of work in me, and today, he raised the trumpet to sound the call to battle and I was ready to strap on the armor and fight.

I was one of about twenty other students in Wyatt's classes for anger management and addiction recovery. I received a solid foundation for dealing with anger and not being consumed by it.

Mr. Mullinax knew exactly from where I had to begin. He knew God was willing to reach a lot further down than I could possibly reach up, and he showed me how to grab hold of the mighty arm of God and hang on and learn.

Not once did Wyatt make me feel ashamed or embarrassed. He never treated me with the disrespect I had placed upon myself. Wyatt had something unique, and I wanted it. He had a way of making me feel like I was important to God, and I wanted to feel that too. God's love was the glue that bonded my trust and friend-ship to the man I tried to scare with my anger. I'm sure God must have smiled at that.

For weeks, God scraped off the miry clay of my old ideas and habits while I learned the steps to walking in peace with God and my fellow man. The more I learned, the more I knew it would be a long time before I even scratched the surface on learning what it meant to be a child of God.

As the months passed, I was learning the error of my thought pro-cess and moved forward with corrected thinking and a more com-mon sense approach to my problems. I was making progress, mov-ing ahead with my life, and making it more and more on my own.

I continued the class sessions with Mr. Mullinax, when one day, he laid another challenge at my feet.

"Donnie, I'd like for you to be my guest at church this Sunday. Whaddya say?"

"Ohhh no! I ain't goin' to no church, dude. I've had my fill of churches and church people. I'll take your classes, but uh-uh! I ain't goin' to no church!"

"Well, okay," was his reply. "I just thought maybe you'd like to sit in a service with me."

A couple weeks later, he approached me again after class.

"Now, Donnie, I know you don't care anything about going to church, and that's okay, but I'd like for some of my friends to meet you. We're hosting a picnic this Saturday at Foster Park. No pressure there. Whaddya say? Let's go have a hot dog together, and if you don't like my friends, you can leave anytime you want." I agreed to go only because he said I would be free to leave when-ever I wanted.

I showed up at Foster Park late. I found Wyatt, and he intro-duced me around. I was in a mix of people from Wyatt's church, and before I knew it, the afternoon turned to evening, and I was having a great time.

From the time I arrived until the festivities were over, I was not asked, even once, about my past. We laughed. We talked. We played games and threw baseballs, footballs, and Frisbees. When I was spoken to, people were concerned about where I was, not where I'd been. Several asked me about where I stood on a spiritual level: did I know God, did I want to know God, was I a believer? They asked me those questions with a true concern in love. I ate it up! I felt love from those people. They obviously had more going for them than just a bunch of pew warmers. I envied them for what they had, and I wanted it.

"Okay, dude. I'll visit your church, but I'm making no promises."

The next week, I was in the pew right next to Wyatt. The love from the congregation flooded over week after week. No one ever asked about my past. I became a regular attendee at the little brick church by the side of the road in Fort Wayne, Indiana.

Then Wyatt was just full of challenges. He approached me one day with this stunning opportunity. "Donnie, how about sharing your testimony with the folks at church?"

"Whaddya mean, 'share my testimony'?"

"I mean, tell the folks a little about yourself."

"You mean just pick out a few people and tell them?"

"That's one way, but not exactly what I had in mind. I was thinking more along the lines of you getting in front of the folks there some Sunday and telling them about your battles with drugs and alcohol. There are folks sitting in that congregation that need to hear and see how God can change a man."

"You mean get up front? Stand up there where the preacher stands and talk? I don't know, dude. I've never done anything like that before."

"Well, you think about it and pray about it. I think it would be a good experience for you and for the folks that know you. It will make them appreciate you even more to know where you've come from."

The only thing I'd ever done before in front of spectators was fight. Early on in our friendship, I shared with Wyatt what Millie said in the courtroom. After he put that opportunity in front of me, I felt her gentle hands cup my face and heard her words again: "Go with God...Become the warrior for him he has called you to be."

Well, I thought to myself, *let's just see if those people are as loving after they hear my story as they are now. That will be the true test of all this love they're showing me.* I told Wyatt I'd do it.

It was the coolest experience I'd ever had!

People that I had been sitting next to in the pews had no clue about my life. I had their full attention from the first word to the last. Their love spilled over even more.

Kelly was adjusting to her new life on her own. She found new strength to tackle things that before would have discouraged her and taken her spirits to the ground. I continued to do what I could to help her in both a supportive and financial way.

The old car she was driving needed some repairs, and I was doing what I could to avoid a mechanic's bill for her. One Saturday afternoon, I needed to go get some parts for the car, so Kelly went with me.

We started the ride in silence, and then Kelly spoke, "Donnie, thank you again for always being here for me. I can always count on you when the chips are down. You stuck by me when I didn't know which way to turn or if I'd even done the right thing by striking out on my own. Whenever I felt beaten down or was made to feel like I was dirt, I knew you were there taking the stabs with me. Living day in and day out with someone drinking every waking hour convinced me I could not live like that the rest of my life.

"Since the kids and I have been on our own and going to church and learning about Jesus, the kids are so much different. I'm so thankful they don't have to hear a violent tongue at home anymore, and I know they would have grown afraid if we had stayed in that environment. It bothers me they have to grow up without their dad in the house, but I have real peace that I've done the right thing. I know if I went back, God would help me, but I just don't have peace about taking my kids into an alcoholic abusive home. What do you think? Tell me the truth; am I fooling myself by being convinced that I did the right thing?"

"Kelly, you know I'm crazy about you and the kids. I love your kids like they were my own. You know I would do anything in the world for you and for them. No, I don't think you should go back. I know what you were living with. I know what's on the inside of an abusive man. I know he's not going to change on his own. It won't happen, Kelly. You can go back to him and waste your life away waiting on something that will never happen. The only way he will ever change is by the power and grace of God. You really don't want the kids exposed to an alcoholic day in and day out, do you? I was raised with an alcoholic father and then an alcoholic step-father. They'll grow up to think that kind of a life is normal, and they'll carry the lifestyle right into their generation and the next and the next. So yes, I am very sure you've done the right thing.

"I remember Brother Bob talking about the sins of the fathers being passed down to the third and fourth generations, and I'm finally beginning to understand that. I want that abusive behavior to stop with my generation. I don't want it to go any farther, and the only way to stop it is to commit it to God; my desire is for the sinfulness to stop here and now. I care for you and the kids very much, and you know I will be here for you for whatever you need. You're the finest lady I've ever known."

I found myself taking a long pause. I knew what I wanted to say for weeks, but my throat cramped up, and my hands broke out in a sweat.

"Who am I kidding? It's more than that. I love you, Kelly. As time goes on, I realize you're stealing my heart."

Kelly just sat there saying nothing and avoiding my eyes.

"Look at me, Kelly."

She lifted those beautiful eyes of a dove, and I could have melted right into my socks.

"Donnie, you don't have any idea how much those words mean to me. I think I've known since the night you stood up for me and protected me that you had something very tender and special under that rough exterior. I'm going to ask you something, and I want the truth. Do you mean everything you just said, because if you don't, if you're just telling me these things to make me feel better about leaving the situation I was in, you tell me right now because, Donnie, I know I'm losing my heart."

"Kelly, I mean every word of it. I'm a long, long way from being any kind of the changed man I want to be, but there's something you need to know. Years ago, in prison, I prayed to know the true love of a woman. I begged God for a tender woman to love and one who could love me. I begged God to help me be the kind of man a woman can respect and never fear. I don't know how it will all work out, but I know if you are that woman, Kelly, God will work it out. I'm not an easy man to love. I come with a ton of baggage and a lot of emotional undercurrents, but somehow, someday, I would hope that you could come to love me, Kelly."

Tears spilled over those big beautiful eyes. "Donnie, I've cared for you since I've known you, and the more I know of you, the more I care for you. I don't know either if we can make it work, but I told you the night you stood up for me that I saw hope in you, and I still believe it."

She slid across the seat, and I held her. It was the warmest, most gentle embrace I had ever experienced. I could feel Kelly's heart in every pore like a gentle quilt of comfort. I knew I loved this woman.

Instead of getting the part for the car, we went for a cup of coffee. We talked freely and laughed openly with no reservations, no inhibitions. I paid our tab, and we left. I opened the car door for her, and just before I pushed the door shut, I got close to her face, and I said, "You think I'm cute too, don't you?" She just shook her head.

"You think you are; why shouldn't I?"

"Very funny!"

Kelly and I became inseparable. We knew we cared for each other, and we knew we had to be cautious and patient.

That devilish imp on my shoulder still kept me convinced it was okay to party with a beer in one hand and marijuana joint in the other. It convinced me it was okay because weed was a natural product, and natural things were okay. It was one of the biggest lies I ever believed, but I believed it because I wanted to believe it.

Kelly had a difficult time accepting that part of me for anything closer than a friend, but our relationship grew. I knew I loved this woman. I knew she was different from every other woman I'd ever known. I knew I wanted to be with her more than anything else. I really thought love should overcome any obstacle, and I thought she would eventually get past my little habits.

I had lived my adult life in a pit of sin so deep there were social issues I never even considered to be wrong or unacceptable. Nor did I realize I needed to change my way of thinking about them. One of them was asking Kelly to live with me. I was free, she was free, and we cared for each other. What more normal thing could there be?

But then I found out just how much the people of Wyatt's church truly cared for us. When they found out Kelly and I were going to live together, I learned real quick they cared enough they were *not* about to approve that decision and let us live in sin. These folks seemed to know what they were talking about and were definitely on the side of God. I wanted their spiritual guidance, so we took their advice.

I wanted my proposal to be special. I wanted the entire world to see.

We were out with the kids on a beautiful evening drive going nowhere in particular. We left Fort Wayne, and I got the kids to playing a game by reading billboards. I would pick the billboard and then call on one of them to read it before we passed it. The kids liked the challenge, and Kelly and I played along. We were coming in on Highway 930 in New Haven. There were two billboards close together, and I had one of the kids read the first. "Okay, Kelly, the next one is yours."

"Oh, my God! Oh, my God! Donnie, are you serious?"

"What's the matter, Mom?" were the shrieks coming from the backseat.

I pulled off on the side of the street.

"Look! Read that billboard!"

Kelly's daughter started to read it aloud. "'Kelly, will you marry me? All my love, Donnie.'"

Kelly was crying. The kids were crying. Finally, she slid next to me. "If you weren't so darned cute, I'd say no."

I screamed; they screamed. Then we did what any normal American family would do after that—we all went out for ice cream!

Well, Kelly said yes, but I hadn't even begun to win the battles Satan had hold of. I wasn't sure she knew what she was getting herself into. The persistence of the enemy lurked behind every corner. I still had a lot to learn about deliverance and submission. God had barely scratched the surface.

When I remember sorrow
my heart still feels the pain;
When I remember gladness
does my heart not feel the same?
When I remember fear and ire
rise up my heart and fly;
Hold not to fear, nor ire retain
lest it pierce my soul and I should die.

AVS 10/13/08

I could not (or would not) break away from smoking weed. No one, not even Wyatt, knew I continued the highs, but I knew it hindered me from walking as closely with God as I could have. I knew God had changed my heart, and I knew my heart became his temple, but there was that one little room that I kept for myself and couldn't submit to the Spirit's house cleaning.

Satan deceived me into thinking it was okay, and he was satisfied. Satisfied, that is, until the opportunity came to entangle Kelly in his twisted order of destructive things. He wormed his way in and turned the screws on Kelly by drawing her into his ring of smoke.

> I acknowledged my sin to you, And my iniquity I have not hidden. I said, "I will confess my transgressions to the Lord," and you forgave the iniquity of my sin.
>
> Psalm 32:5 (NKJV)

One devastating weekend, Kelly decided to try marijuana, and she fell in love with it. At first, I was excited about her participation, but it wasn't long until I realized I was taking her down with me, just as I had done in every other relationship I'd ever been in. We'd make our appearances at church and church events and then go home and get high. I was drawing Kelly right into the demon's web.

I believe Wyatt knew something was not right in my life, but I was convinced he really couldn't put his finger on it.

One night, he asked me to go with him and participate in his mentoring program.

Why not? I thought. I tagged along for several weeks, faithful to accompany him as he shared truth from the Word of God with inmates, drug addicts, and alcoholics.

Wyatt's wife, Carolyn, also had a mentoring program for women with similar problems, and Kelly asked if she could be in her mentoring classes. Kelly began to spend a great deal of time with Carolyn, sitting under her Bible studies.

After accompanying the Mullinaxes on their mentoring visits, Kelly and I would return home and get high. The discontent in my heart was a bitter sting on my conscience. I knew it was wrong, and I know Kelly knew it was wrong. But did we make any effort to change? Not until one cold and wintry New Year's Eve.

I always looked at the end of the year as the perfect time to usher out the old and ring in the new with all the celebrating I could do.

I arrived home on New Year's Eve, and Kelly met me at the door.

"Hey, Mama. Get your party clothes on! We're gonna celebrate tonight!" I grabbed her and spun her around on the floor.

"Donnie! What are you doing?" We laughed and danced to imaginary music, and then I reached in my pocket and held up a small bag of white powder.

"Know what this is?" I asked her as I danced around her.

She was feeling giddy and said, "I'll bite. What is it?"

"It's better than chocolate candy on a rainy day!"

"Oh yeah?"

"Yeah, and there's enough here for us to bring the New Year right to our doorstep. Are you with me?" She stopped dancing.

"I don't know, Donnie. I think smoking marijuana is as far as I care to go. What if someone comes by and catches us?"

"Well, darlin,' I got plans for that too. We'll get a motel room away from here where no one knows us, and you'll have the time of your life. I promise. What's in this little bag will light up your world like a roman candle. It will be the best New Year's Eve celebration you ever had. Now come on. I'll get a sitter for the kids while you throw whatever you need for overnight in a bag, and let's start celebrating."

We spoke very little as we drove to the motel. I'm sure Kelly was thinking along the same lines as I was thinking. I checked us in. It was a quaint little room with a hot tub, but we weren't there for luxury. All we needed was privacy.

What was going on in my head is next to impossible to explain.

I knew where this was leading.

I knew if I went through with this, it wouldn't be long until I was stealing again to support my addiction.

I knew, beyond a shadow of a doubt, I was plunging full speed back into a lifestyle that would put me right back behind bars.

I knew God had every right to throw his holy book of truth and judgment right through the back of my disobedient and self-ish heart.

I knew it!

And *I knew* I was taking Kelly down with me.

We unlocked the door to our room and threw the bag on the bed. Kelly sat down and kicked off her shoes. She lay back on the bed with her hands behind her head.

"I don't know, Donnie. I have a really bad feeling about this."

I lit a joint for both of us.

"Here. This will take the edge off and get things off to a good start."

I knew after a couple drags of marijuana, the whole guilt trip I was on would drift right out with the smoke. I was afraid if Kelly had too much time to think about it, she might back out of this great evening I had planned.

I was right. The edge disappeared, and the high was working its magic. I'd brought in all the beer I had, which was more than enough. We drank a few ales, and then I showed her how to snort cocaine. We snorted coke, drank, and smoked weed into the night, partying ourselves silly. We were so high on cocaine that there was no sleeping, so we left the motel early the next morning.

As Kelly was coming down off the high, I could tell she was terribly disturbed about what we had done. I was hung over and in a fog of misery. My head felt like a bale of cotton, and my eyes were so sensitive to the light that I had to fight to keep them open.

"Kelly, do you feel like driving?"

"Driving? I guess."

"Good, because it's all I can do to stay upright without throwing up my socks."

"Just get in the car, and let's go home." I could tell by the tone of her voice she was having deep, deep regrets.

Kelly drove us home, and neither of us spoke. All I wanted to do was vegetate somewhere dark and quiet.

Kelly, on the other hand, was dealing with not just her guilt of disobedience but mine as well, and once we got home, I could tell she was riding a guilt trip that wasn't going to go away.

God was letting us feel the full effect of our selfish and sinful disobedience. God was letting us know he was not going to let either of us relish in our *good* time, and he was not giving up on us. Finally, Kelly came to me in tears.

"Donnie, how can I ever face Carolyn after what we did last night? She is my mentor, and she has no idea about my sins. I can never share my testimony with anyone because I am living a lie, Donnie. I'm living a horrible, dirty lie! How could I let you talk me into doing something so wrong? Look at us! I feel so dirty before God. Donnie, I am too ashamed to show my face back at church. We totally ruined everything God has accomplished in us. I'm living a lie, and you're living a lie, and I don't want to do this anymore." She fell into my arms and sobbed. It was a gut-wrenching cry from the very heart that God had inhabited. His spirit was washing out the sin and the rubbish while she laid it all on the altar before him. Her heart was truly repentant.

I knew she was right. We were both living a lie, and her pain was burrowing into my own heart and eating away at my already raw conscience. I saw what my sin had done to Kelly, and I knew I was responsible for her grief before God. I took her hands in mine, and we wept together. Finally, I spoke.

"Kelly, I am so sorry for what I brought on us last night. I can't tell you how sorry I am! I don't know what came over me.

No, that's not true. I do know. Satan dangled the bait in front of me, and I let him gain a little control by temptation, and when he saw I was tempted, he ran amuck with it. It's my fault, Kelly. It's my fault." I took her in my arms and held her. Together we cried to God, confessing what we had done. Finally, Kelly looked me square in the eyes. "Donnie, I need to talk to Wyatt and Carolyn. If anybody can help us through this, it will be them."

I wasn't sure I was ready to do that, but I said okay. We called them and asked if we could stop by. They were more than gracious to our request.

"Come on, Kelly. Let's go."

It was still early on New Year's Day when we drove to their house. I knocked on the door, and Carolyn answered the door. She knew something was desperately wrong, and she immediately asked us in.

Kelly spoke first. "We need to talk to the two of you. We've done something terrible, and we need help."

"Well, come in, come in. I just made some fresh coffee. Wyatt's in the front room, so go on in, and I'll be right there."

Wyatt came to meet us and took our coats. We sat next to each other on the sofa, and Wyatt asked, "What's going on? You two look pretty devastated."

I started talking, and the words just tumbled from my mouth. I told him exactly all I arranged for us to do, where we went, what we did, and how God drew us into his light this morning.

When I finally quit talking, Wyatt asked, "What do you think we ought to do about all this?"

"That's why we're here. We need you to tell us."

"Well, the first order of business is to get rid of the temptation. Where's the stuff you have left?"

Kelly and I looked at each other. Rarely does an addict leave himself with nothing. If possible, you always save a little until you get the opportunity to make your next buy. I had tossed the little bag of weed under the driver's seat when we left the motel.

"It's in the car," I said.

"Go get it." I got up and started toward the door. "You bring all of it in, Donnie. Every last speck, you hear?"

"I will."

I trudged through the snow to the car and reached under the seat for the bag. There, on my shoulder, was that little tap of demonic temptation.

Hey, there, my friend, are you sure you want to do this? Better think it over. Just go back in there and tell your friend you took it in the house. Who's going to know? You've had so many bigger sins in your life than this. This is nothing. All you did was snort a little coke and smoke a little weed. Besides, think about the guys you used to hang around with. You're not nearly as bad as they are. Right, Donnie? Come on. It's just a little weed, just enough for one more good night of entertainment.

I realized I was sitting in fifteen-degree weather without so much as a jacket, and sweat was pouring from my face. My hands were shaking as I tried to reason against the evil one clinging to my back, dangling the bait in my face. My chest felt tight, and I was breathing in short, shallow breaths.

"Donnie, are you all right?" I looked up, and Kelly was standing there, her arms folded tight around her, and she was shivering from the cold. "What's wrong, Donnie? Why aren't you coming in?"

It didn't take her long to put two and two together and know I was struggling with what I'd come out here to do. I was both angry and embarrassed at being caught in my temptation, so I snapped at her.

"Get back in the house, Kelly. Go on! Get back in the house!"

"No, Donnie, I won't! What are you doing? Come on! Get the stuff and bring it in."

I didn't look at her, and I didn't move. My anger was rising.

"Donnie! Come on! You're not going to back out on this, are you? Because if you are—

"Stop it, Kelly! Stop it! Just back off and don't crowd me!" I'd never talked to her like that before. *Oh God, what's happening?* I thought. "Look, Kelly. Okay, I'm sorry. Kelly, look."

She walked around and got in on the other side of the car. I was clutching the bag of joints so tight my hand began to cramp.

"Now, you listen to me, Donnie Foster! We're going through with this! Do you hear me? Look at me! That bag is as much an enemy to me as it is to you. Now, give me that bag!" She started to grab it from my hand. I grabbed her wrist and lifted my eyes to hers. There was a fire of determination in those hazel eyes.

"Look, just give me a minute, Kelly. Baby, I'm sorry. I'm sorry I snapped at you."

I took a couple of deep breaths and laid my head on the back of the seat. "Why is this so darn hard?"

She didn't respond. Was she listening or was she just too mad?

"Kelly, I was ready to lie to Wyatt and tell him I must have left this at the house. *Why can't I give this stuff up?*"

"Give me that bag, Donnie. C'mon, give it to me!" I released my death grip on it, and she took it from my hand.

"I'm not having this stuff in my home anymore. Every time you light one up, you widen the crevice between you and me and between you and God. The contents of *this bag* are part of *my sin,* and I'm getting rid of it. Now, you can choose to be part of the victory or you can continue to wallow in your defeated pity party, but this bag is not going home with us." She twisted the bag so hard the joints all crushed. "Now, you make up your mind because I'm tired of messing with this!"

When did she become such a strong woman? This was a side of Kelly I had not seen. She was right. I knew she was right. In my head, God replayed the remorse we both experienced just a couple hours ago when we both repented of our actions the night before.

"What were you going to do with this, Donnie? Keep on living your little lie?"

"Kelly, I'm an addict. It's a crutch, and I can't give it up. Come on, let's go in."

"No, we're not going in until you decide it's really something you want to give up, or do you plan on enjoying the little game you play with it?"

"I want to give it up. God as my witness, I want to give it up. When I'm tempted, I just don't see what the big deal is; why is it so wrong?"

"Get out and go in the house and ask Wyatt Mullinax that question. I'm going in. Are you coming?"

I got out of the car and followed her in. Before we opened the door, Kelly turned and said, "Donnie, if we don't do this together, it's not going to happen. Wyatt and Carolyn are there to help us, and I know God is waiting to wash this all away if you really mean what you're saying. Do you, Donnie?"

I really don't think she understood the power of the battle going on in my head, but I nodded.

"Then come on. Let's go in and tell Wyatt and Carolyn the whole story."

Wyatt was still in his big chair when we walked in.

"Did Satan try to pull the wool over your eyes out there, Donnie?"

I shook my head. "How'd you know?"

"I know."

Kelly and I spent the morning with the Mullinaxes. Wyatt suggested we bury the remains of our sin fest as though it were a dead enemy. We prayed, and we talked.

Their advice to us was simple: we had to work together to be successful. If we agreed before God and to each other never to use drugs again, we needed to make a pact then and there stating that if it ever happened, whatever measures were needed, we would both adhere to the consequence. Did we agree to do that? Kelly was ready. I reluctantly said yes. I knew it was the right thing to do, but I also knew my own weaknesses. After what I put Kelly through the night before, I had to do this for her. She knew she had to do it for me. The pact was this: if either of us fell into the temptation to use illegal drugs of any kind again, the other one had the right to dismiss the user from coming home. We decided we did not want drugs in any shape, condition, or form to penetrate our home or family. We also agreed that measures of tough love could and would be implemented as needed as a means of accountability to each other and before God.

I knew we did the right thing and even had a sense that we were winning the war one battle at a time, but I could also feel the scratchy noose dangling close to my scalp. I knew, beyond a doubt, I was my own worst enemy.

Wyatt and Carolyn took us out for a late breakfast. I felt good about what we had done and the pact we made, but I was afraid to get too excited over the victory that was trying to brew in my heart. I was becoming familiar with the deceptive measures Satan uses. He stays out of sight until the hype is over and real life settles back in. In my heart, I wanted to be free from the bondage of coke, marijuana, and alcohol, and in my heart, I truly felt I was winning. Wyatt told me over and over, "Donnie, you can't do this by yourself. God is the only true source of strength you can depend on to keep the victory. You have to pray and trust."

WHERE THE RUBBER MEETS THE ROAD

THE CATALYST: **THE TASTE OF VICTORY**

Who can find a virtuous and capable wife? ...
Her husband can trust her
and she will greatly enrich his life.
She will not hinder him
but help him all her life ...
she is clothed with strength and dignity ...
She carefully watches all that goes on
in her household ...
Charm is deceptive ... but a woman who fears the Lord
will be greatly praised.

Proverbs 31 (NLT)

So Christ has really set us free.
Now make sure that you stay free
And don't get tied up again in slavery to the law.

Galatians 5:1 (NLT)

With the holidays over, our normal routine returned. I was thrilled to realize I was not facing temptation to snort any more cocaine. But there was still that lifelong ogre in my face to smoke marijuana. I was reneging on the pact Kelly and I made on New Year's Day. I knew it had to go. But those familiar lies continued to justify my continuation: Was I hurting anyone? Didn't everybody do it? Who's going to know? Just one more buy and *then* I can kick the habit. There are so many other bigger sins. I'm not as bad as … And then I fell for the granddaddy of all lies, the over-the-line-lie. I figured if Kelly didn't know I still smoked weed, it wouldn't hurt her, so I hid it from her.

I now had another job that included a delivery route for a supply company, and I continued to smoke marijuana with the guys at work. At home, I was the obedient man. Every day, God was at the helm of my ship telling me, *Donnie, don't do it. Donnie, don't go there.* Some days his voice was so loud it was almost annoying because I continued to enjoy my little sin behind the woodpile like a disobedient little boy. I thought for weeks I was hiding all this from Kelly. But Kelly was no dummy. Because I had introduced her to marijuana, she could identify the aroma, and she smelled it on me. She knew what I was doing, but she continued to let me carry out my little charade.

Now, in the midst of all this, there was another issue going on in my heart and in my head. I was having great remorse for the children I had fathered as well as those I had been a father figure to. I knew I had failed them as someone they could trust or depend on to be a good influence in their lives. I knew the rebellion and struggles they were facing in their lives was a result of the sin they mimicked in me. I gave them nothing on which to build a firm foundation, and they lived their lives the way they saw me live mine. I guess they thought it was the norm.

Many were the hours I wept over them in remorse and repentance, so I began to ask God for another chance. I told Kelly how I felt and asked her if she would be willing to give me another chance if God would allow me to father one more child and raise it up to his glory and according to his Word. She said, "Of course." Time and again I told God I would really like a little girl with silky brown hair and blue or green eyes. I even had her name picked out, and God heard the desire of my heart. God gave us a beautiful little girl, yet Kelly continued to allow me to live my little lie.

God was giving me another chance at raising a child for him, and here I was, a continual bad example as a father and husband. I knew it. God knew I knew it. Kelly knew it, but she also knew she didn't want to raise the child alone, so she tried to maintain peace in our home by keeping her mouth shut.

Now, because my job involved courier service, I would make nightly delivery runs, and this eventful night, I was to make a delivery to Indianapolis. I generally stopped by the house before leaving for a run just to check in with her and the kids. She was in the kitchen preparing dinner when I got home. The baby was playing on the floor, and the two older kids were watching cartoons under the pretext of doing homework.

Kelly was ready for me. She knew I would be pretty high on marijuana, like I was most evenings. The look on her face when she met me at the door stopped me cold. She had not had a good day, and I was always trying to play the pacifist. It was my way of covering up my guilt. I don't remember what started the heated discussion, but peace was not to be maintained that night. We finally ended up exchanging very harsh words. I stomped out and slammed the door.

I went out, crawled in my truck, and headed south on Highway 69. It was about a two-hour trip to Indianapolis, and I knew Kelly would be counseling with Carolyn about our big fight. I also knew she would try to call me on my cell phone, but I refused to answer.

When I arrived at my destination, I completed my job and crawled back in the truck to head home. I decided to check my voice mail before getting on the road, and there was a text message from Kelly. It read, "All your stuff is at the church. Don't call me. Don't come home. Don't contact me until you get help."

What does she think she's doing?

I was mad. Whatever I had gained in anger management to that point went right out the back of the truck, because I was almost frothing-at-the-mouth mad. The first thought that pierced through the defensive lobe in my head was fired from the demonic little fiend hanging onto my shoulder. *So that's the way she wants to play, huh? Okay. I can play her little game.*

I thought I had Kelly under my control, and that whole idea just blew up in my face. I certainly never expected her to do anything like this. Well, we'll see about that. I wasn't about to give her the upper hand over this.

In my heart, I made up my mind; I wasn't going down without a fight. The enemy on my shoulder knew I had not yet got past my old solution for dealing with life going bad. He was right there, urging me to take care of this just like I had always taken care of everything. *Donnie, you need to just tie on one more good high. That way, you'll be sharp when you get back to Fort Wayne. You'll have the courage to put that woman and her cohorts in their place. One more high, Donnie, just one more. I can show you where to buy the good stuff. You need it. You won't be sorry. Nobody can deny you the right to have the power to claim what is yours.*

One thing about addicts is they always know where to go to do a deal. I drove to a bar, and within twenty minutes, I found a guy who told me where I could make a cocaine buy. At this point, God must have grabbed this temptation and spun it by the tail because the more information I was given, the less I wanted to go to the trouble to run it down. I crawled back in my truck. They'd have to deal with me, as I was, clean, sober, and angry!

A few miles out of Indianapolis, I called the pastor at our church.

"Hello, church office."

"Hey, Pastor. It's Donnie."

"Hi, Donnie. I was hoping you'd call. Where are you?"

"Heading back to Fort Wayne. I'm about an hour out. I just wanted to let you know I'll be there to get my stuff. I'm sorry Kelly involved you. I don't know what my wife thinks she's doing anyway."

"What do you think she's doing, Donnie? Tell ya what. I'll wait here at the church for you tonight. Why don't you come on down when you get back into town and we can at least talk about this. Okay?"

"Yeah, I'll be there."

I had no clue that Kelly would have the courage to take measures such as this to get me clean. When I arrived at the church, I saw the pile of my clothes and personal belongings in the vestibule. I went directly to the pastor's office. There, the pastor and assistant pastor were waiting.

"Come on in, Donnie."

"I'm just here to get my stuff and get out."

"Are you sure that's the best thing to do right now?" I knew he'd want to talk and then pray, and I was in no mood to do either.

"Yeah, I'll load up my stuff and be out. Sorry Kelly got you involved. I'll talk to her about that. It won't happen again."

"Donnie, you know Kelly did this because she cares about you. What do you think the kids would say about this if they knew?"

"Hey! Don't bring the kids into this. They don't need to know anything about this! They're just innocent bystanders! You and Kelly have no right to make me look bad in front of them!"

"How long do you think you can keep it from them? Kelly said the two of you made a pact about keeping drugs out of the house. According to her, you can't go home tonight. How long before they start asking, 'Where's Daddy? Why isn't Daddy coming home?' They love you, Donnie. You're an intricate part of their life."

"And they're part of my life, but you and Kelly are not telling me what to do, and you're certainly not keeping me from those kids. You got that? You're not telling me what to do."

In my heart, I knew they were right, but my mind was so full of anger. I was going to do it my way.

I threw my things in the truck and went to a motel. For the next couple of days, I went to work as usual.

The pastor's comments about the kids kept nagging me, and I knew I had to see them. I was still angry at Kelly. I made up my mind that she was just like all the rest. A woman was a woman, and they were all alike. In the back of my mind, I knew I was going to have to come to terms with Kelly and deal with her, but the imp on my shoulder kept telling me she wasn't going to tell me what to do.

Also, somewhere in some secret corner of my heart, I was truly afraid my anger would overtake the conviction I was carrying. I honestly did not want that to happen. Conviction for my sin was definitely there, and in some strange and bizarre way, it gave me assurance I was still in the battle. The contention mounted between these two emotions.

After dealing with this a couple days, I knew I had to see the kids and at least be assured in my own mind they still cared for me. I wanted to see Kelly too, but I knew that would have to be more than just walking in and saying, "I'm back!" I kept pushing that thought away; I knew before this was over, I would have to come to terms with what I had done.

Anger and conviction were vying for first place when I decided to call Kelly.

"Hello."

"Hi, Kelly. It's Donnie."

"I know."

"How are you and the kids?"

"We're okay, Donnie."

"Have the kids asked about me?"

"They wonder why you're not home."

"What do you tell them?"

"I tell them Daddy's just working on some things."

"I'd like to see them. Would that be okay?"

"Yes, but you can't come here to see them."

"Kelly, those are our kids, and that's my home, and you can't keep me from coming there to see them! You're making me look bad to them!"

"Donnie, I'm not keeping you from seeing them. *You* are keeping yourself from coming home to see them, and if you look bad before them, who's responsible for that, Donnie? You're behavior is bad as their father and disrespectful as head of this home. You are choosing to do things that make you a bad example before them. We made a pact, Donnie, remember? You and I, for the good of our home and family. We made a pact, and this is the consequence for breaking that pact."

I slammed the phone down. I started out the door to fix things the way I always fixed them. One more fix. I needed just one more high to get my thinking straight. I stopped short of crossing the threshold. Maybe I should try Kelly one more time. I picked up the phone and dialed her number.

It rang and rang. Why didn't she answer? I went out to the truck and crawled in behind the wheel. I put the key in the ignition when conviction began its awesome rise over the anger that had been consuming me. I could see Kelly's beautiful eyes and knew that I was responsible for taking the sparkle from them. I knew she was right. At that point, I found extreme joy in the yoke of conviction laying across my shoulders because it was squeezing the life out of the devilish imp vying for my attitude.

I went back to my room and dialed her number one more time. I was willing to come halfway with whatever was necessary to see her and the kids, but cinders still burned to maintain some type of control.

"Hello."

"Kelly, I'm sorry I hung up on you. I really need to see you and the kids. I'll do whatever I need to do. Just let me know when and where."

"It has to be done the right way, Donnie, or it's not going to happen. Are you willing to submit to that?"

"Yeah, whatever. Where do you want me to meet you?"

"I don't know yet. Call me back in an hour or two, and I'll let you know."

"One hour, Kelly. I'll call you back in one hour."

I heard her hang up.

One hour, I thought. That would give me enough time to get my head in order. I still had some marijuana cigarettes in the truck. One more would give me courage and put me back in a good mood.

I took about five steps to the truck when the strangest phenomena transpired. From somewhere in my head, someone hit the rewind button. "*You* are keeping yourself from coming home to see them, and if you look bad before them, who's responsible for that, Donnie? *You're* behavior is bad as their father and disrespectful as head of this home. *Your* choices are making you a bad example before them. It has to be done the right way, Donnie, or it's not going to happen. Are you willing to submit to that? *You* are keeping yourself from them. *Your* choices, Donnie; *your* choices." Then a chill started at my feet, and the shudder erupted through the collar on my jacket. Again I heard the mysterious voice of Millie from behind the bar in the courtroom as she shared the vision she received on my behalf. "Donnie will be my servant, and his story will touch the quick of the spirits enslaved as Donnie was enslaved ... I find it more important for me to be obedient ... It is more important that I obey God."

I shook myself back to my senses, running my hands through my hair, trying to clear my head.

Then came this mind-boggling lecture from somewhere: "Donnie, when was the last time you made a decision without being under the influence of mind-altering dependency? You might be surprised at what good choices the real Donnie could make. Do you even know the real Donnie? Truthfully, all you really know is the Donnie that depends on deadly crutches to get through life. How pitiful is that? That's weak, Donnie. You're defeated as soon as you take that first step toward weed, cocaine, or alcohol. If that's the Donnie you want to be, then just roll yourself up in a fetal position and let those things take you to a defeated grave. Kelly has more guts than you do. She's at least willing to stand and take the bull by the horns and has the courage to do what's right. Go ahead. Fall on your face again ... and again ... and again. You've got a whole hour to show the kids how pitiful you are. For once ... just once ... let the real Donnie face reality and see what happens."

Whoa! Where did this come from?

Yeah, okay! I'll do this. I can face the music without a high. She might as well see the real Donnie.

I walked off the rest of the hour, right down to the second, and I picked up my phone and dialed her number.

"Hello."

"Your hour's up, Kelly. Where do you want me to meet you?"

"Come to the church office tomorrow at 10:00 a.m."

"At the church? Come on, Kelly. How about a park or someplace besides the church?"

"Donnie, I will be at the church tomorrow morning at ten. You can either choose to be there or not be there."

"Okay. I'll be there."

I wasn't sure I liked where this seemed to be going. What's come over her?

I walked in the door a little after ten. I could have been on time. This was just my selfish, stubborn way of keeping as much control over the situation as I could. She could have the pleasure of waiting a few minutes.

From the door, I saw the pastor and assistant pastor and their wives. Stepping in, I saw Wyatt and Kelly all waiting on me.

Wyatt spoke first. "Come in, Donnie. Have a seat."

"What's going on? I just came by to see the kids and get the rest of my stuff. I don't see the kids. Where are the kids, Kelly?"

Those questions were ignored. Wyatt continued, "I know. But, Donnie, everyone in this room is here because we love you and we care about what happens to you."

"Yeah, well, this is between me and Kelly. Kelly, get your stuff and the kids. We're going home."

Kelly spoke up with a confidence I had not seen in her. "No, Donnie, we're not going home."

How dare she talk to me like that? I was on my feet and headed for the door. Wyatt stepped up and stood between my exit and me.

"Donnie, what's it going to take? What are you willing to commit to in order to save your family and get your life clean and stay clean? Kelly's not going to put up with it anymore. You have three young impressionable children who need their father, but they need a clean father. They need a father who will love *them first,* not himself. They need a father who will make sacrifices for them and teach them and train them. They need all those things you were never privileged to have, and God has given you the opportunity to be their daddy. Do you really want them to grow in the kind of atmosphere you have in your home right now?"

I was beginning to wish I hadn't listened to the convicting thoughts I had the day before. "Look! You, none of you, can keep my family from me! That is my wife and my family, and nobody's taking them from me."

Kelly stood up and took a couple steps in my direction. "They aren't keeping us from you, Donnie. *You* are keeping us from you. I am making a conscious decision to take the children and myself from you unless you get some help, pure and simple, Donnie. I'm not living like this anymore. You make the choice."

My anger was seething through my pores. I turned and busted through the doors and walked out of their little holier-than-thou meeting.

I drove to St. Mary's River. Before I got out, I lit up one more marijuana joint—you know, just to get my head thinking right, *the lie in the pit from which I could not crawl free!* I started to walk. A good fifty yards away from the truck, I sat down on the bank. The air was very crisp, and I remembered seeing my breath in the winter chill and realizing at that moment my anger was that of a raging bull. I quickly put the thought out of my head, telling myself I had a right to be mad.

I was devastated. I lost control of my family. How dare the bunch of them gang up on me *with my wife?* They could not do this to me, and I would see to it they didn't.

Tonight, the marijuana wasn't taking the edge off.

What will you do in the day of punishment, and in the desolation which will come from afar? To whom will you flee for help?"

Isaiah 10:3 (NKJV)

For all this ... His hand is stretched out still!

Isaiah 10:4 (ESV)

Between the anger in my head and the conviction in my spirit, I lashed out and blamed the ultimate one I could lash out at.

Are you up there, God? Are you seeing all this? Why didn't you just let me die back in California? You could have taken my life any number of times in the last thirty years. Is this some kind of sick joke you enjoy with guys like me? When are you going to let it end, God? Huh? When? Ever?

I was so angry that I started to weep. I couldn't go back to Wyatt. I couldn't show my face among the people who had become my church family after this. And Kelly? I was sure Kelly wouldn't take me back under any circumstances. And there were the three kids that lovingly called me Daddy.

Okay, God! I've had it! Is this the kind of sick entertainment you enjoy by allowing me to father another child, only to let me destroy her life like you've let me destroy everyone else who ever came into my life?

I wept until I couldn't weep anymore.

I started to get up when this gentle spirit moved over me and filtered through my anger and confusion. "Donnie, why can't you trust me? I'm your Father, and I love you. Why can't you trust me?"

"Trust! Ha! I've never found anyone in my life I could trust but myself!" I squatted down on my haunches on the riverbank and flipped splinters of small sticks in the dirty, half-frozen water. I watched them float on down St. Mary's River, getting hung up along the debris at water's edge. I knew what that felt like.

I forgot that it was cold. I don't know where my thoughts were taking me. I just remember an awesome spirit of peace flood over me, and the words of Brother Bob, Millie, and Wyatt surged through my mind, all of them desperately wanting to take root in my heart. I knew there were people who loved me, and I thought they were people I could trust. That brought about somewhat of a sense of peace.

"Seek me *first*, Donnie. If you seek me first and my righteousness, I will add to your life all things you will ever need. But you don't, Donnie. You continue to rely on yourself and solve things the way you always have—with fists, fire, fury and a fix—and you fall, and you'll keep on falling unless you take to heart Wyatt's instruction and do as I've told you in my Word. Renew your mind and the way you think. It's not my way to just step in and take over. It's a choice that must be made, Donnie. Choose today, who you are going to serve."

That sounded good, but I didn't know how to do that.

The spirit of God nudged my heart and prompted questions in my mind about myself so I audibly started asking the One who brought me to this point.

"What is it you want, God? I try and I try. What is it you want? I've chosen you, God. You know I've chosen you, but where are you? Where are you when I need you, when I light up that joint, when I'm mad and everything falls apart? Huh? Where are you? Look at me, God. It's me, Donnie Foster. I'm a failure. I'm your big, fat failure, and that's all I'm ever going to be."

"Donnie, I am with you always. I will never leave you. I am with you to the ends of the earth."

I read that somewhere, didn't I?

"Then why don't you stop me? You know I don't have the will-power to stop smoking pot! And my temper! What about my temper? When are you going to change that? Huh? When? I'm losing here, God so when are you going to stop me? Oh, God, *why don't you stop me?*"

"You can do all things through me who will give you of my strength."

Again, I started to weep. I was beginning to realize how weak I was. Oh, God, I never wanted to be thought of as weak. I controlled everything and everyone around me, and now I was beginning to see that *I couldn't even control my own life.* I was a failure all right, and as long as I continued on in my own pitiful power, that's all I would ever be. The tears ran, and my heart began its journey.

"God, you have to know that in my heart I want to do what's right, but in my mind I'm still the same old Donnie!"

God used Wyatt's mentoring to stir thoughts in my head. "You lived and grew up in this world, and this world formed your way of thinking. Don't copy the behavior of this world anymore. Let me transform your mind by helping you change the way you think.

If your heart is truly changed, your mind-set must also change.

Stop shooting from the hip! It's okay to give yourself time to stop and think and pray."

If you put any other desires before God, you will fail. God demands first place.

"God, I've been an addict so long. Like a pig in a sty, I'm always wallowing in my own filthy mess!"

"Brother Bob told me 'God can't look on sin, Donnie, and when you sin, God extends his hand of deliverance but turns his face. His hand is there, but you must choose to take it.'"

I threw a few stones and started back to my truck. I wasn't sure what to do.

I'd served the demons of hell so long I had to trust God to set me free.

Instead of getting back in my truck, I again walked along the bank.

I began to think about the newness I felt in my spirit during the time Abby and I spent with Brother Bob in Oregon. I knew then something unnatural had taken place that I couldn't explain. I wanted to understand. I began to think about that part of me that would live forever—my soul, my spirit, the living person inside this shell of flesh. I remembered Brother Bob talking about death, and I tried desperately to get a handle on the idea that the body would have to die to set my spirit free. As long as I lived and breathed, my spirit was confined to this shell.

Until I received forgiveness, I always had a feeling of emptiness. I tried to fill that emptiness with the only things I knew—drugs, alcohol, and taking whatever I wanted for myself. I took what I wanted, trying to bring satisfaction to that dying spirit, but feeding it with more dead and destructive waste.

Jacob DeBaine's words returned. "Man is born with the nature to satisfy the pleasures of his flesh. From the time he is an infant, he puts himself first. Putting yourself first is what destroys your spirit."

The spirit of man is what God created for himself, "*but you must choose to return it to him.* Your spirit will always be governed by the force that owns it. When you were born into this world, you were born to the world and it's authority. Only God can create a new, clean, and acceptable spirit worthy of his acceptance.

Only the shed blood of the Son of God can destroy the spirit the world gave you and create in you a new spirit. But it has to be God's way, and it has to be your choice, Donnie."

I don't know how long I walked. God had so gently yet miraculously touched my spirit there in the cold on the banks of the St. Mary's River. I kicked a couple more rocks before I walked back to my truck. What should I do? Go home and see if Kelly will let me in? Call Wyatt and apologize for my anger? Call my pastor and tell him I was ready to listen? I had so much to learn and so much going on in my head; I needed time to process what just took place in my heart, so I did none of those things.

I drove myself to a Fort Wayne Recovery House. I knocked on the door and told the gray-haired gentleman who answered, "I need a bed."

He took me in and gave me a bed. For the first time in a long time, I felt safe there. For some reason, I wasn't feeling like a failure. I knew I made the right choice, and my comfort level allowed me to sleep. But I had no clue what I should do next.

Whoever drinks of the water
that I shall give him
will never thirst.
But the water that I shall give him
will become in him
a fountain of water
springing up
into everlasting life.

John 4:14 (NKJV)

The next day, Wyatt showed up. I didn't bother to ask how he knew where to find me; I was just glad to see him. He came every day. He gave me Scripture to look up and study. He became my soul brother, and I was clean and feeling the love. He brought me material to help me study the Word, and he prayed with me. I knew he and Carolyn were covering my family and me in prayer. I could feel it like I could feel the warmth of a new garment.

Wyatt gave me a passage in Matthew 12 to study. He said he thought it would help me understand some of what had taken place in the past. I identified with the passage the first time I read it through. I was astonished that it spoke about me.

The passage tells us that if an unclean or evil spirit goes out of a man, it will find it has no place to go, so it will seek for a place to rest. When it finds no place to rest, it will return to the man from whom it departed. When he finds that man, he finds the man's life is in order and his heart is clean, but it's empty of God, so the evil spirit goes out again and gathers seven other spirits more evil than himself, and they all return with him and enter back in to the man, and he is seven times worse off than he was before. I knew that was true. How many times did I not renounce my sinfulness to follow God and then find myself back in the clutches of addiction, lying, and evil habits worse than I was before?

Then it was time to leave the recovery house. I had to make it this time. I knew I had people around me who would be there to encourage me and keep me on the straight and narrow path. My biggest struggle was to shake the marijuana monkey on my back.

I needed to go home and talk to Kelly. Wyatt came to the recovery house to pick me up and drive me home. Before I got out of the car, he said, "Be honest with her, Donnie. She's having a hard time with this. She loves you, but she needs to know that you are serious about making it this time."

When I walked up to the door, she was there to meet me.

"Kelly, I'm clean. I've been clean since I've been in recovery."

I stepped through the door and put my arms around her. It felt special because I was embracing her with a clean body and mind. The real Donnie was embracing her. There was nothing to hinder or enhance the way I held her. We held our embrace for a while when she said, "Donnie, you even feel clean."

"I have to make it this time, Kelly. I have to make it, and you have to help me. I was so angry when you threw me and my stuff out, but I know why you did it, and I'm glad you did. It was my wake-up call. Kelly, I realize you and I *have to be* on the same page. God has to be leading us in the same direction together. I have to know what it is God wants from me as a husband, as a father, and as a member of God's church family."

"And, Kelly, I have to know what God wants from me as a son."

Oh brother! How did my mother fit into all of this? That thought scared me. Could I do it? I didn't know. There was a lot of baggage between Mom and me that I found difficult to carry. That issue would remain to be seen. I wasn't sure I was ready to deal with it just yet. But then I didn't have to fix everything in one day. I just had to be willing.

A lot was riding on my shoulders. I knew the next time I was faced with temptation we'd see what I was made of. I determined in my heart to be made of love, joy, peace, patience, kindness, goodness, faithfulness, gentleness and self-control. I'd learned in my study these were the evidences of the spirit of God in my heart. I also learned there was no law against any of them. Wasn't that an interesting concept? I'd run from laws all my life.

Just think how much more the blood of Christ will purify our hearts from deeds that lead to death so that we can worship the living God. For by the power of the eternal spirit, Christ offered himself to God as a perfect sacrifice for our sins.

Hebrews 9:14 (NLT)

As I look back at this period of my life, I have a very vivid picture of how deceiving Satan is. He's a pusher of lies. Some of the most destructive lies seemed to make the most sense. Disobedience to the things of God caused me to look for ways to justify the choices I was making and the demons of hell were right there to support me.

As the father of lies, the enemy continued his prodding me, keeping me from victory over sin. Some of his favorite little lies are: Nobody's getting hurt; everybody does it; who's going to know; it's just this one time; there are so many bigger sins; well, at least you're not as bad as ... and on and on. As long as he could keep a foothold on the disobedient issues in my life, he remained satisfied. In an effort to justify my behavior, I realized it was of my own doing to choose to believe the enemy's lies.

I learned if I listened, God would speak to my heart in the quiet of my delivery runs. That became my time with God, and I wanted more than anything to be in total submission to the God that loved me. Every day was a struggle. Every day I cried out to God for victory for just one more day! I was right; the demons of hell were deployed at every turn. They were in the battle to control my anger, my tongue, and my love for marijuana. I knew in my heart what I needed to do, but the demonic voice from my shoulder kept saying, "You can't do it. You're a failure, Foster. Forget it. You've tried, and you've failed every time. So you might as well keep your little weed smoking secret to yourself and play the game. That's all you're ever going to be able to achieve. You'll never be able to give God a total surrender, Foster. You've been a druggie so long, it will never happen. You're a loser, Foster! You're a loser, and God ain't gonna use no loser."

I screamed out to deny his blasphemous statements in the name of God's Son. The enemy was shouting in my ear, giving it all he had to convince me I could not come under total surrender or submission to God. He was firing with both barrels to convince me I would fail if I tried to commit to a life of serving God.

Lies! Lies! Lies! Satan's biggest lie held to the flame of a sinner is "You're going to fail. Don't bother trying to change, because you're going to fail ... *again!*"

Well, my friend, God was not idly sitting by. While the enemy tried to fill my head with doubt, the spirit of God was standing by to fill my heart with hope.

I could almost feel the Holy Spirit stand up to speak. He met me face to face and penetrated my heart. I was about to see the revelation of the person of God because my heart was ready.

He presented a loaded question to my heart. "Donnie, what have you been looking for your whole life?"

I had to stop and think about that for a moment. What had I been searching for? I went to my early childhood, through my adolescent and teen years. As a young adult, I was never satisfied, so what was it I searched for but never found? As a very small child, I remembered thinking many times that I didn't want to always be afraid. Then, as I got older, I wanted to experience love, real love, the kind you can always depend on to be there. The kind you don't have to fight for. That person is just there always no matter what.

God picked up that thought for me and allowed me to think it through in his spirit. From the time I was a child, love was the missing link. God revealed to me there on the banks of the St. Mary's River how much he loved me and still does after all I've done and after all the times I failed him.

I remembered the first time I truly trusted him and told the truth about my past and saw his power spare me from man's prison. God began to prompt questions to me concerning his compassion and sovereignty that I was beginning to learn about. *Who do you think was ultimately in control of that situation? Who do think was in control that day in the courtroom when you were facing one hundred and four years for your crimes and the testimony from a lady you could not recall spoke on your behalf? Who do you think gave her a prophetic heart and a spirit of forgiveness? Who do you think it was that led you to live a normal life in Cave Junction and led you to find a friend there who knew you were a wanted man but never arrested you because he trusted in me to show him when the time was right? His name was Phil, remember?*

I began to see how God had placed his servants in my path throughout life. I never recognized them because I didn't know to look for them. I had only to seek, to open up *all* of my heart to know how much I was loved and watched over, cared for.

God *had been there* all along and I was too absorbed in myself to know it. God did love me enough to spare my life time and again. Perhaps it was for a time such as this. The miles were passing, and my heart felt good. As long as I depended on God and his strength, we were winning battles, one day at a time.

> The earth, O Lord, is full of Your mercy; Teach me Your statutes. You have dealt well with Your servant, Oh Lord, according to Your word. Teach me good judgment and knowledge for I believe Your commandments.
>
> Psalm 119:64 (NKJV)

The most difficult battle I faced was my endurance to subject myself to whatever discomfort I would experience so that I could be free from dependency on the crippling things that were destroying my life, my family, my home, and most importantly, my walk with God. I soon learned it was not going away overnight, and every day of my life would be a test, but if the Son of God could endure the cross and die for me, I could certainly withstand some suffering to free myself from the slavery to drugs I depended on to be my quick fix for everything. God was not responsible for my discomfort that came when I surrendered my dependency on marijuana and alcohol, but I was convinced he would help me through the withdrawal if I trusted him. He was there to be the healing balm that would see me through symptoms of surrender. He promised he would be all I would need, and I was ready to lay it all on the altar. I was ready to cast aside my old methods for good and start making choices, moment by moment, to first seek God's strength that would give me victory.

I turned onto our street. I pulled into the driveway and saw the light left on for me and knew Kelly and the children lay sleeping behind the door. My heart melted with gratefulness because I understood what an awesome gift they were from God. It was a gift of love I didn't deserve. I went in and went to bed. As I lay next to Kelly, I felt extremely thankful for her courage to take charge. Kicking me out and taking my stuff to the church was exactly what needed to be done. She had every right, and I was truly grateful. It brought me face to face with the dead things I had been playing with.

As I lay there in the quiet, I prayed, "God, I want to be that light in the darkness. I want to be a lighthouse to troubled youth, to struggling addicts, to the abused child, to the alcoholic, to the inmate, anywhere you choose to use me. Oh, God, let me be your servant as the Susies, the Brother Bobs, the Abbys and Phils, the Wyatts and my local church family have been to me. I want to be your servant, and I commit my service to you."

I reflected on the rare and precious treasure of memories. I drifted off, recalling stepping stones of grace that brought me to this point. I rested knowing I wasn't doing this alone. I had the power of God, the spirit of peace, the all-consuming love of God to see me through. I had the tough love of a godly woman and God's servants placed all around me who prayed for me and held me accountable before God. The victory was mine. I would claim it based on the promises of the one who loved me and gave himself for me, one day at a time.

Don't you realize that whoever you choose to obey becomes your master? You can choose sin, which lead to death, or you can choose to obey God and receive his approval.

Romans 6:16 (NLT)

The recovery period of an addict is an ongoing struggle. There were so many who were playing such important roles of ministry to me as well as being supportive in my recovery.

Temptation taps me on the shoulder every day. I was still clean, but part of dealing with addiction withdrawal affects all areas of life. Anger and depression would set in, creating distress in our home, on the job, and in my social life. Kelly and I still had our moments of marital trials and moments of strained communication. I still had eruptions of anger over silly things.

One day, it dawned on me Kelly wasn't pushing my buttons like she used to. She was living in a light that was a shining testimony to me, so one day I asked her, "What's come over you, Kelly? Why won't you argue with me anymore? Are you afraid?"

"Afraid? No, Donnie, I'm not afraid. I've just learned that our marriage is not about you, and it's not about me. You and I together have a far greater purpose than just getting along. God has shown me some very valuable techniques when conflicts come between us."

"So what's your solution, Miss Kelly?"

"Okay, I'll tell you. When we start screaming at one another, I shut up and pray."

I sat there, and I waited for her to continue. She said no more.

"Yeah, okay. You shut up and pray, then what?"

"That's it. I shut up and pray. And then while you're ranting and raving, I pray some more."

Was she trying to mess with my head or what? I wasn't sure what to say or ask. Maybe she was trying to rile me now.

"That's it, Donnie. Some of the best advice I've ever received—shut up and pray. It does no good for us to mouth off to each other. Fighting back does nothing more than stoke the flames of anger until we have a roaring, out of control inferno. While I pray, I find the kindling splinters. Anything I say to you in anger will bounce right back at me like a ball off a racket because that's exactly what happens when you mouth off to me. When we're both angry, anything said in the spirit of anger is worthless, so I shut up and I pray and let God do the work only God can do. I can't change your heart anymore than you can change mine. That's a God job. I can't do his job, Donnie."

"Come on. Don't give me that. There has to be more to it than that."

"I'm serious, Donnie. When I close my mouth, God opens my heart, and my prayer is that he will open yours."

"You're praying right now, aren't you?"

"Look here." She stepped to the counter. Picking up her Bible, she turned to Ephesians 6:12. "Carolyn showed me right here. 'For we do not wrestle against one another but we wrestle against principles and powers and rulers of darkness. We fight against wicked spirits.' It makes so much sense, Donnie. It's the power of Satan that arouses anger and selfishness, and he uses that to try and destroy the principles of God in our marriage and in our home, in our lives! Whenever angry words come between us, I just close my mouth to you and whisper a prayer that the enemy will be bound in the name of Jesus. Then I remain quiet, and I leave it there. Once I pray and leave the anger for God to deal with, my words would be nothing more than noisy, clanging cymbals. Since I started doing this, I can see changes taking place, Donnie, in both of us. You know, Jesus showed us how to live. If we know him, we know life as it should be."

She started shuffling pages in her Bible again, and this time, she turned to the First Epistle of Peter 2:23.

"When Jesus had anger shown against him, he didn't retaliate with more anger. He said nothing and left the outcome to his Father. God is the only one who knows how to judge the inner most thoughts and motives of all men.

"When Jesus was threatened, he didn't come back with counterthreats. He could have called heaven's angels to protect him or do battle for him, but instead, he remained quiet and put himself in the righteous hands of his Father. He simply prayed for God to deal with those who were angry. That is what we need to do. I've decided if I let myself get sucked into a battle of words, first of all, no one's hearing me, and second, I'm just getting in God's way."

I couldn't argue with her logic. I could hear Wyatt and Carolyn's instruction from the Word of God in what she was learning. She was the most important light of God in my world, and her outward faith and trust encouraged me to follow after her kind of faith. Kelly and I had been granted a new start. Undeserving as I was, God had my life and my heart, and Kelly had her hands full!

> You, (Oh Lord)
> Have turned my mourning into dancing;
> You have put off my sackcloth
> and clothed me with gladness
> to the end
> that my glory
> may sing praise to You
> and not be silent.
> O Lord, my God,
> I will give thanks to you
> *forever!*
>
> Psalm 30:11–12 (NKJV)

Well, here I am, fully alive in the spirit of God. I have been clean and sober for four years and out of the prison system for ten. God—and God alone—has set me free, both physically and spiritually. I look back at the multiple opportunities the creator had to take me out, to throw up his hands and say, "I give up! How many times do I have to bail you out, Foster? Forget it! I'll find somebody else!" *God never says that!*

Countless were the times God could have turned his back and said to Satan and his demons, "Take him! He's yours! I'm done! No more! I'm not messing with this guy any longer! You want him, you can have him!" *God never says that!*

I did not in the past, nor do I today, deserve any of the gifts God has given me. Yet he makes all his blessings available to me and all he has is mine. This story of my life will not have a final chapter because my life will never end. Therefore, as long as I have breath *in this life*, I will carry on in the power and spirit of the one I serve until this body is laid down in death. Then the real living starts!

EPILOGUE

BASED ON **ECCLESIASTES 3:1-8**

There is a season for all things. There is a time for every purpose under heaven.

A time to be born, a time to die:

> A time to be born, and I was; a time to die, and I did—to myself. That was the same instant I was reborn in the spirit of God. Someday, my body will shut down in physical death, but my spirit has new life, and it will live forever.

A time to sow; a time to reap:

> I sowed seeds of sin and wrath for forty-plus years, and I reaped the wrath of God through the laws of man. Now, I sow toward the harvest of heaven, and I will reap according to the riches of God.

A time to destroy; a time to heal:

> I was on the road of self-destruction of my body, my mind, and my soul, and I reaped the pain and torment of my effort.

Now my body, my mind, and my soul continue to heal more deeply every day because I made the choice to give up my self-destruction and became a new man by the forgiving grace and mercy of God and his Son.

A time to break down; a time to build up:

I not only broke down my own life but so many relationships because of my past life. Now God is giving me strength to build up a new life through the power of his Word and the leading of his Spirit.

A time to weep; a time to laugh:

I've wept oceans of salty brine because of my past, but God has covered my weeping with his mercy and fills my heart with laughter and joy at what he has done.

A time to mourn; a time to dance:

I have mourned for the loss of days given to my addictions and anger. Now I claim the words of the psalmist: "You, (Oh God), have turned my mourning into dancing; You have removed my rags of oppression and covered me with gladness."

A time to cast stones away; a time to gather them up:

I have cast so many stones of anger and rebellion at those who dared to step into the path of my past, but today my heart is doing all it can to gather them up and mend the wounds they inflicted and remove the scars and bruising of spirits because of the evil force that held my heart captive to destruction.

A time to embrace; a time to refrain from embracing:

There were so many times I should have embraced those around me who offered me the love and the will of God upon my life, but I didn't know it was God; neither did I know what they offered. Then there were times I should have turned away from embracing the influences of people that weakened my character and stole my integrity, but I didn't even know I could possess those things.

A time to gain; a time to lose:

I had forty-plus years to gain for myself. I was given chance after chance to make a good living, make something of myself; it was my opportunity to gain, but I lived under the power of drugs and alcohol, and nothing would ever be gained from that. Now is my time to gain in the knowledge and wisdom of the one who saved me and delivered me from the things that held me captive.

I guess there can be a time to lose good things or lose bad things. I have to look back and say that God allowed me to lose over and over so that I could be found by his mercy. I lost the deadly grip of addiction when I lost *myself* to live for him.

A time to keep; a time to throw away:

I held on to the security I thought my addictions gave me until I realized I was hanging on to dead sources of comfort. Once I decided to throw them away, God threw them even farther than I could have imagined. He threw them so far into the east that they will never return from the west.

A time to rend; a time to sow:

My body and spirit were violently torn apart by the evil that ravaged through my flesh, but now God has picked up the pieces of the pitiful creature I was and is stitching back together a brand-new garment fit for the new creation he is making of me.

A time to keep silent; a time to speak:

All the years that I fed my addictions and my anger, silence was the word in the circles of my acquaintances. I had nothing to speak out because whatever I said could and would be used against me in a court of law, so I was self-incriminating, but now God has given me a proclamation of *his love* to make to anyone who will listen and a voice to speak for the only thing worthy of carrying my words.

A time to love; a time to hate:

As a child, I wanted all those around me to love me. All I felt was fear from abuse and hateful minds. As an adult lost in the world of addiction, I wanted to love somebody but loved only myself to the point of where I hated myself and everyone around me. Now, God has given me my time to love and be loved because he is love, and I learned to love because *Jesus loves me!*

A time of war; a time of peace:

I was engaged in a war for forty-plus years, daily fighting on the frontline of every battle. The enemy was the worst enemy to encounter—myself, marching to the drum of Satan and his demons. The battle could not be won; it had to be surrendered. Once surrendered to the King of all the ages, he took up the battle for me and put my enemy to death. His peace now floods my soul and *is my hope!*

CPSIA information can be obtained
at www.ICGtesting.com
Printed in the USA
FFHW020332080319
50890643-56294FF